A Master Pilot's Manua

CW00797102

Avionics and
Flight Management Systems
for the Professional Pilot

David Robson

Air Pilot Publishing Ltd

Nothing in this handbook supersedes any legislation, rules, regulations or procedures contained in any operational document issued by Her Majesty's Stationery Office, the Civil Aviation Authority, the manufacturers of aircraft, engines and systems, or by the operators of aircraft throughout the world.

Copyright © 2006 Aviation Theory Centre

ISBN 1 84336 086 1

First edition (UK) September 2001 – Airlife
Reprinted 2006 – Air Pilot Publishing Ltd

Published by Air Pilot Publishing Ltd
Mill Road, Cranfield
Bedfordshire MK43 0JG, England

Email: sales@appltd.net

Acknowledgements
Thanks to Ansett Worldwide Aviation Services for permission to reproduce extracts from their B767 Operations Manual; Condor Flugdienst, Germany, for the cover photograph of the B767 instrument panel; and Honeywell Inc. for permission to use extracts from their publications.

Graphics:
Rob Loriente

Typesetting and index:
Catherine Jeffreys

Printed and bound by Antony Rowe Ltd, Eastborne

The APP Master Pilot's Manuals

Air Pilot's Manuals (APMs)

The Air Pilot's Manuals have gained the respect of student pilots and instructors alike for their depth of information, veracity, currency and user friendliness. The Civil Aviation Authority also recognises these manuals and has included them in LASORs as recommended reference texts for student pilots. The APMs are also published by Air Pilot Publishing Ltd at Cranfield, with Peter Godwin as technical editor. Peter brings over 15,000 hours of flying and instructional experience to this task.

Master Pilot's Manuals (MPMs)

Most of our terminology in aviation was handed down from ancient mariners (especially French) – *echelon*, *aileron*, *squadron*, *line astern*, *port* and *starboard*, *rudder*, *keel* and even the term *pilot*. Another nautical term is *master*.

A master can be defined as 'a skilled practitioner of an art or activity' (*The New Oxford Dictionary of English*, s.v. "master"). A *master mariner* is a seaman capable and qualified for the role of captain. The term was used for a seaman whose experience, skill and attitude was a class above the norm. The essence was learning, observing and paying attention to detail. The same criteria apply to airmen.

A *master pilot* is a pilot worthy of distinction – a pilot who has continued to question, to develop, to strive for excellence and to explore and extend the boundaries of the aircraft and his or her personal flight envelope. The Guild of Air Pilots and Air Navigators recognises the term – as does the RAF and USAF. There is also a category of *master instructor* in the US. Master pilot is a universal expression for an exceptionally skilled and knowledgable aviator. We have rightly adopted the term for these manuals because they seek to motivate and to take the pilot's skills and knowledge to a higher level and a broader base – into such areas as aerobatics, multi-engine, night flying and turbine aircraft.

All professional pilots strive to be masters of their craft – and being professional is an attitude, a state of mind, not a salary.
Welcome Aboard!

Series Author: David Robson QTP
Series Technical Advisor: Peter Godwin

Contributors

David Robson (Editor)

David Robson is a career pilot with over forty years of experience in military and civil aviation. He holds an ATPL, Grade One Instructor's rating and Command Instrument Rating. He had over twenty years' service in the RAAF and is a graduate of the Empire Test Pilots School (UK). For three years he was editor of the Aviation Safety Digest, then Manager (Business Development) for the Australian Aviation College.

Jim Rhind

Jim joined the RAF in 1951 and transferred to the RAAF in 1967 as a flying instructor until joining the Department of Civil Aviation in 1971. He served as an Examiner of Airmen (RPT). He flew the F27, F28, DC-9, B727, B737 and B767 until 1989, when he became Chief Pilot for IPEC, Australia's largest airfreight carrier.

Mick Vaughan

Mick began flying as a flight engineer with Tasman Empire Airways. After a period in the RAAF, which included time as a flying instructor at the RAAF Central Flying School, he joined the Department of Civil Aviation in 1971 as an Examiner of Airmen. He went on to become Senior Flying Operations Inspector (B737).

Bruce Byron AM

Bruce had twenty years' service in the RAAF, including a period as flying instructor at the RAAF Central Flying School. While in the RAAF, he wrote several technical and training manuals. In 1985 Bruce joined the Department of Aviation as an Examiner of Airmen. Since 1989, he has flown jet aeroplanes engaged on corporate operations and currently serves as a safety adviser to the board of CASA.

Table of Contents

Introduction

In producing this handbook, our aim has been to provide a basic understanding, in generic terms, of the avionics, instruments, displays and flight management systems used in modern transport category aeroplanes. It must be emphasised that we are not providing training for a type endorsement. This is the task of the individual airline/company.

This book has been prepared to meet the demands of the aviation training industry for a suitable reference text for students who are preparing for a transition to a wide-body jet. It is also a very useful introduction to typical modern aircraft avionics systems.

Throughout the text, reference has been made to the systems and equipment fitted in the B767. The material has been drawn from operation manuals used by various international airlines operating the B767-300ER.

Although avionics has traditionally been covered under the subject of navigation, the transport aeroplane of today uses its flight management system to integrate navigation inputs from various sources with the electronic flight instrument systems, the autopilot/flight director system and the various warning and recording systems.

Avionics and Flight Management Systems for the Professional Pilot

The subjects covered in this book are summarised below.

Area Navigation Systems

This deals with both short-range and long-range area navigation (RNAV) systems, with particular emphasis on inertial reference systems (IRS) and GPS. The IRS is covered in some detail, with the latest strapdown system used in aeroplanes such as the B767 as the main reference.

Flight Instrument Systems

Following a brief review of conventional flight instruments, including data transmission systems, the air data computer, and the flight director, this chapter deals in detail with electronic flight instrument systems (EFIS) and the engine indicating and crew alerting system (EICAS). The chapter concludes with an examination of the attitude heading reference system (AHRS).

Flight Management Systems (FMS)

This chapter deals with the FMS as fitted to the B767. It covers the flight management computer (FMC), which is the heart of the FMS and where the integration of all the inputs from other systems takes place. To conclude the chapter, we show the operation of an FMS as controlled by a pilot using the control display unit (CDU) on a typical flight.

Automatic Flight Control Systems

This discusses the basic autopilot and associated control systems, the yaw damper and fly-by-wire systems. The chapter concludes with a detailed description of the autopilot flight director system (AFDS), including the autothrottle and automatic pitch trim – followed by an example of a typical autoflight operation.

Warning and Recording Systems

Finally, we deal with the various warning systems, and include detailed descriptions of the ground proximity warning system (GPWS) and traffic alert and collision avoidance systems (TCAS). The chapter concludes with descriptions of the flight data recorder (FDR) and cockpit voice recorder (CVR).

We hope you find this volume a practical and valuable basis for understanding modern systems and we welcome your constructive feedback.

Chapter 1

Area Navigation Systems

Area navigation (RNAV) is defined as a method of navigation permitting aircraft operations on any desired track within the coverage of station-referenced navigation signals, or within the limits of a self-contained navigation system (but not necessarily bound to one track between navaids). RNAV therefore includes:

- short-range self-contained systems that rely solely on the reception of VHF/UHF radio-navigation aids like VOR and DME, and TACAN (which is a military system providing both range and bearing); and
- long-range navigation (LRN) systems using technologies such as inertial navigation, satellite navigation, and, more commonly these days, multiple sensor systems.

Multiple sensor systems employ one or more LRN navigation sources in combination and, when within range, VHF signals to update or establish position, e.g. the computer of a typical multiple sensor system could process navigation data from dual inertial and satellite sensors, and up to three VHF/UHF navigation receivers.

Short-Range Area Navigation Systems

Traditional short-range navigation systems are based on line-of-sight reception of a ground signal (typically from a VOR or DME), and the display of that signal as a single position line on a cockpit instrument. The position line may be in the form of an arc from a DME with the distance displayed numerically, or as a position line from a VOR displayed either by a needle on a radio magnetic indicator (RMI) or a course deviation indicator (CDI) on a horizontal situation indicator (HSI).

The key features of these systems are that:

- they are limited to line-of-sight range; and
- the information from each station is displayed as a single position line.

As the electronic processing of information became easier in the 1970s, avionic manufacturers were able to design systems that combined the received signals from more than one ground station to present it in a more user-friendly format. Rather than having a needle showing a single position line in relation to one of the ground stations, these systems could be programmed to show position in relation to any point (a waypoint), using several navaids to establish current position. The term *area navigation system* was coined to describe these 'smarter' short-range navigation systems.

In addition to displaying position in relation to a waypoint, RNAV systems were able to interface with the new electronic flight instrument systems (EFIS), and display track and waypoint information pictorially. Groundspeed, drift and time data could be easily computed and displayed.

The processing ability of the system enabled position line information from a variety of received stations and other navigation sources to be converted to a position in latitude and longitude, and then as position-to-waypoint track/distance information.

The features of a short-range RNAV system are:

- dependence on short-range VOR/DME stations; and
- ability to insert and display waypoint data using latitude and longitude coordinates.

Area Navigation System Inputs and Outputs

The key elements of a short-range RNAV system using only line-of-sight signals from VOR/DME stations are:

- the ability to receive multiple stations (normally at least four);
- airspeed (TAS) input from the air data computer or TAS computer;
- a computer database of station positions and frequencies together with non-aid airway waypoints, e.g. turning points (the database is normally updated at regular intervals by computer disk);
- the computing capability to integrate various input signals and computer database;
- a display method, normally a cathode ray tube; and
- a full alphanumeric (figure 1-1) or abbreviated (figure 1-2) keypad to enter the required operation mode and extra waypoint data (the examples are representative of both short- and long-range RNAV systems).

A system with these features can be used either as a stand-alone unit, or linked to an HSI to display RNAV track information and have the ability to connect to the electronic flight instrument system displays and automatic flight control (autopilot) systems.

Before flight, the system must be initialised to confirm the present position. This is a simple procedure of entering the identifying letters for the aerodrome using the keypad and verifying the input as displayed on the cathode ray tube (CRT). UTC time is confirmed by the same method. With this information the RNAV computer scans its database to compare the known latitude and longitude of the aerodrome with the coordinates of VOR/DME stations in the area.

Having located nearby stations in the database, the various receivers scan the appropriate frequencies and identify the stations. Normally, at least three stations must be tracked (three position lines) for the system to operate in the NAV mode. The system interprets these position lines to compute a present position lat/long.

Once airborne, track made good and groundspeed are determined from the continuous processing of position information. These are then compared with heading and TAS inputs to register actual wind velocity and drift. With the present UTC time in the computer memory, it is then an easy step to calculate an estimate for the next waypoint. All this information can be accessed on the display by using the keypad. By inserting a sequence of waypoints, which may be navigation aids, aerodromes or random lat/long positions, the computer can store a flight plan. When activated and interfaced with an automatic flight control system, the autopilot will fly the planned route with system monitoring by the pilot (this must be an active checking process).

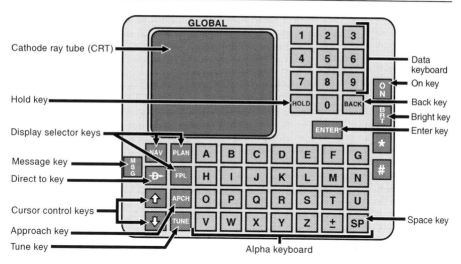

Figure 1-1 **Typical full alphanumeric keypad**

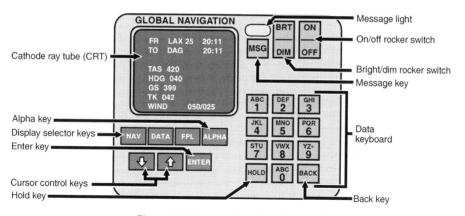

Figure 1-2 **Typical abbreviated keypad**

Short-range RNAV systems are extremely popular in North America where the density of ground stations provides excellent coverage at medium altitude.

Short-Range Area Navigation System Performance

Being totally dependent on received VOR/DME signals, a short-range RNAV system is subject to the same types of signal interference, range and errors that affect VOR and DME stations. VOR stations that are subject to scalloping will give less accurate position line information. Offset against this, however, is the ability of the computer to assess the received signal integrity and reject a station from the computation if necessary.

Where station density is low, rejecting a station because of poor signal quality may reduce the number of position lines below that required by the system to guarantee certified accuracy. In such a case, the system will revert to a dead-reckoning (DR) mode (alerted to the pilot by a warning annunciator), but will still compute position based on the most recent information available before the reversion to DR occurred.

When operating in the normal NAV mode, with at least four acceptable stations (four good position lines), the accuracy of the system will be better than ±2 nm, although far better accuracy is the norm. Figure 1-3 shows how various position lines from VOR/DME stations allow the computer to calculate a present position, or fix.

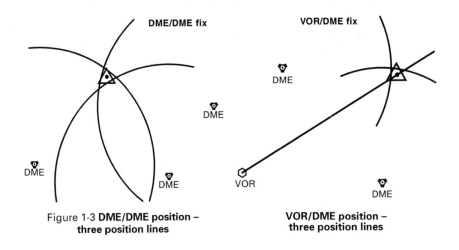

Figure 1-3 **DME/DME position –**   **VOR/DME position –**
three position lines   **three position lines**

Long-Range Area Navigation Systems

Development of Long-Range Navigation Systems

At the same time that RNAV systems using VOR/DME signals were being developed, long-range RNAV systems, not dependent on short-range transmissions, were being refined. These systems used long-range transmissions or internal reference data together with data from the aircraft's air data computer.

Contemporary LRN systems use an input from any of the following:

- inertial navigation system (INS or IRS);
- very low frequency (VLF) stations; and
- global navigation satellite systems.

Note: LRN inputs that were common in earlier days included Loran (still available over parts of the Pacific) and Doppler.

The key feature of an LRN system is its independence from short-range navigation aids. Initially, LRN systems used either Doppler, Loran or an inertial navigation system (INS). INS describes an inertial system that is used primarily as a navigation reference. However, modern set-ups employ one or more inertial systems that are capable of providing the navigation computations as well as heading and attitude references for flight instruments and autopilot modes.

In the 1970s, the US military's VLF and Omega network came online and avionic manufacturers were soon producing receivers for civilian use. More recently, access to the US military satellite navigation system known as Navstar Global Positioning System (GPS) has been made available for universal use. Most recently, full system accuracy of the system has been made available for civilian use. Other satellite navigation systems were in operation or under development, e.g. the Russian Glonass (global navigation satellite system) and Inmarsat (International Maritime Satellite).

Multi-sensor systems have the ability to generate blended position information (an average position from the various sources) and automatically update position when within range of VHF/UHF navaids. Such systems were known as *navigation management systems* (NMS), but other sensors were then added providing engine and aircraft performance data and fuel management information, and thus the *flight management system* (FMS) was conceived. The aim of FMS is to reduce cockpit workload and improve operating efficiency with more precise navigation and aircraft performance settings. When FMS is combined with appropriate autoflight systems, route and performance data can be programmed to provide automatic navigation and aircraft operation for virtually the entire flight.

Inertial Navigation Systems

The inertial navigation system (INS) is considered to be an ideal form of automatic navigation since it operates independently of external stations and provides a high level of accuracy for en route navigation given correct initialisation and alignment. More widespread use of the system is limited only by the cost of the equipment, which is high compared to other navigation options today. In smaller aircraft, the weight of the hardware is also a consideration. Early INS systems needed to be realigned (like a DG) every 20–30 minutes by input from a navaid. As a stand-alone navigation system (automatically compared with other navigation sources), INS required three systems to be fitted (three so that, if there was disagreement between the other two, the third would act as the arbitrator). System integrity was accomplished by checking and comparing the INS position displayed on each unit.

The inertial platform, the heart of the INS, is used for many purposes other than navigation and has multi-sensor outputs such as aircraft attitude fed to the flight management system. As we will see later, the input from the inertial sensor is combined with other navigation sensors, such as DME and VOR, and a composite, more accurate position is computed.

Rather than referring to inertial navigation systems, we now talk about *inertial reference systems*, or IRS. The term IRS generally indicates that a combined inertial reference unit (IRU) and computer is fitted to provide the various outputs. Invariably, more than one IRS is fitted to transport aircraft, and in aircraft equipped for autoland procedures, it is a requirement to have three IRSs fitted to allow for redundancy.

The IRS consists of an inertial reference unit (IRU) and associated inertial reference mode panel (IRMP), and, as shown in figure 1-4, has outputs to the various flight deck displays and, through a system interface, outputs and inputs to various computers and other facilities, all of which will be described in later chapters.

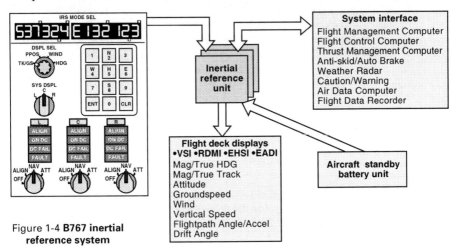

Figure 1-4 **B767 inertial reference system**

Principles of Inertial Navigation

The basic inertial system consists of a group of accelerometers which sense movement along three axes and feed that information to a computer. The accelerometers are mounted on a platform that is free to move relative to the aircraft. Being gyro-stabilised, the platform maintains a constant level relative to the earth as the aircraft attitude changes.

An inertial navigation system can provide all the necessary data for an accurate, self-contained navigation system. Previously this data was supplied from separate sources that had to be used by the pilot to interpret aircraft attitude, performance and position. This is illustrated schematically in figure 1-5.

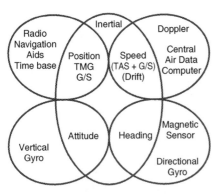

Figure 1-5 **Navigation data supplied by inertial systems**

Once the inertial navigation system has been provided with initial position information, it is capable of providing continuous and extremely accurate outputs of aircraft position, groundspeed and aircraft attitude and heading. In addition, the system is able to provide guidance or steering information to the autopilot and flight instruments.

Inertia

In order to understand the basics of an inertial navigation system, we must consider both the meaning of *inertia*, and the basic laws of motion as described by Newton over 300 years ago. Inertia can be defined as follows:

> *A body remains in a state of rest, or continues in uniform motion in a straight line, unless acted upon by an external force.*

This is also known as Newton's first law of motion. Newton's second law of motion states:

> *Acceleration of a body is directly proportional to the sum of the forces acting on the body.*

Newton's third law of motion states:

> *For every action, there is an equal and opposite reaction.*

Using these laws, we can mechanise a device that is able to detect minute acceleration (changes in direction and velocity). This ability is necessary in the development of an inertial system.

Velocity and distance are computed from sensed acceleration by the application of basic calculus. The relationship between acceleration, velocity and displacement is shown in figure 1-6.

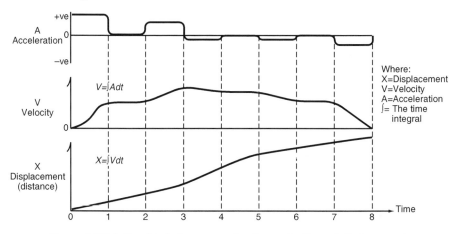

Figure 1-6 **Relationship between acceleration, velocity and displacement**

Note that velocity (speed and/or direction) changes whenever acceleration exists and remains constant when acceleration is zero.

Pendulous Accelerometers

Inertial accelerometers contain a pendulum that swings off its null position when it is exposed to an acceleration or deceleration. Pendulous accelerometers have exhibited very good performance and reliability at an acceptable cost. A pickoff device is positioned so that it can measure the size of the swing and generate an electrical signal proportional to the swing (figure 1-7). This signal is amplified proportionately into a current that is used to torque the pendulum back to the null position. The net result of this control loop is that the pendulum remains in the null position, and a current has been generated proportional to the acceleration that the accelerometer is experiencing. This current is the output of the accelerometer.

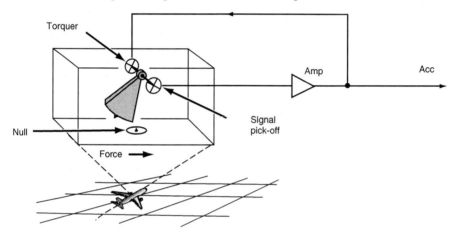

Figure 1-7 **Operation of an accelerometer**

Unlike the inherently digital output of a laser gyro (discussed later), the current output of the accelerometer is an analogue signal. The current is converted into a voltage, that in turn is converted into a digital signal by a high-precision analogue-to-digital (A/D) converter. This digital signal is supplied to a microprocessor that uses this acceleration measurement in the navigation computations, integrating that measurement once more over time to give distance travelled.

Integration

The acceleration output signal from the amplifier is also sent to an integrator (figure 1-8), which is a time multiplication device. It starts out with acceleration (velocity change) which is measured as metres per second per second (m/sec²). In the integrator, it is literally multiplied by time and the result is a new velocity in metres per second as was shown in figure 1-6 ($V = \int A dt$).

The signal from the accelerometer is then sent through a second integrator (figure 1-9), and again it is a time multiplier. With an input of metres per second, that is then multiplied by time, the result is a distance (or displacement) in metres ($X = \int V dt$), as was shown in figure 1-6.

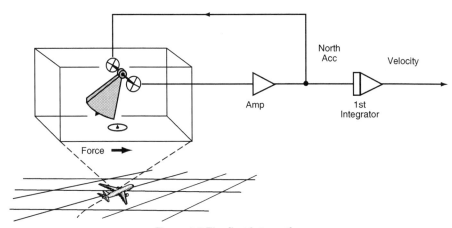

Figure 1-8 **The first integration**

This distance, in metres, can be converted in the computer into nautical miles by using the international value of 1 nm = 1,852 m. The computer associated with the inertial system knows the latitude and the longitude of the take-off point and now calculates the distance the aircraft has travelled in the north–south direction.

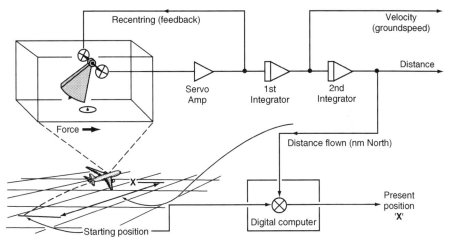

Figure 1-9 **The second integration**

Dual-Axis Navigation Computation

So far, we have discussed only the north–south accelerometer. In the unlikely event that this is the only direction in which the aeroplane flies, then one accelerometer would be sufficient to determine distance travelled from the starting position. However, since the aircraft will invariably fly in other directions, two accelerometers mounted to sense acceleration 90 degrees apart are required for navigation.

The accelerometers are stationary relative to the aircraft frame. To determine how much the acceleration is causing horizontal movement over the earth, the outputs of the accelerometers have to be compensated by the IRU computer to take account of the aircraft attitude and earth curvature.

The compensated outputs from the accelerometers are vectorially added to determine the actual direction of travel and the amount of travel horizontally. In general, the accelerometers are not oriented north–south and east–west, but their output signals can be related to a north–east coordinate system, and the present position can then be determined in terms of latitude and longitude, as shown in figure 1-10.

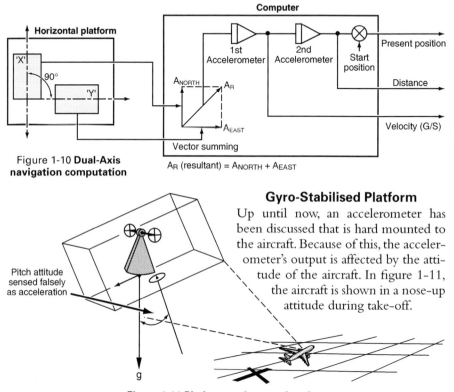

Figure 1-10 **Dual-Axis navigation computation**

A_R (resultant) = A_{NORTH} + A_{EAST}

Gyro-Stabilised Platform

Up until now, an accelerometer has been discussed that is hard mounted to the aircraft. Because of this, the accelerometer's output is affected by the attitude of the aircraft. In figure 1-11, the aircraft is shown in a nose-up attitude during take-off.

Figure 1-11 **Pitch sensed as acceleration**

This pitch angle makes the pendulum swing off the null position due to gravity. The accelerometer would send an erroneous signal that would result in an error in the velocity and distance travelled.

From this, we can see that there is a false acceleration problem caused by this pitch angle, and the solution is, of course, to keep the accelerometer level at all times.

The accelerometers are mounted on a gimbal *platform* (figure 1-12). The platform is a mechanical device that maintains the accelerometers level regardless of aircraft attitude. The inner element of the platform, where the accelerometers are mounted, also carries the gyroscopes used to stabilise the platform. The gyros provide signals to motors that control the gimbals of the platform.

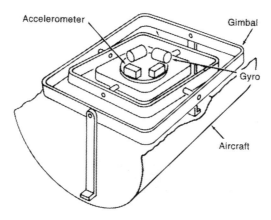

Figure 1-12 **The gyro-stabilised platform**

Figure 1-13 shows how the gyro is used to control the level of the platform. The gyro and accelerometer are mounted on a common gimbal. When the gimbal tips off the level position, the spin axis of the gyro remains fixed. The case of the gyro moves with the gimbal, and the amount of movement is detected by the signal pickoff in the gyro. That signal is then amplified and sent to a gimbal drive motor, thus restoring the gimbal back to a level position.

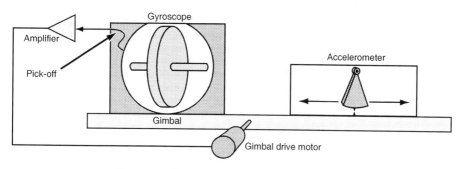

Figure 1-13 **Gyroscopic levelling of the platform**

Since the accelerometer is just being kept level, it does not sense a component of gravity and is able to sense only true horizontal accelerations of the aircraft. Here we have illustrated a single-axis platform. In reality, movement can occur in three axes of the platform, pitch, roll, and yaw.

Earth Rate Compensation (Due to Earth's Rotation)

The gyro-stabilised platform we have described would remain pointing to the same fixed point if operating in space outside the earth's atmosphere. However, the aircraft is not operating in outer space; it is operating over a planet that is round and rotating. In order to keep the accelerometers level with respect to the earth and ensure that they sense acceleration of the aircraft in a horizontal direction only, some compensation must be made.

Take the example of looking down at the earth from a point in space over the North Pole as shown in figure 1-14. At noon, the platform is levelled so that the accelerometers sense only horizontal accelerations. Now, as the earth rotates, the platform would maintain the same orientation in space; however, from an earth vantage point, the platform would appear to tip over every 24 hours.

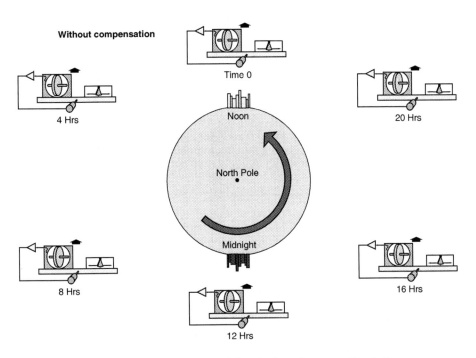

Figure 1-14 **Apparent tipping of the platform due to earth rotation**

To compensate for this apparent tipping, the platform is forced to tilt in proportion to the earth's rate of rotation. From our vantage point over the North Pole, the platform appears to tip over every 24 hours, while from an earth vantage point, it remains fixed and level as required for proper operation (figure 1-15).

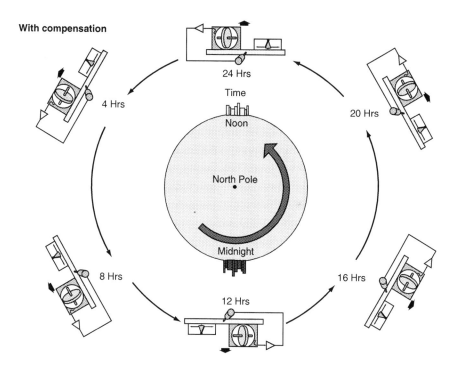

Figure 1-15 **Platform with earth rate compensation applied**

The required earth rate compensation is a function of latitude, since what is being compensated for is the horizontal component of earth rate that is felt by the gyro platform. At the equator this value is 15.04°/hr, and with travel north or south of the equator, it reduces until it becomes zero at the poles.

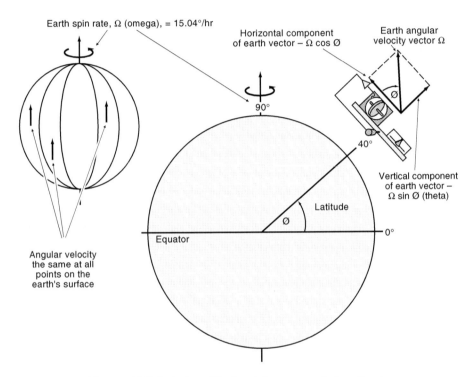

Figure 1-16 **Calculation of horizontal component of earth rate**

From figure 1-16, we can see that:
- at latitude 0°, i.e. the equator, the horizontal component of earth rate is $\Omega \cos \Phi$ = 15.04 × cos 0° = 15.04 × 1.0 = 15.04°/hr;
- at latitude 40°N, the horizontal component of earth rate is $\Omega \cos \Phi$ = 15.04 × cos 40° = 15.04 × 0.7660 = 11.52°/hr; and
- at latitude 90°, i.e. at either pole, the horizontal component of earth rate is $\Omega \cos \Phi$ = 15.04 × cos 90° = 15.04 × 0 = 0.

Transport Rate Compensation (Due to Aircraft's Change of Position)

The purpose of the gyro platform is to maintain correct orientation, and hence ensure that the accelerometers remain level with the earth for proper measurement of the aircraft accelerations.

In figure 1-17, we can see what happens to the platform as the aircraft takes off and flies to its destination. The uncompensated platform maintains its fixed space orientation, and appears to tip in relation to the aircraft as it travels from A to B. This will lead to incorrect measurements of acceleration, and is known as *transport rate error.*

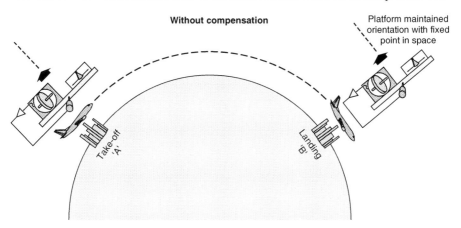

Figure 1-17 **Transport error**

Compensation for transport rate is carried out in much the same way as for earth rate. The platform is forced to tilt so that it maintains the accelerometers level during the whole flight, as shown in figure 1-18.

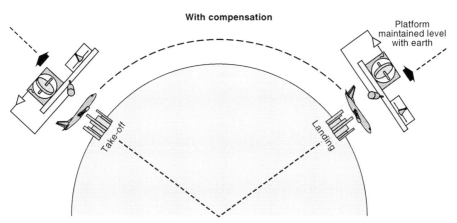

Figure 1-18 **Transport error compensation**

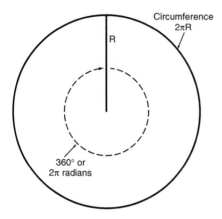

Figure 1-19 **Geometry of a circle**

Transport rate compensation is achieved by using the velocity signal, which is derived from the first integration of the accelerometer output.

Geometry can be used to show how the transport rate can be calculated. The circumference of a circle is equal to $2\pi r$, where r is the radius, and the total angle bounded by the circle is 360°, or 2π radians (see figure 1-19). The relationship between the circle's angle in radians and its circumference is $2\pi/2\pi r$, or $1/r$.

Using this relationship, the angle through which a body (in our case the aeroplane) has rotated can be calculated given the distance travelled. If we now divide both distance and angle by time, the relationship can be extended to relate tangential velocity (i.e. horizontal) to angular rate. When applied to inertial navigation, the result is that the transport rate can be found by multiplying the velocity v found from the first stage integration, by $1/r$, giving us an angular velocity (i.e. transport rate) about the surface of the earth (see figure 1-20).

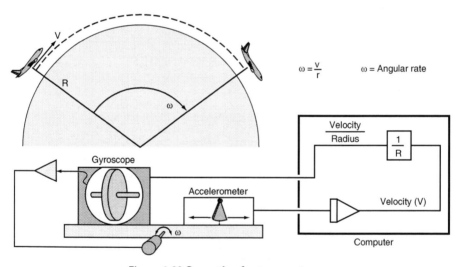

Figure 1-20 **Correcting for transport error**

This angular velocity signal is then used to torque the gyro and cause the platform to precess about the surface of the earth at the same rate that it is being transported over the surface by the aircraft, thus maintaining the platform normal to the local vertical, i.e. horizontal. This action is known as *Schuler tuning*, and you will frequently come across the term *Schuler tuned platform*.

Note: Because the aircraft is flying at altitude (usually above 30,000 ft), an allowance has to be made, and the multiplying factor is actually 1/(R + h) where:
- R = the radius of the earth in metres; and
- h = height of the aircraft above the surface of the earth.

Of course, both earth rate and transport rate compensation are simultaneously and continuously in effect.

Gyro Torquing
Rather than making individual corrections for both earth rate and transport rate, they are carried out simultaneously in the INS computer by torquing the gyro as in figure 1-21.

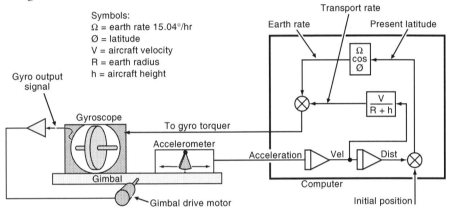

Figure 1-21 **Gyro torquing**

As can be seen, the transport rate and earth rate components, v/(R + h) and $\Omega\cos\Phi$ respectively, are summed and sent to the gyro torquer. This causes the gyro to tilt with respect to its case. When this happens, an output signal is generated. This signal is then amplified and used to drive the gimbal motor causing the gimbal to tilt the platform to its level position.

Schuler Tuning
Although not necessary for a basic understanding of transport rate compensation, the following is a brief explanation of Schuler tuning. A pendulum is a suspended mass, free to rotate in at least one axis in a horizontal plane, and whose centre of gravity is not on the rotational axis. Any pivoted mass which is not perfectly balanced is, by definition, a pendulum. Unfortunately, perfect balance is a non-achievable aim, and this fact applies to inertial platforms which are designed to provide a vertical reference. These platforms behave like all pendulums in aligning with the

dynamic vertical when at rest. The Schuler theory assumes the pendulum bob (mass) is at the centre of the earth, and suspended from a point (the aeroplane in our case) above the surface, as shown in figure 1-22.

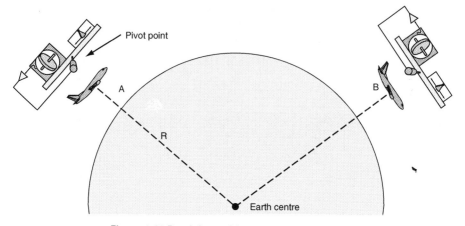

Figure 1-22 **Pendulum with mass at earth's centre**

If the suspension point is accelerated around the earth, i.e. the aeroplane moves from A to B, then, since the mass of the pendulum is assumed to be at the earth's centre, it will theoretically always remain vertically below its suspension point. This means that our inertial platform will remain horizontal irrespective of any acceleration.

As we said to begin with, perfect balance is not possible, and if for any reason the pendulum bob became displaced from the earth's centre, it would start a natural period of oscillation. In the case of a pendulum, this can be found from the formula:

$$T = 2\pi\sqrt{\frac{L}{g}}$$

Here, T is the period of oscillation in seconds, L is length of the pendulum and g is the gravitational constant.

With the *Schuler pendulum,* L in the formula is the radius of the earth, and this can be taken to be 6,378,163 metres, and *g,* the acceleration due to gravity of 9.815 m/sec^2. From this we can derive the period of oscillation to be 84.4 minutes.

$$T = 2\pi\sqrt{\frac{6,378,163}{9.815}}$$
$$= 5,065 \text{ seconds}$$
$$= 84.4 \text{ minutes}$$

Thus, by mechanising the INS platform to remain horizontal (as was shown in figure 1-20), an analogue of the Schuler earth pendulum is produced. The platform is then said to be Schuler tuned.

Summary

So far, in explaining the principle of inertial systems, we have used a simple pendulum accelerometer to illustrate the various stages of operation.

In practice, there are today many different types of accelerometers, which are classified as either mechanical or electrical depending on how the restoring force operates. Yet, for an understanding of inertial systems, a detailed knowledge of accelerometers is unnecessary.

It is enough to know the general principles involved and, regardless of the type of accelerometer used, recognise the following desirable characteristics:
- low threshold sensitivity (i.e. small accelerations that can be sensed);
- wide sensitivity range (i.e. from small to large accelerations are able to be handled);
- linear output (i.e. an output varying in direct proportion to the input); and
- high resolution (i.e. the ability to detect small increments of change).

With the gyroscopes and associated platforms, we have discussed the conventional spinning gyroscopes and gimballed platforms. Modern systems such as fitted to the B767 make use of laser gyros and strap-down inertial systems. These systems are described in the next section.

Laser Gyro

Principle of the Laser Gyro

The laser gyro is among the most remarkable on the ever-growing list of laser uses. The laser gyro is a device that measures rotation by using the properties of two laser beams rotating in opposite directions inside a cavity.

In a laser cavity, photons are emitted (or light is radiated) in all directions. However, only the light that radiates in a straight line between two or more mirrors is reinforced by repeated trips through the gain medium, which consists of a mixture of helium and neon gases at a very low pressure. This repeated amplification of the light reflecting between the mirrors soon reaches saturation, and a steady-state

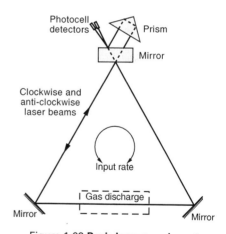

Figure 1-23 **Basic laser gyro layout**

oscillation results. This light oscillating between the mirrors is typically called a laser beam. To obtain useful laser light outside the laser cavity, a small percentage of the laser beam is allowed to pass through one of the mirrors.

A laser gyro operates much like any ordinary laser, but rather than just two mirrors it contains three so that the laser beams can travel around an enclosed area. Such a configuration allows the generation of two distinct laser beams occupying the same space. One beam travels in a clockwise direction, and the other in an anticlockwise direction (see figure 1-23, page 19).

Laser Gyro Operation

Laser gyros are not gyros at all, but sensors of angular rate of rotation about a single axis. As exemplified in the Honeywell design (figure 1-24), they are made of a triangular block of temperature-stable glass weighing a little more than 1 kilogram. Very small tunnels are precisely drilled parallel to the perimeter of the triangle, and reflecting mirrors are placed in each corner. A small charge of helium-neon gas is inserted and sealed into an aperture in the glass at the base of the triangle. When high voltage is run between the anodes and the cathode, the gas is ionised. In the energy exchange process many of the atoms of the gas are transformed into light in the orange-pink part of the visible spectrum. This action is abetted by the *tuned cavity* effect of the physical dimensions of the light path inside the glass block.

The randomly moving particles resonate at a single frequency resulting in a thin, high energy beam of coherent light travelling through the triangle of tunnels. The mirrors serve as both reflectors and optical filters, reflecting the light frequency for which they were designed and absorbing all others.

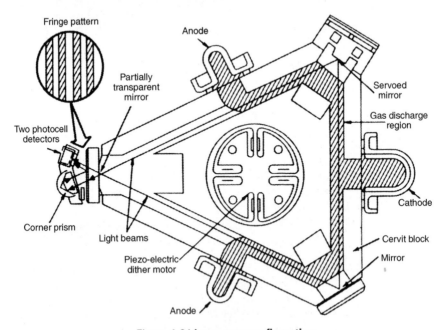

Figure 1-24 **Laser gyro configuration**

In a laser gyro, two beams of light are generated, each travelling around the cavity (in this case a triangle) in opposite directions, and the operation of the laser gyro is based on the effects that rotational motion has on the two laser beams.

The laser beams, even though in the light spectrum, have coherent wave-like properties, undulating between zero and a peak in sine-wave fashion. The light is said to be a pure frequency. In the Honeywell helium-neon laser gyro, as defined by its wavelength (the reciprocal of frequency), the light is 6,328 angstroms.

Although the frequency is determined by the gas that is *lasing*, it can be varied somewhat by changing the path length over which the waves have to travel. For a given path length there is an integral number of waves (cycles that occur over the complete path). If the path length is altered, the waves will be either compressed or expanded, but there always will be an integral number of cycles that occur over the complete path. If the waves are compressed, more cycles occur per unit time. Hence, the frequency increases. If expanded, the opposite is true.

Measurement of Rotation

In figure 1-25, the triangular path ABC is non-rotating, and since both contrarotating beams travel at the same constant speed (the speed of light), it will take each beam exactly the same time to complete its circuit. In this case, the opposite beams cancel each other, and no movement around the axis is detected.

If, however, the triangular path is rotating, say, anticlockwise as shown, light leaving point A will arrive at B_1 rather than B. The distance AB_1 is longer than AB. For light travelling in the opposite direction, the distance of each leg will be less. Thus the transit times of light travelling in opposite directions will differ.

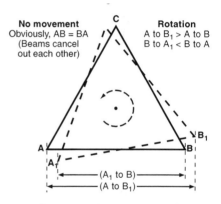

Figure 1-25 **Measurement of rotation by laser gyro**

Devices known as gain elements are placed in the path of the moving beams and allow measurement of the frequency change that results from the change in time taken. Measuring the difference in frequencies of the opposing beams allows the rate of rotation to be calculated.

Measurement of Frequency Difference

As was shown in figure 1-24, the three corner mirrors are not identical. One is servoed so that it can make micro-adjustments to keep the physical path always the same. Another (the one at the apex of the triangle in the diagram) is partially transparent to permit a small amount of light to pass through so as to impinge on the photocell detectors. The prism, as can be seen, flips one beam around, causing it to meet and interfere with the beam aimed directly at the photocells.

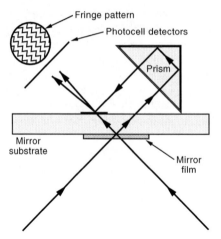

Figure 1-26 **Fringe pattern in a laser gyro**

The interfering beams alternately cancel and reinforce each other, thus generating the fringe pattern, as shown in figure 1-26.

The difference in frequency between the two beams is measured by counting the fringes of the fringe pattern generated by the interference of the two beams.

The change in the pattern will move in one direction or another, depending on which way the laser gyro is rotating. The photocell detectors read both the direction and rate of movement which are then converted to signals used by attitude or navigation systems.

Limitations and Accuracy

One potential problem with a laser gyro is a phenomenon known as *laser-lock*. At very low rotation rates, the output frequency (i.e. the frequency difference between the two beams) can drop to zero. This is due to small amounts of energy from one beam being back-scattered into the opposite beam, causing the two frequencies to be pulled together until they synchronise – that is they can no longer indicate the rotation. Since extremely low rotation rates – in the order of $0.001°/hr$ – are required to be measured in inertial systems, a remedy is required. The most common method of eliminating the effects of laser lock is a vibration device known as a *piezo-electric dither* motor as was shown in figure 1-24. This breaks the laser lock and permits these very small rotations to be measured.

The accuracy of a laser gyro is influenced by the length of its optical path. The longer the path, the greater the accuracy. The relationship between length and accuracy is non-linear, and a small increase in length, say 10%, will result in a significant improvement in accuracy of 25%.

As with a conventional spinning gyro, the major source of error in a laser gyro is random drift. While in a conventional gyro, the root cause of this problem is imperfect bearings and mass imbalances, in the laser gyro it is *noise*, due almost entirely to imperfections in the mirrors, including the mirror coatings. Notwithstanding these limitations, laser gyros with exceptionally high performance and reliability are now commonplace, and have demonstrated performance accuracies of better than 0.01 degrees/hour.

Note: The triangular arrangement is often called a *ring laser* because the light is travelling around an enclosed area, and you will come across the term *ring laser gyro*. The term *laser gyro* is more specific (a ring laser may have additional applications besides sensing rates) and is equally correct.

Strapdown Inertial Reference Systems

Principles of Strapdown Inertial Navigation

Inertial navigation is the process of determining a vehicle's location using internal inertial sensors rather than external references. A microprocessor calculates velocity, position, and attitude from the acceleration and angular rate measurements derived by the inertial sensors. Three accelerometers and three gyros are needed because in a three-dimensional world an aircraft can simultaneously accelerate in three directions and rotate about three orthogonal axes – pitch, roll and yaw (heading).

In a strapdown inertial reference system (IRS), the gyros and accelerometers are mounted solidly to the chassis that is mounted solidly to the airframe. There are no gimbals to keep the sensors level with the surface of the earth, and the laser gyros are used as rate sensors rather than displacement sensors. The accelerometers are mounted such that the input axis of one accelerometer is always in the longitudinal aircraft axis, one is in the lateral axis, and one is in the vertical axis. In other words, the gyros are mounted such that one gyro senses roll, one senses pitch, and the other senses yaw.

In a typical strapdown IRS, such as the Honeywell system used in the B767, the inertial sensors, coupled with high-speed microprocessors, allow the system to maintain a stable platform reference mathematically rather than mechanically. This results in a significant increase in accuracy and reliability over the older, gimbal stabilised platforms described previously. Figure 1-27 shows a comparison between a gimballed INS and a strapdown IRS.

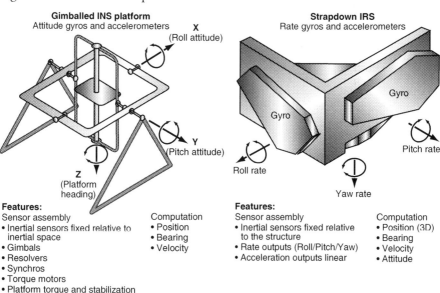

Features:
Sensor assembly
• Inertial sensors fixed relative to inertial space
• Gimbals
• Resolvers
• Synchros
• Torque motors
• Platform torque and stabilization electronics
• Attitude outputs
• Acceleration outputs

Computation
• Position
• Bearing
• Velocity

Features:
Sensor assembly
• Inertial sensors fixed relative to the structure
• Rate outputs (Roll/Pitch/Yaw)
• Acceleration outputs linear

Computation
• Position (3D)
• Bearing
• Velocity
• Attitude

Figure 1-27 **Functional comparison of gimballed INS and strapdown IRS**

Operation of a Strapdown Inertial Reference System

The accelerometer produces an output that is proportional to the acceleration applied along the sensor's input axis. The microprocessor integrates the acceleration signal to calculate a velocity.

Integration is a function that can be viewed as a multiplication by time. For example, a vehicle accelerating from rest at three metres per second per second (3 m/s^2) would be travelling at a velocity of 30 metres per second after 10 seconds have elapsed. Note that acceleration was simply multiplied by time to get velocity.

The microprocessor also uses the calculated velocity to determine position. For example, a vehicle travelling at a constant velocity of 30 metres per second for 10 seconds will have changed position by 300 metres. The velocity was simply multiplied by time to determine the position. This is called *integration*.

Although it is used to calculate velocity and position, acceleration is meaningless to the system without additional information. For example, consider an accelerometer strapped down to the longitudinal axis of the aircraft and measuring a forward acceleration. Is the aircraft's acceleration north, south, east, west, up or down? In order to navigate over the surface of the earth, the system must know how this aircraft acceleration is related to the earth's surface and from where the flight began. Because the accelerometers are aligned to the axes of the aircraft, the IRS must know the relationship of these axes to the surface of the earth and to north.

The laser gyros in a strapdown system make the measurements necessary to describe this relationship in terms of pitch, roll, and heading angles. These angles are calculated from the angular rates measured by the gyros through an integration – similar to the manner in which velocity is calculated from measured acceleration. For example, suppose a gyro measures a yaw rate of three degrees per second for 30 seconds. Through integration, the microprocessor calculates that the heading has changed by 90 degrees after the 30 seconds.

Given the knowledge of pitch, roll, and heading that the gyros provide, the microprocessor resolves the acceleration signals into earth-related accelerations, and then performs the horizontal and vertical navigation calculations. This can be illustrated in the following scenarios.

- Suppose the gyro signals have been integrated to indicate that the aircraft's heading is 045°T and the pitch and roll angle are both zero. The only acceleration measured has been in the longitudinal axis, and it has been integrated into a velocity of 480 kt. After flying at a constant heading and attitude for one hour, the microprocessor has integrated the velocity to determine that the aircraft has flown to a latitude and longitude that is 480 nm north-east of the original location. In doing so, the inertial reference system has used the acceleration signals in conjunction with the gyro signals to calculate the present position.

- Consider an inertial reference unit with sensors measuring a heading of 090°T, a pitch of 10 degrees, a zero roll angle, and only a longitudinal acceleration. The pitch angle indicates that the longitudinal acceleration is partially upward and partially eastward. The microprocessor uses the pitch angle to accurately separate the acceleration into upward and eastward components. The vertical portion of the acceleration is integrated to get vertical velocity that, in turn, is integrated to get altitude. The eastward portion of the acceleration is integrated to get the new east velocity that, in turn, is integrated to get the new longitude.

Under normal flight conditions, all six sensors sense motion simultaneously and continuously, thereby entailing calculations that are substantially more complex than shown in the previous examples. A powerful, high-speed microprocessor is required in the IRS in order to handle this additional complexity rapidly and accurately.

Strapdown Inertial Reference System Errors

In addition to the basic strapdown concepts that have been discussed, there are some additional details that must be considered in order to navigate with respect to the earth's surface. These special considerations are necessitated by the earth's shape, gravity and rotation. A strapdown IRS compensates for these effects entirely within the software.

Gravity

Vertical velocity and altitude are calculated using the acceleration that is measured perpendicular to the earth's surface. However, an inertial accelerometer cannot distinguish between gravitational force and actual aircraft acceleration. Consequently, any accelerometer that is not perfectly parallel to the earth's surface will measure a component of the earth's gravity in addition to the true aircraft acceleration. Therefore, the microprocessor in the IRS must subtract the estimated local gravity from the measured vertical acceleration signal.

Earth Rate

As with the conventional INS, the strapdown system has to compensate for the earth's rotation rate of 15.04°/hr, and the microprocessor does this by subtracting this value, which is stored in memory, from the signal measured by whichever gyro or gyros are pointed eastward. Without this earth rate compensation, an IRS operating at the equator would mistakenly think that it is upside down after 12 hours of navigation. At other places on the earth, the system would develop similar errors in pitch, roll, and heading.

Transport Rate

Schuler tuning of the strapdown system to compensate for transport rate is performed by the microprocessor. It carries out the calculation of $v/(R + h)$, and then subtracts the resultant transport rate from the laser gyro's measurements.

Automatic Calibration

Automatic calibration improves system performance and reduces component replacement during line maintenance by automatically maintaining the calibration of all three gyros and the longitudinal and lateral accelerometers. Automatic calibration is mechanised using computer programs that estimate the long-term bias drift in the sensors, and adjust the sensor calibration coefficients accordingly.

Gyro

The effects of gyro bias errors are very predictable, and given a particular gyro bias error and a particular flight profile, the position error that will result can easily be forecast. Gyro automatic calibration uses this relationship in reverse – it measures the end-of-flight position error, records the flight profile, and estimates the gyro bias errors that would have caused the measured position error.

Position errors are measured by comparing the end-of-flight calculated IRS position against the actual position entered by the pilot at the beginning of the next flight. Reasonableness checks, details of which will be covered later, and Kalman filtering (a special software data sampling routine) ensure that all measurements and estimates are scrutinised and appropriately weighted for optimal performance.

Accelerometer

Accelerometer automatic calibration takes advantage of the fact that velocity errors during taxi are almost entirely due to accelerometer bias errors. Under normal taxi conditions the actual lateral velocity of the aircraft is zero, so any lateral velocity detected is considered to be an error caused by bias errors.

By recording the heading profile of the aircraft and the lateral velocity error during taxi, automatic calibration estimates the accelerometer bias errors.

It may seem impossible to calibrate the longitudinal accelerometer with this technique, because only a lateral velocity error is measured. However, due to the manner in which the alignment procedure is mechanised, each accelerometer bias error introduces velocity errors in two directions simultaneously – in the direction that the accelerometer pointed during alignment, and in the direction that it points during taxi.

For example, consider an aircraft that aligns with north and then turns and taxis to the east. Part of the lateral (north) velocity error during taxi will be caused by the lateral accelerometer because it is pointing north during taxi. The other part of the lateral velocity error will be caused by the longitudinal accelerometer because it was pointing north during alignment. It follows that any heading change after alignment causes both the lateral and longitudinal accelerometer bias errors to induce lateral velocity errors. The heading profile is required to determine how much of the velocity error was caused by each accelerometer.

As in gyro calibration, Kalman filtering and reasonableness checks ensure highly reliable accelerometer calibration.

Inertial Reference System Alignment

Inertial navigation depends on the integration of acceleration to obtain velocity and distance. In any integration process one must know the initial conditions, which, in this case, are velocity and position. The accuracy of the IRS depends greatly upon the accuracy of the initial conditions. Therefore, system alignment is of paramount performance.

Gyrocompass Process

Inside the inertial reference unit (IRU), the three gyros sense the angular rate of the aeroplane. Since the aeroplane is stationary during alignment, the angular rate is due to earth rotation. The IRU computer uses this angular rate to determine the direction of true north (figure 1-28).

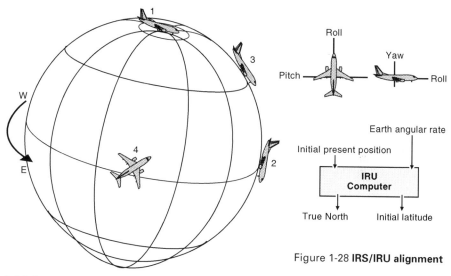

Figure 1-28 **IRS/IRU alignment**

Initial Latitude

During the alignment period, the IRU computer has determined true north by sensing the direction of the earth's rotation. The magnitude of the earth rotation vector allows the IRU computer to estimate latitude of the initial present position. This calculated latitude is compared with the latitude entered by the operator during initialisation.

Alignment Mode

For the IRU to enter ALIGN mode, the IRS mode selector switches on the inertial reference mode panel (IRMP), shown in figure 1-29, are set to ALIGN or NAV position. (It is preferable to set the switch to NAV.)

During ALIGN, the system software performs a vertical levelling and determines aircraft true heading and latitude.

The levelling operation brings the pitch and roll attitudes within 1.0 degree accuracy (coarse levelling), followed by fine levelling and heading determination. Initial latitude and longitude data

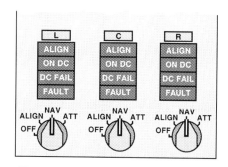

Figure 1-29 **IRS mode selectors on IRMP**

must be entered by manually entering the actual present position via the IRMP keyboard (figure 1-30) or by entering it by the FMS CDU as described in chapter 3.

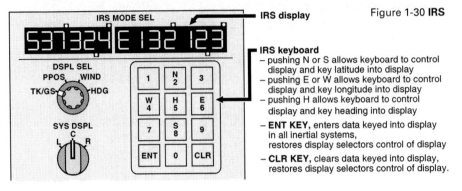

Figure 1-30 **IRS**

Upon ALIGN completion, the IRS will enter NAV mode automatically if the mode select switch is set to NAV during alignment. If the mode select switch is set to ALIGN, the system will remain in align until the pilot selects NAV mode.

There is a disadvantage in leaving the switch in ALIGN in that the IRS system remains vulnerable to upset by excessive motion while the system remains in this mode.

Alignment Time

The IRU completes alignment in 2.5 minutes at the equator and up to 10 minutes at 70° latitude (figure 1-31). During alignment, the ALIGN annunciator is illuminated.

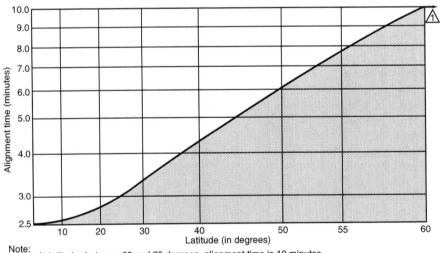

Note:
⚠ At latitudes between 60 and 70 degrees, alignment time is 10 minutes.
   At above 70 degrees, additional time may be required.

Figure 1-31 **Time of alignment**

High-Latitude Alignment

Under normal circumstances, alignment should be initiated only within the latitudes of 70° north to 70° south. If necessary, alignment above 70° may be attempted, but system accuracies may be degraded to an extent that will prevent NAV mode engagement. To improve navigation performance for high-latitude alignments, the alignment time can be increased beyond the normal 10 min by leaving the mode select switch in the ALIGN position.

Alignment Requirements

During alignment, the aircraft must remain stationary. If the IRU detects excessive aircraft motion, the ALIGN annunciator will flash and the FAULT annunciator will illuminate. If this occurs, the mode select switch on the IRMP must be set to OFF for a minimum of 3 seconds and then set back to ALIGN or NAV to restart alignment.

Note: *Normal passenger-loading activities and wind gusts will not disturb alignment.*

If the pilot does not enter present position within the normal alignment time, the ALIGN annunciator will flash, and the IRU will not enter the NAV mode until it receives a valid input of present position. The pilot may update the current latitude and longitude entry any number of times without delaying alignment as long as the IRU has not entered the NAV mode. Each successive latitude and/or longitude entry overwrites the previous entry. Only the latest entry is used for navigation.

Alignment Tests

To ensure that the alignment is correct, the IRU conducts a reasonableness test and a system performance test on the position that the pilot has entered.

Reasonableness Tests (Does It Make Sense?)

The IRU conducts a reasonableness test on latitude and longitude immediately after each has been entered, as follows.

- The IRU compares the entered latitude and longitude with the latitude and longitude stored at the last shutdown. If the entered position does not agree within a given limit of the stored position, the entered latitude or longitude fails the test, and the ALIGN annunciator on the IRMP flashes.
- The IRU will accept additional latitude and longitude entries, although each entry must also pass or override the reasonableness test. To override the test, the new entry must be identical to the last entry. For example, if S 37° 32.4 was entered and failed the test, then this latitude must be entered again to override the test. If a new entry passes or overrides the reasonableness test, the flashing ALIGN annunciator will become steady.
- A correct latitude and/or longitude entry may fail the reasonableness test if a new IRU has been installed or if the aircraft has been moved to a different location without operating the IRU. In this case, identical coordinates should be entered twice to override the test.

System Performance Test

At the end of alignment, the entered latitude must pass a system performance test. This test requires that the latitude entered by the pilot be within a given limit of the latitude computed by the IRU. If the entered latitude passes this test, alignment is completed.

- A flashing ALIGN annunciator at this time indicates that the entered latitude has failed the system performance test. The IRU will not enter the NAV mode until the entered latitude passes the test.
- Additional latitude entries are still allowed until the test is passed. However, new latitude entries must also pass the reasonableness test. If two consecutive, identical latitudes are entered and the system performance test fails, the flashing ALIGN annunciator goes steady, and the FAULT annunciator will illuminate.
- When one entry of the correct latitude passes the test, the FAULT and ALIGN annunciators will turn off, and allow entry into the NAV mode.

Sine and Cosine Latitude Comparisons

Figure 1-32 shows that the maximum errors possible occur when alignment is made near the equator. The error at the equator is most closely checked by the sine test.

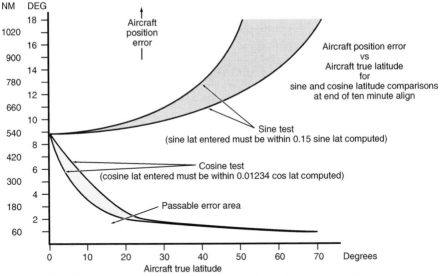

Note: The sine test is effective only in establishing whether the aircraft is north or south of the equator. (The cosine is positive for both north and south latitudes.)

Figure 1-32 **Sine and cosine latitude comparisons**

Whenever alignment is done at a latitude that is greater than approximately 1° N/S the cosine test takes over and the sine test is then only used to indicate whether the aircraft is north or south of the equator. A passable error occurs (basically) below the cosine curve. The maximum error is 60.6 nm at 45° latitude and is approximately 518 nm at approximately 1° from the equator.

The view shows a band for both sine and cosine curve. In each test, the error could be at either a higher or a lower latitude than the true latitude. The two directions (above or below in latitude) give two curves for each test.

The maximum error of approximately 518 nautical miles shows that the sine/cosine test is a very coarse test. The comparisons with stored latitude and longitude that are made when latitude and longitude are first entered could reflect a maximum error of 84.8 nm (for 1 degree in latitude and 1 degree in longitude). However, the flashing ALIGN annunciator for either entry (that is in excess of 1 degree from the stored value) can easily be cancelled and made steady, by a second, consecutive, identical entry. Therefore, this check can easily be overridden.

It remains the responsibility of the pilot in command to ensure
that correct latitude and longitude is entered into the IRS.

Summary of Strapdown Inertial Reference Systems

The modern strapdown inertial system is very accurate and generally reliable but, as with any system, there are certain limitations that should be borne in mind.

* Correct alignment is the key to success, and keying in the correct initialisation coordinates is absolutely essential.
* All inertial systems will drift with time. A system is performing poorly if it drifts 1 nm/hr, or more. An average of 0.3 nm/hr is considered to be normal. For this reason, on long flights, the system should be updated whenever possible.
* As with any form of automatic navigation system, errors can easily be induced by the operator, particularly during the initialisation process, and the loading of route navigation data such as waypoints.

Global Navigation Satellite Systems

Global navigation satellite system (GNSS) is the generic term used to describe a global position and time determination system. The system includes one or more satellite constellations, aircraft receivers, system integrity monitoring, and augmentation as necessary to achieve the *required navigation performance* (RNP) for the particular phase of operation. GNSS is the term now used in discussions and policy development forums related to satellite navigation by ICAO and leading aviation authorities.

The satellites and other components of the system broadcast signals that aircraft receivers can interrogate to establish accurate position and time reference. Since GNSS primarily broadcasts signals from space, direct rather than reflected transmissions can be used, allowing the use of higher frequencies. This in turn provides very high quality signals and thus high levels of accuracy. By the use of multiple satellites, GNSS has the potential of generating very precise position information.

In this section, we focus on the United States' military system known as the *Navstar Global Positioning System* (GPS). It should be regarded as just one element of the ultimate global architecture that we call GNSS. However, it is a system that has reached a mature stage of development and is in widespread civilian use.

Other Systems

There are other systems evolving or being planned which use similar technology. The Russian military system known as Glonass is operational and has been offered for civilian use. Inmarsat (International Maritime Satellite Organisation) is a satellite system used to detect rescue beacons and proposes to launch satellites equipped with navigation transponders. Receiver technology will continue to develop rapidly such that signals from more than one satellite system can be processed for navigation purposes.

Future Developments

Regardless of which system, or combination of systems, is used by the GNSS, certain accuracy, reliability and redundancy criteria will need to be met before authorisation is issued for independent (sole means) navigation for civilian operations, i.e. fail-safe criteria must be demonstrated before certification is granted. To this end, ICAO has established a Global Navigation Satellite System Panel to develop standards and recommended procedures (SARPS) for the future of civilian air navigation using satellite technology. There are big issues to be considered, such as the replacement of ageing ILS equipment for precision instrument approaches, the decommissioning of certain en route and terminal radio navigation aids, and the introduction of a system of en route air traffic management known as *automatic dependent surveillance* (ADS).

Useful Definitions

Before moving on, it is useful to list some of the more important definitions related to GNSS/GPS. The definitions can be referred to as the various terms arise later in this chapter.

Sole Means Navigation System

Sole means navigation system is a navigation system which, for a given phase of flight, must satisfy the required accuracy, integrity, availability, and continuity performance requirements.

Primary Means Navigation System

This is a navigation system which, for a given operation or phase of flight, must satisfy accuracy and integrity requirements, but not necessarily the availability and continuity of service requirements. With respect to the latter, safety is achieved by either limiting flights to a specific time or by imposing operational requirements and restrictions.

Supplemental Means Navigation System

This navigation system must be used in conjunction with a sole means navigation system.

Availability

Availability is an indication in percentage terms of the ability of the system to provide useful and acceptable service within a specified area of coverage.

Required Navigation Performance (RNP)

RNP is a statement of the navigation performance accuracy necessary for operation within defined airspace. It prescribes the required track containment standard, i.e. the maximum allowable track deviation in nautical miles, within which an aircraft must be contained with a 95% probability for the route. For example, RNP 4 means that the aircraft's RNAV system must be capable of navigating the aircraft within 4 nm of track.

Integrity

Integrity refers to the probability that the system will provide accurate navigation as specified, or the ability to provide timely warnings to the user that the system should not be used for navigation.

Pseudorange

Pseudorange is the determination of position, or the obtaining of information relating to position, for the purposes of navigation by means of the propagation properties of radio waves, i.e. the distance from the receiver/processor to a satellite plus an unknown clock offset distance. With four satellites in view, it is possible to compute position and clock offset distance.

Receiver Autonomous Integrity Monitoring

Receiver autonomous integrity monitoring (RAIM) is a technique whereby a civil GPS receiver/processor determines the integrity of the GPS navigation signals using only GPS signals or GPS signals augmented with altitude. At least one satellite, in addition to those required for navigation, must be in view for RAIM to operate.

Almanac

Almanac is a set of parameters, providing orbital data for the entire GPS constellation, which is used by the GPS receiver to predict the satellites in view and their estimated pseudoranges.

Ephemeris

Ephemeris is the data that defines the current position of each satellite in the constellation. Ephemeris data is transmitted as part of each satellite's unique navigation data message.

World Geodetic Standard

World Geodetic Standard (WGS) is a constant set of parameters describing the size and shape of the earth, i.e. an earth model.

Navstar Global Positioning System

The Navstar GPS has three functional elements: a space segment, a control segment and a user segment (the airborne receivers).

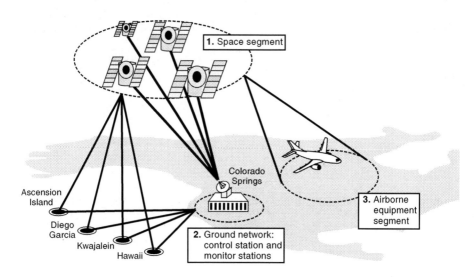

Figure 1-33 **The GPS consists of three basic segments**

Space Segment

The space segment consists of a constellation of 24 satellites orbiting the earth at an altitude of just over 20,200 km (10,900 nm) in six strategically defined orbital planes. Three of the satellites are operating as spares, with the remaining 21 in the constellation sufficient to provide global navigation coverage. The objective of the GPS satellite configuration is to provide a window of at least five satellites in view from any point on earth.

The satellites orbit at an inclination angle of 55°, taking approximately 12 hours to complete an orbit, and the orbital position of each satellite is known precisely at all times.

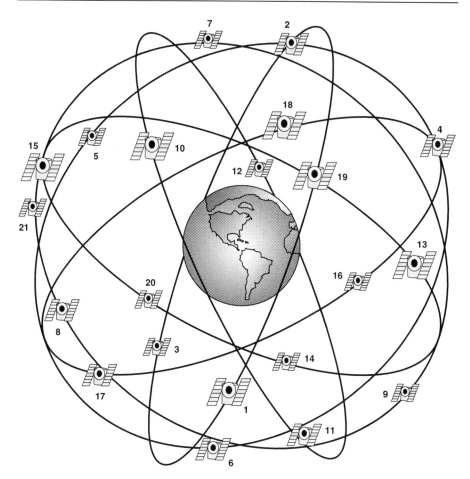

Figure 1-34 **The orbital configuration of the 21 GPS satellites**

Pseudo-Random Code

Each satellite transmits its position and precise time of transmission, and a separate signal used by the receiver to establish range from the satellite. This is achieved by the satellite carrier wave being modulated with a 50 bit/sec navigation message and a unique encoded signal known as a *pseudo-random code*. It repeats itself every millisecond and is used by the GPS receivers to recognise and track individual satellites for ranging purposes. There are two types of pseudo-random code providing for two types of services:

- A *precise positioning service* (PPS) accessed by the precision (P) code that is only available to authorised military users, and which permits extremely precise position resolution and full access to the total capacity of the satellite system.

• A *standard positioning service* (SPS) accessed by the *coarse acquisition* (C/A) code is made available for general civilian use. Previous to mid-2000, it had been a degraded signal having its accuracy reduced to the order of 100 m in lateral position and 140 m in altitude (95% of its capability) given a quality receiver. This deliberate degradation, known as *selective availability* (SA), has since been switched off and the accuracy of the system is greatly improved, now universally providing a precision that had only been available to the military.

As will be discussed later, a minimum of three satellites is required to determine a two-dimensional fix if altitude is known. For a three-dimensional fix, four are required. The navigation message contains information on satellite ephemeris, GPS time reference, clock corrections, almanac data and information on system maintenance status.

Control Segment

The controlling authority is the United States Department of Defense. By letter of agreement between the United States Government and ICAO, civilian access is permitted on a no-cost basis for the foreseeable future. It remains, in the end, a US military system but with an increasingly utilised civil component.

The control segment includes monitoring stations at various locations around the world, ground antennae and up-links, and a master station. The stations track all satellites in view passing information to a master control station which controls the satellites' clock and orbit states, and the currency of the navigation messages.

Satellites are frequently updated with new data for the compilation of the navigation messages. Assuming the current level of space vehicle technology, the planned life span of a GPS satellite is seven to eight years.

User Segment (The Receiver)

As previously mentioned, the receiver identifies each satellite by its unique pseudorandom code. It then starts to receive and process navigation information. Ephemeris data takes about 6 seconds to transmit, but almanac data takes about 13 seconds.

For this reason, almanac data is stored in the receiver's memory. During operation, almanac data in the receiver is changed on a continuous basis. On start-up, the receiver recalls the data that was last in memory on the preceding shutdown.

From this information, and the stored almanac data, the receiver determines which satellites should be in view and then searches for their respective codes. It then establishes ranges to the satellites, and by knowing their position, computes aircraft position, velocity and time. This process is known as *pseudoranging*.

Range determination is a simple matter of measuring the period between the time of transmission and the time of reception of each satellite C/A code and multiplying that time interval by the speed of light in free space. The GPS receiver in fact does this by emitting its own code at the same time as the satellite's, and uses it, and the time the signal from the satellite is received, to establish the time interval. Timing is critical. This is why time reference is provided by synchronised high-precision atomic clocks in the satellites.

Fixing Position

A three-dimensional position in space (position and altitude) is accomplished by the receiver determining where it must be located to satisfy the ranges to four or more appropriately positioned satellites. A two-dimensional fix requires only three satellites to be in view if altitude is known. The synchronisation of the receiver's time reference with that of the satellites' is vital.

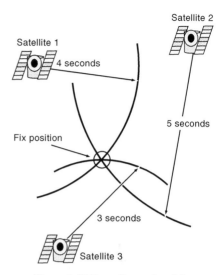

Figure 1-35 **Two-dimensional fix established with perfect timing**

Timing errors are detected and eliminated by the receiver's computer. Figure 1-35 shows a two-dimensional position established assuming the respective clocks are synchronised perfectly. However, if the receiver's clock is, say, one second fast, as is the case in figure 1-36, then the period between transmission and reception with respect to each of the three satellites interrogated will be sensed initially as taking one second longer. This will be represented as a gross error in all three ranges and thus, rather than producing a precise fix, will create a very large area anywhere within which the receiving aircraft could be positioned.

The receiver's computer senses this and immediately begins a trimming process until it arrives at an answer which allows all ranges to arrive at the one and only position possible. This process automatically eliminates the effect of receiver clock error for subsequent tracking and position fixing.

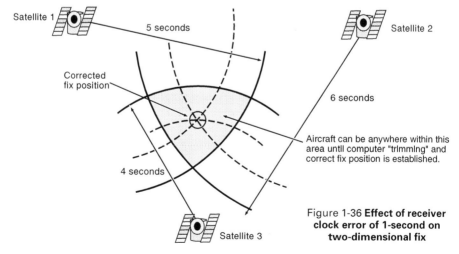

Figure 1-36 **Effect of receiver clock error of 1-second on two-dimensional fix**

Receiver Design

The capability of making range calculations to three, four or more satellites has an impact on the design, cost and accuracy of GPS receivers, i.e. whether they are single-channel receivers operating sequentially or the more expensive and accurate receivers providing multiple channels operating simultaneously. GPS receivers approved as a supplemental or primary means navigation aid have multiple channels and come under the provisions of an FAA Technical Service Order (TSO C129). IFR/primary navigation certification specifications for GPS equipment include a requirement for multiple receiver channels and a navigation integrity monitoring system known as *receiver autonomous integrity monitoring* (RAIM).

Receiver Autonomous Integrity Monitoring

Receiver autonomous integrity monitoring (RAIM) is a special receiver function which analyses the signal integrity and relative positions of all satellites which are in view, so as to select only the best four or more, isolating and discarding any anomalous satellites. At least five satellites must be in view to have RAIM find an anomalous situation, and six to actually isolate the unacceptable satellite.

When operating, RAIM ensures that the minimum acceptable level of navigation accuracy is provided for the particular phase of flight. In the process, it ensures that a potential error, known as

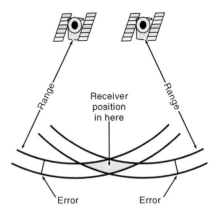

Figure 1-37 **Poor satellite geometry resulting in high PDOP**

the *position dilution of precision* (PDOP) or *geometric dilution of precision* (GDOP), is minimised. The PDOP depends on the position of the satellites relative to the fix. The value of PDOP determines the extent of range and position errors.

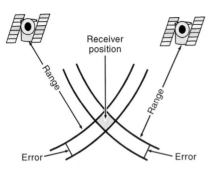

Figure 1-38 **Good satellite geometry resulting in low PDOP**

When the satellites are close together the tetrahedron formed covers a large area, and results in a high PDOP value (figure 1-37).

However, when the selected satellites are far apart, the area covered by the tetrahedron is much more compact, resulting in a lower PDOP value and therefore greater accuracy. A PDOP value of less than six is acceptable for en route operations. A value of less than three will be required for non-precision approaches.

Barometric Aiding

Barometric aiding is the process whereby the digital data of the pressure altimeter is used by the GPS receiver as, in effect, the range readout of a (simulated) additional satellite. It is only applicable when there are fewer than five satellites in view and RAIM alone cannot be effective. Barometric aiding provides additional back-up and RAIM capability, and therefore increases the navigation coverage of GPS.

Masking Function

The masking function in the GPS receiver software ensures that any satellites in view that lie below a fixed angle of elevation relative to the receiver are ignored. This is due to the range errors that will be generated because of the greater distances that their signals will have to travel through the ionosphere and troposphere to reach the receiver. The fixed angle stored in the receiver is known as the *mask angle*. In some receivers it is selected automatically by the receiver, depending on the strength of the transmitted signals at low angles of elevation, receiver sensitivity and acceptable low elevation errors. When fixed, it is typically set at 7.5° (figure 1-39).

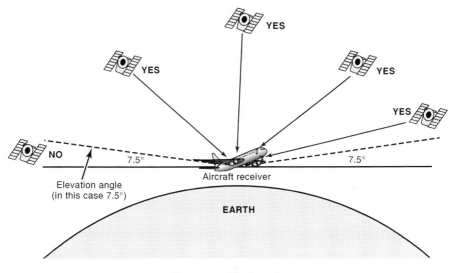

Figure 1-39 **Mask angle**

Receiver Displays

Displays for the pilot vary from one GPS unit to another. Flight planning data is usually entered via an appropriate keypad on a control display unit (CDU) or control panel. The usual navigation information – i.e. position, track, groundspeed, EET, and, with a TAS input, TAS and wind – is displayed. The unit must also be capable of showing satellite status, satellites in view and being tracked, the value of PDOP, RAIM status and signal quality.

Operating Modes

GPS receivers normally provide three modes of operation:
- navigation with RAIM;
- navigation (two- or three-dimensional) without RAIM; and
- loss of automatic navigation (annunciated as DR in some receivers).

Differential GPS

For GPS to be of any value as a primary navigation source for precision approach/ departure operations, an extremely high order of accuracy is required. Furthermore, the high accuracy standard should be available 99.99% of the time. Although the accuracy of the standard positioning service has improved greatly now that selective availability has been switched off, GPS itself, as yet, is not capable of providing that standard of accuracy or reliability – even when used with P-code access to the precise positioning service. However, with such accuracy having been previously denied to civilian users, enhancement methods were devised to increase the accuracy above the 95%.

An additional means of improving the accuracy for approaches is by using an enhancement known as *differential GPS* (DGPS). A GPS receiver is installed at a ground station located in the terminal area. The station compares the GPS computed position with the actual (surveyed) position of the station and determines the difference, if any, which of course would be common to other GPS receivers operating in the area. The station transmits the appropriate error correction signal by data link to the aircraft, with the result that an accuracy in the order +1 to −10 metres is achievable. Figure 1-40 shows the simplicity of the concept.

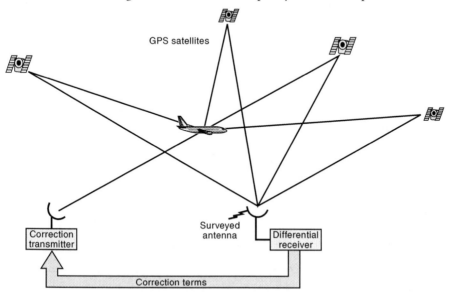

GPS satellites

Correction transmitter

Surveyed antenna

Differential receiver

Correction terms

Figure 1-40 **Differential GPS**

This enhanced standard of accuracy is acceptable for non-precision instrument procedures but not for precision approaches. However, much research and development work is being undertaken, particularly by the FAA, to improve the accuracy even further. In fact, the FAA have confidently predicted that Category II and III precision approach navigation capability using GPS will be possible by the year 2002.

As well as developing differential GPS for precision operations, a much wider network of ground receivers, with geostationary navigation receiver and communication satellites and relays, is being developed for en route operations. The enhanced network is known as a *wide area differential GPS* (WADGPS).

Note: It is important to point out that GPS (GNSS) is still a developing technology as far as civil air operations are concerned. At the time of publication, GPS equipment meeting system integrity standards and operated in accordance with specified limitations and procedures is approved as a primary means navigation aid for IFR en route operations, specified IFR arrival procedures and certain non-precision approaches.

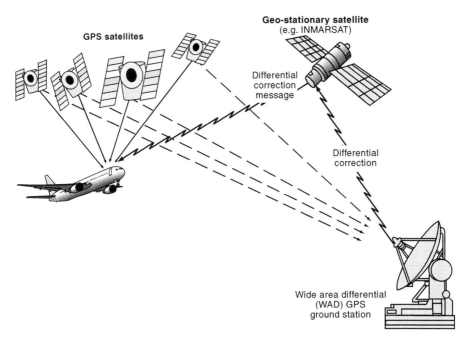

Figure 1-41 **Concept of Wide Area Differential GPS**

GPS Errors and Limitations

So far the errors we have covered are receiver clock error and how it is resolved, the effect of PDOP on position accuracy, the accuracy (or errors) associated with receiver design. However, there are other errors which can affect GPS performance that we must examine briefly.

Ephemeris Error

Ephemeris error is the error inherent in the data that defines the satellite's current position, which, in turn, is transmitted to the receiver.

Multi-Path Error

In a similar manner to the behaviour of signals used by other radio navigation systems, it is possible for some of the satellite signals, i.e. the pseudo-random code signals, to reach the receiver antenna after bouncing off the earth's surface, as well as directly from the satellite. Thus the receiver can receive signals from different directions. This can lead to distortion of the C/A and P-coded pulses which in turn can induce a ranging error.

Ionospheric Propagation Effects

The ionosphere, which we know is the band of charged particles which lies between 80 and 120 miles above the earth's surface, affects the propagation speed, and thus the travel time of the GPS signals, thereby degrading the accuracy of the position. Ionospheric propagation effects can be offset by the receiver with data received from several satellites.

Tropospheric Propagation Effects

The lower region of the atmosphere, the troposphere, contains significant amounts of water vapour. The effect of this is to slow down the satellite signals, inducing ranging errors. This tends to degrade accuracy. However, tropospheric propagation effects are minimised by appropriate compensation in the receiver.

Receiver Error

This is simply a small ranging error brought about by the difficulty of matching precisely the receiver's emitted digital pseudo-random code with that of the satellite's.

Interference

Because GPS (GNSS) signals are relatively weak, interference can cause significant degradation in navigation or, under certain conditions, complete loss of navigation capability. With more and more extensive use of all bands of the electromagnetic spectrum, the potential for interference problems has increased.

Interference to GPS operation can occur from electromagnetic influences on board the aircraft, e.g. insufficient shielding from VHF transmitters and other equipment, and from external sources, e.g. high-powered radar, TV and FM stations in the vicinity of the receiver. Minimisation techniques and shielding systems offset these problems. However, where GPS integrity is suspect, or there is a loss of RAIM, or interference is experienced, occurrences should be reported with comprehensive details of the circumstances so that the matter can be properly recorded and investigated. GPS system verification sheets are available for this purpose.

Tracking Accuracy and Collision Avoidance
Tracking accuracy should not really be classified as an error; rather it is a testament to the precision of GPS. Its very quality of precision track-keeping highlights the increased potential for collision, particularly head-on collision, with other GPS-equipped aircraft operating on the same track, or approaching the same turning point. As will be discussed later, this problem is not helped by the propensity of some pilots to have their heads always in the cockpit.

It is essential to maintain the required separation procedures and to maintain thorough lookout. However, this problem is considered to be so significant that there have been discussions in the US and Europe about the notion of requiring airline operators to flight plan with small track offsets as a safety measure in addition to ATS separation, when navigating by GPS.

GPS Errors

Sources of GPS Error	C/A Code	DGPS	P-code
Clock error	2 metres	0	2 metres
Ephemeris error	4 metres	0	4 metres
Ionospheric propagation error	8 metres	0	1 metre
Tropospheric propagation error	3 metres	0	3 metres
Receiver noise error	1 metre	1 metre	1 metre
Total pseudorange error [square root of sum of the squares of (a) to (f)]	10 metres	1 metre	6 metres
Maximum position dilution of precision (factor)	3	3	3
Total position error [(g) × (h) approximately]	29 metres	3 metres	17 metres

Figure 1-42 **Sources of GPS error**

Operations Without RAIM

If RAIM is lost, the accuracy of the system is considered unacceptable for both navigation and ATC separation purposes. Therefore, the following procedures apply:
- tracking must be closely checked against other navigation systems; and
- if in CTA, ATC must be advised when:
  - RAIM is lost for more than ten minutes, even if GPS is still providing position information; or
  - RAIM is not available when ATC request GPS distance, or if an ATC clearance or requirement, based on GPS distance, is imposed; or
  - the GPS receiver is in DR mode or loses navigation function for more than one minute; or
  - indicated displacement from track centreline exceeds 2 nm.

ATC may then adjust separation.

If valid position information is lost (2D and DR mode), or non-RAIM operation exceeds ten minutes, the GPS information is to be considered unreliable. Other navigation techniques should be used until RAIM is restored. If RAIM is restored, the appropriate ATS unit should be notified prior to using the GPS for primary navigation, to allow ATC to reassess the appropriate separation standards.

Human Factor Considerations

We know that in its fully operational mode, GPS has the capability of providing precise navigation information and guidance. However, like all forms of advanced computer technology, its capability, and therefore ultimately the safety of the flight, is governed largely by the manner in which the equipment is operated and monitored. This can be especially so when the equipment interfaces with an autopilot, flight director or advanced autoflight system.

Regardless of equipment design and ergonomic factors, ultimately, the pilot in command must shoulder the responsibility for the safe performance of any aviation system under his or her control.

Accident and incident history shows, however, that an alarming number of pilots tend to be too trusting when using advanced aviation technology. GPS operation is a case in point. There are some who are quite happy to allow the equipment to 'drive the ship' without questioning its accuracy, or applying basic airmanship principles such as cross-checking the steering data it provides. Put simply, some pilots operating equipment like GPS can and often do lose situational awareness, i.e. they allow themselves to drop out of the loop.

Generally, the tendency develops as the result of complacency since GPS seems to perform so admirably for most of the time. However, GPS is subject to a number of errors and limitations. It can also fail or, in some cases, lose its power supply However, there are also important human-factor-related errors and procedures applicable to GPS (and, for that matter, all automated systems) that need to be addressed.

Mode Error

Incorrect mode selection is a very significant problem, and one which has come more into prominence now that fully integrated autoflight systems and flight management systems are commonplace, e.g. a tracking error occurs because the autopilot controller has been left in HDG instead of NAV mode.

In the context of a GPS, it is not possible to discuss specific modes because of the differences in the design of the various receiver CDUs and control panels. However, suffice to say that, when a GPS mode or function switch is operated, a positive check should always be made to ensure that the action or function desired has actually been selected.

Data Entry Error

As the term implies, this is the error caused by inserting incorrect information, usually via the CDU or panel keyboard, into the GPS computer. It applies to all RNAV systems and can have catastrophic consequences. In the overwhelming majority of cases, incorrect waypoint position coordinates are inserted, i.e. a human error caused by either inattention, unfamiliarity, or a simple typographical error when transferring data from a navigation chart to the GPS.

However, ergonomic factors can contribute to the problem, e.g. some GPS receivers have complicated CDU keyboards or control panels, or alphanumeric displays which are difficult to read. Also, it is not unknown for databases to carry mistakes, either through transcription errors by the provider or incorrect navigation data being supplied by the relevant aeronautical information service – all the more reason for using only current databases, checking NOTAMs and adopting rigid data validation procedures.

Data Validation and Cross-Checking

Validation and cross-checking procedures are designed to detect data entry errors and, in the broader sense, confirm GPS reliability and accuracy by comparing the navigation output with other navigation sources. The following procedures are recommended:

- All data entered, either manually or from a database, should be checked carefully by the pilot against the relevant and current navigation chart. This check should include a second crew member in the case of a multi-crew operation.
- To reduce the chance of data entry error, navigation data should be derived from a current database which cannot be modified by the crew.
- Only data from a validated, current database should be used for navigation below LSALT.
- All GPS generated tracks and distances of the flight plan (waypoint string) should be checked against the current chart and flight plan for accuracy before flight, and at any time in flight prior to embarking on an amended route, e.g. prior to 'direct-to' tracking or a diversion to an alternate, i.e. a check for reasonableness should be carried out.
- If the navigation data is derived from a database, the database should be checked to ensure that it remains current for the duration of the flight.

- Radio navigation aids, other RNAV systems if fitted, and where appropriate DR and visual navigation techniques should be used to cross-check and backup the GPS navigation data (keep it honest).
- When within coverage of conventional radio navigation aids, the navigation performance of the GPS should be checked to ensure that track is maintained within the tolerances as defined for the most accurate aid being received. If there is any discrepancy, the navigation information provided by the radio navigation aids must take precedence.

Automation-Induced Complacency

Automation-induced complacency is a man-machine interface problem which we have already touched on. It is one which could be characterised by the question, *'Who's in charge, Captain?'* It is a condition whereby pilots become complacent and overdependent on the automatic features of the aircraft. It has come more into prominence in recent years with the advent of glass cockpit aircraft with fully integrated automatic systems.

It is usually an insidious process whereby, over time, complacency sets in – the magic machinery is really in control and not the pilot. The pilot is usually blissfully unaware of what is really going on. It is a condition which is highly relevant to GPS operators.

As mentioned previously, there is a tendency for pilots to drop out of the loop. They allow the machine, in this case the GPS, to work on its own without considering its limitations or potential to get things awfully wrong. The effects of automation-induced complacency can be particularly significant when the cockpit workload is high. There seems to be a reluctance to intervene and take control away from the machinery even when something is obviously not going according to expectations.

Pilots lose sight of the fact that GPS is only a tool and cannot think for itself. It works well for most of the time, albeit within defined limitations and subject to certain errors. However, it needs to be set up correctly, monitored continuously, and its data validated by appropriate cross-checks and backup procedures. Like any other aviation technology, GPS can occasionally let you down. Some of the cockpit disciplines necessary to combat the problem have already been discussed. Here are a few more tips, which are relevant to GPS operation as well as the operation of other automatic systems:

- Know exactly what the system's operating modes, limitations and errors are.
- Be clear in your mind beforehand what you wish the system to do.
- Be suspicious. Look for errors. Always double-check data output against data input and against other data sources.
- Always know what the equipment is doing. Manage it. Don't let it manage you.
- Reject the assistance of a system that is not performing to your expectations or which is providing conflicting information. Either resolve the ambiguity properly, or ignore the system altogether.
- Arrange your cockpit priorities. Flying the aircraft must always come first.

Keep in the loop. Stay in command even if you delegate control.

Non-Standardisation of GPS/Pilot Interface

Non-standardisation of GPS keyboards or control panels, functions and displays is a factor which significantly increases the potential for pilots to make errors. The proliferation of GPS types contributes to the problem, making it difficult for pilots to transfer from one type to another. Hence the regulatory requirement for GPS type training for IFR pilots. Clearly, some form of standard design code for controls and displays of advanced avionics would be desirable, but is unlikely to be realised. With some GPS receivers, it would appear that marketing and engineering considerations have taken precedence over the operating needs of the user. What looks neat and nice in the glossy brochures can end up having many shortcomings when situated in an aircraft cockpit, i.e. ergonomic (man-machine interface) considerations have not been properly addressed. Some GPS receivers are not user friendly.

A further important factor is the placement of the equipment in the cockpit. Poor design combined with poor placement can make it extremely difficult for pilots to interface with the equipment with confidence. Here are a few of the considerations that are causing concern:

Size

As is the trend in mobile telephone and computer markets, we are told by the marketers that small is good, tiny is better. Consequently, some GPS equipment is unsuitable for aircraft. Tiny keyboards and miniature displays in a cockpit might look neat but are quite impractical, contributing in a large measure to data entry error.

Control Knobs and Switches

This is a significant area of non-standardisation. There is also considerable variation in the types of knobs and switches, their size, the direction in which they operate and their functions. To aggravate the problem, there is a growing trend towards providing multi-functional controls in the interests of neatness and compactness, e.g. providing knobs which control more than one function, depending on the mode selected. The trade-off is usually added complexity. Therefore, the potential for mistakes increases correspondingly, especially when workload is high. A GPS receiver with simple, unambiguous controls and switches is clearly the best choice, all else being equal.

Data Display

The problems here have already been touched on. Screen size can be critical, particularly having regard to the placement of the unit in the cockpit. However, the size and definition of characters and symbols are also important issues. The data must be clearly discernible within the general cockpit scan, but not too prominent so as to be a distraction diverting the pilot's attention from the primary task of flying the aircraft. Generally, with monochrome displays, CRTs are superior to liquid crystal, especially under varying cockpit light conditions. However, the technology in this area is improving rapidly and colour displays are becoming more common, highlighting a need for standard colour codes as well as standard symbology.

Position In the Cockpit

This consideration can be influenced by the previous three. Ideally, the GPS should be located within the NAV/COM group on the main instrument panel or centre pedestal panel, depending on the aircraft type and the information displayed, e.g. some receivers can display a CDI on the data screen. The position must ensure that parallax errors and potential physiological effects, such as spatial disorientation, are avoided.

Human Information Processing and Situational Awareness

Human information processing and situational awareness are complex human behavioural issues which have challenged academics, psychologists, and human factor experts over the years. It is extremely relevant to GPS operation and monitoring. Literally hundreds of technical papers, study references and books have been written on these matters. Some of these are available in technical libraries for the keen minded to pursue. For our purposes, a brief and simple overview will suffice.

Information Processing

The human brain can be likened to an information processor or computer. The healthy brain is designed to act logically to incoming stimuli, and like the computer, follows a programmed path to a programmed result (often for pilots, this means a decision).

The process can be influenced by past experiences, training and knowledge (stored data). Under certain circumstances, these influences can be very compelling indeed.

Any stimuli first have to be sensed by one or more of our sensory organs, e.g. sight, hearing, touch, smell, muscular, etc. Our interpretation of what is sensed will either be related directly to the stimuli, or more often than not, modified significantly by past experiences and knowledge, e.g. everyone has experienced an odd sensation of stepping up or down an escalator which isn't working; and most of us understand that the command 'right engine' means the one on the right, not the one that isn't wrong!

The brain generally is a serial processor, or single-channel system, in which information passes through sequentially. In other words, we cannot concentrate on more than one thing at a time. This is why we have in the cockpit, information displays, warning and caution systems, and lights and bells, to shift our attention immediately should the need arise.

The final part of the process is to convert the stimuli that have been interpreted (and modified) into a decision, i.e. some kind of action. The important consideration here is that the quality or correctness of the decision will depend to a great extent on the amount of information obtained (the number of stimuli) and the extent to which past knowledge and experience has been used in making it. Also, the implementation of the decision, i.e. the action, requires the pilot to adopt the correct response and, importantly, to perceive and interpret the feedback to validate the process which led to the decision and action in the first place.

Accident statistics show how easy it can be for pilots to rush into decisions based on insufficient information. There is also a condition known as *false hypothesis* whereby in relation to processing stimuli, the pilot's past knowledge and experience become so dominant that a high expectancy of outcome is raised (is assumed).

Information is either incomplete or misinterpreted and, as a result, false conclusions are drawn. For example, a pilot reports that a piston engine aircraft's cruise performance is down by around 10 kt. The CHTs are low, therefore the engines must be running rich, affecting power. But, after landing the cowl gill C/B is found popped. Both cowls had been fully open for the entire flight, causing extra drag, low CHTs and lower than expected cruise performance. The message from this simple example is that more information should have been sought. Therefore the keyword in the whole process is *information*. To gain information, the pilot must be in a situation to receive it. This means that the pilot must be situationally aware.

Situational Awareness

Situational awareness can be described as the degree to which a pilot is conscious of the constituents which make up the environment in which she or he is operating. Put simply, it characterises how closely one is in touch with what is going on. It requires conscious effort and attention, i.e. the pilot must expend time and energy in order to stay in touch, and it is fundamental to the information-processing mechanism previously described.

It is an orderly process, and in the context of aircraft operations, includes the disciplines of system monitoring, regular checks, cross-checks and procedures, to ensure that the pilot or crew is completely aware of how the aircraft and its systems are performing, the factors which influence its operation, e.g. weather, traffic and ATC, and whether operations are proceeding in accordance with plans.

Compulsive Fiddling

Since we are examining human factor issues, it is appropriate to have a final word about a disease with which many pilots are afflicted. It is called *compulsive fiddling*. It is especially common whenever new technology is introduced into the cockpit. The attraction to fiddle with the new equipment is, for some, overwhelming. The symptoms include excessive tapping, switching and adjusting, usually with the pilot's head down and eyes focused on the new toy and little regard for how the aircraft is performing or what is happening in the real world outside the cockpit. As we have mentioned, the potential for collision has increased markedly with the advent of GPS. Clearly, compulsive fiddling is a danger that must be recognised and avoided. The importance of maintaining situational awareness when operating GPS cannot be overemphasised.

Authorisation and Documentation

Pilot Training

It is a requirement that prior to operating GPS equipment for primary navigation, the pilot must undertake training with an approved organisation and in accordance with a syllabus set down in the CAOs. Satisfactory completion of the course and competence must be demonstrated and certified in the pilot's logbook by an approved person (FOI, or chief pilot, or CFI of the organisation or their representative).

Aircraft Equipment

Under current policies, GPS receivers approved for IFR primary navigation purposes must have the US FAA TSO C-129 authorisation or its approved equivalent. Installation must meet airworthiness requirements, demonstrate accuracy and reliability, and must include the connection of the automatic barometric aiding function.

Automatic Dependent Surveillance

Along with the advancements in GNSS has been the development of automatic dependent surveillance. Automatic dependent surveillance (ADS) is simply a system whereby an aircraft's current GPS position can be transmitted automatically and on a continuous basis by data link, either directly or via communication satellites to the relevant air traffic service centre. The aim is that the flight crew will no longer be required to report position. The aircraft's position will be displayed in real time and on a continuous basis on a controller's screen.

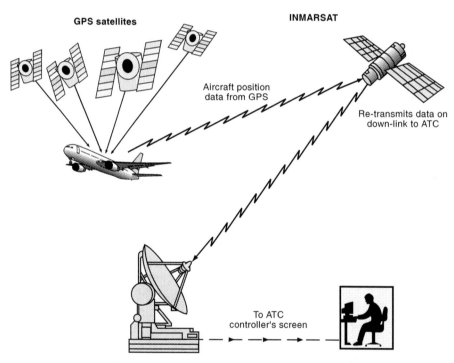

Figure 1-43 **Automatic dependent surveillance**

With appropriate development, this technology has even been suggested as a substitute for radar. Unlike other long-range navigation systems, use of GPS for ADS will allow significantly reduced separation standards for participating aircraft without compromising safety. This in turn will permit greater optimisation of the airspace and airways, resulting in very substantial fuel savings. Also, more aircraft will be able to use the airspace.

Geodetic Considerations

We know that the earth resembles an oblate spheroid (flattened sphere). However, this is too gross an approximation for precision mapping purposes since the earth has a much more irregular shape. In other words, the shape of the earth at a particular locality will differ somewhat from the shape of the earth at another. Consequently, as shown in figure 1-44, it is common practice to adopt a local ellipsoid (mathematical model) which provides the closest approximation to the shape of the earth, or geoid, over the particular area of interest.

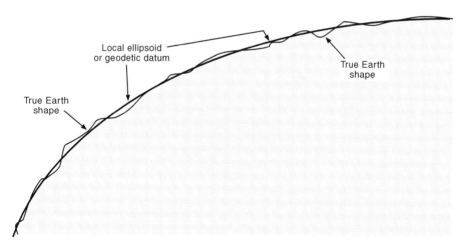

Figure 1-44 **In mapping, It is common practice to use a local ellipsoid**

GPS receivers and data banks use a global datum known as World Geodetic System (WGS) 84. Glonass uses a Russian datum known as Parameters of the Earth (PE) 90.

The problem is that the coordinates for a position from one datum, e.g. the touchdown point on the centreline of a runway, on an aeronautical chart could result in a different position using a map based on a different geodetic datum. For example, the runway touchdown point coordinates extracted from, say, an aerodrome chart might in fact represent the position of an adjacent taxiway if keyed into the GPS (WGS 84 database). The differences can be significant, with errors as high as hundreds of metres.

GPS (GNSS) is now an international navigation reference. ICAO has formally adopt the WGS 84 geodetic datum for its aeronautical charts and data banks.

Chapter 2

Flight Instrument Systems

Before discussing modern flight instrument systems, we need to have a brief discussion about the principles and development of such systems. This will help in understanding the complexities of fully integrated automatic flight control systems, and what we nowadays refer to as the *glass cockpit*.

Principles and Development

Simple Flight Instruments

Simple instrument panels, such as that shown in figure 2-1, give basic information about aircraft attitude, heading, airspeed, altitude, vertical speed, and perhaps relative bearings from radio beacons. These instruments are subject to error, and are vulnerable to failure, both of the power supply (usually suction) and of the sensing system (e.g. the pilot).

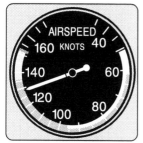

Figure 2-1 **Simple flight instruments**

Air Data Instruments

The air data instruments – the altimeter, the airspeed indicator and the vertical speed indicator – use pitot and static pressure fed directly to the instrument, with individual bellows responding to the changes in pressure, driving the indicating needles through suitable systems of cranks and levers. However, to meet the demands of modern aircraft performance, more reliable and accurate measurement and display of air data is required, and this has led to the development of the *air data computer* (ADC) which will be described in this chapter.

Attitude Indicator

Attitude indicators of the simple type shown in figure 2-1 are prone to gross errors when subjected to acceleration, particularly during and immediately after take-off. The necessity to keep the instrument small, so that it will fit into the limited space available on the instrument panel, imposes limits on the gimbal support system for the vertical gyro, which could topple if the pitch and roll limits were exceeded.

The introduction of electrically driven gyros provided higher gyro rpm, a more stable reference and allowed for duplicated power supplies, but there are still problems with the gyro installation within the instrument case. The development of remote vertical gyros in an installation elsewhere in the aircraft, transmitting an accurate vertical reference to an indicator on the instrument panel, has solved most of these problems.

Heading Indicators

The directional gyro (DG) is particularly error prone and requires frequent alignment with the magnetic compass, which itself is also subject to errors. To improve reliability, electrically driven gyro compasses were developed. This gyro, however, is still contained in the instrument case, and it is still necessary to synchronise the indicator with the magnetic compass. This should only be attempted with the wings level, and in unaccelerated flight. What is needed is some way of removing the heading reference system from the cockpit environment, i.e. a remote sensing system, together with a means of supplying this reference to a gyro-stabilised platform. This would automatically ensure that the heading indicator is continuously synchronised to the magnetic heading reference, and at the same time, provide a stable indication to the pilot. It was this need to transfer data from a remote source to a display in the cockpit that led to the development and use of synchronous data transmission systems.

Synchronous Data Transmission Systems

A simple synchronous data transmission system – *synchro* or *selsyn* system as it is generally known – consists of two matching elements, a transmitter and a receiver, each consisting of a coil (the rotor) mounted within a stator core of three coils at 120° to each other. When an alternating current is applied to both rotors, an alternating magnetic flux will be set up in the respective stator segments, which are wired to each other, as shown in figure 2-2.

When the rotors, R1 and R2, are aligned with each other, with respect to their stators, S1 and S2, the voltages induced in each stator will be equal and opposite, so that no current will flow between the stators. If R1 is turned, the voltages induced in the stators will be out of balance, and current will flow between the transmitter and receiver stators. This current can be used, after suitable amplification, and sensing of direction of current flow, to rotate the receiver rotor R2 until the voltages are balanced and realignment between R1 and R2 is achieved. By attaching the transmitter to a remote sensor, and the receiver to the moving part of a flight instrument, say the pointer, the position or attitude of the sensor can be displayed in the cockpit.

Synchro systems are used to transfer data from remote vertical gyros, to provide attitude information to an attitude indicator. A similar synchro system is used to transfer data from remote magnetic heading sensors to a gyro-stabilised platform and then to a heading display in the cockpit.

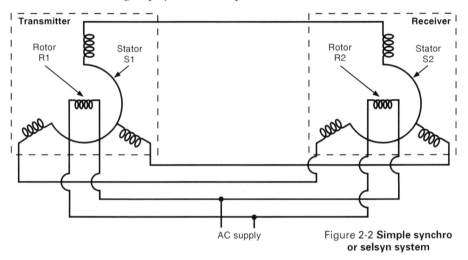

AC supply

Figure 2-2 **Simple synchro or selsyn system**

Air Data Computer

While the simple air data instruments receive pitot and static pressures directly, the more advanced instruments are driven by the outputs from an air data computer (ADC). The ADC takes inputs from the pitot and static pressure sources, converts them to electrical signals, and then transmits them via a data bus to the various flight instruments. In addition, input from the outside air temperature probe is used to enable the true airspeed to be calculated. In some later models of ADC, angle of attack (α) sensor inputs are also provided. Normally, there will be two ADCs (to provide redundancy), the pilot being able to switch to the output of the other ADC. Outputs from the ADC go to the altimeters, VSI, and ASI/Mach-meter, as shown in figure 2-3.

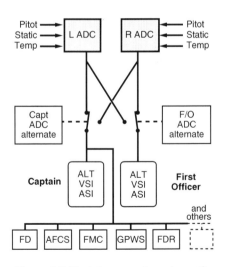

Figure 2-3 **Air data computer schematic**

In addition, outputs are fed to such systems as the flight director (FD), automatic flight control system (AFCS), flight management computer (FMC), ground proximity warning system (GPWS), the flight data recorder (FDR). A typical air data system is shown in schematic form in figure 2-4.

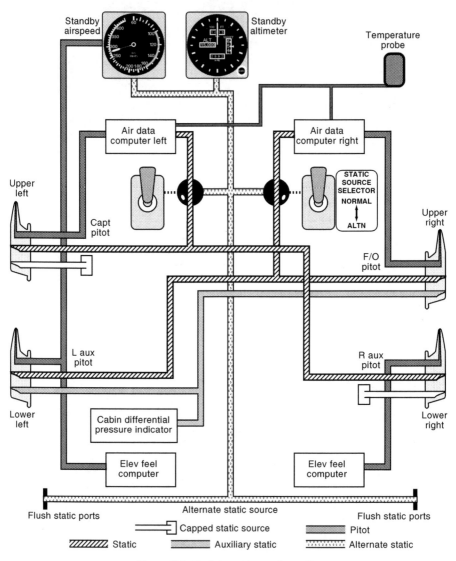

Figure 2-4 **Air data system schematic**

Note the direct supply of pitot and static pressure to the standby airspeed indicator and altimeter. There is also a provision to switch static sources from normal to alternate. The capped static sources are redundant to allow standardisation of the pitot heads.

Conventional Modern Flight Instruments

As a result of the developments in data transmission systems and air data computers, modern flight instruments became both more accurate and reliable. A typical instrument panel such as can be found on early model transport aeroplanes like the B737-200 and B747-200, as well as some corporate jets like the older Citations and Learjets, is shown in figure 2-5.

The flight instrument display depicts the basic six instruments, plus some peripheral indicators such as DME, radio altimeter, and mode annunciators. Also present on the captain's display will be a clock, an altitude alert control, an instrument comparator, and standby instruments such as a self-contained attitude indicator and pneumatic altimeter. The attitude and the heading indicators are electrically driven by signals from remote sources, while the airspeed indicator, the altimeter and the vertical speed indicator are electrically driven by signals from the air data computer.

Power sources for the pilot's instruments vary from type to type, but the instrument buses always have alternative power supplies, either automatically or manually selected. Failures of power supply or data sensing are typically shown by a flag across the display, or by blanking of the display, as described later when discussing the instruments in more detail.

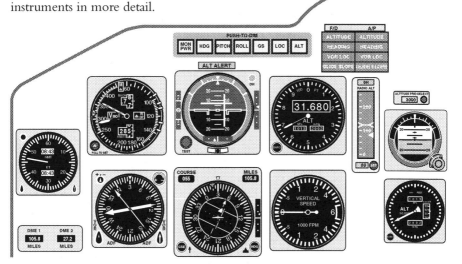

Figure 2-5 **Conventional flight instrument panel**

Magnetic Heading Reference Systems (MHRS)

In the development of an improved heading reference system, the sensing element (flux detector) was positioned in an area comparatively free from unwanted magnetic influences, usually a wingtip or on top of the aircraft fin.

The output from this remote heading sensor was fed to a compass card mounted on the instrument panel, though later systems have a gyro-stabilised platform remote from the cockpit instrument.

Detector System

A typical remote heading reference system uses an inductive element to sense (detect) the aircraft heading with respect to the earth's magnetic field, in the form of voltage changes induced within the detector that then can be transmitted via a synchro system to a receiver within a heading indicator.

The sensing element, which we call a *flux valve,* consists of a pendulous element which is mounted horizontally, with three segments (spokes) forming a wheel. At the hub is a coil which, when fed with an alternating current, will excite magnetic flux in the spokes. The legs of the spokes carry coils to pick off the induced flux. The induced flux in a particular spoke will be affected by its orientation within the earth's magnetic field; any difference in flux can be detected and used to drive a heading indicator (see figure 2-6) using a synchro.

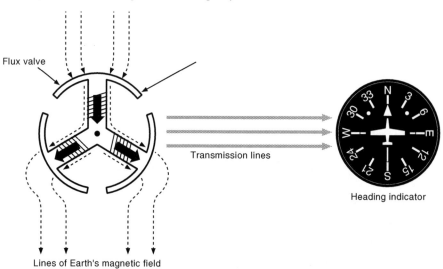

Figure 2-6 **Simple remote heading reference system**

The flux valve can be likened to the transmitter of the simple synchro system, where the transmitter rotor field is represented by the horizontal component of the earth's magnetic field. The voltage induced in the flux valve pick-off coils 1, 2 and 3 causes a current to flow along the transmitter lines to the receiver stator (figure 2-7).

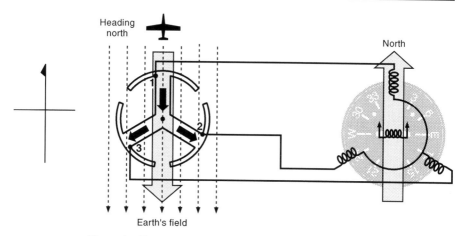

Figure 2-7 **Receiver rotor aligned by the flux valve currents**

A field is set up across the receiver stator, which can be regarded as the heading indicator, in a direction determined by the resolution of the current flowing in each of the stator coils.

When the aircraft alters heading, the direction of the induced field in the flux valve will change. The rotor will follow this change, and hence the heading indicator needle will follow the aircraft heading change, until the turn stops. At this time, the rotor will be realigned with the current flow from the flux valve (figure 2-8) and the heading indicator will be synchronised.

Because the flux valve is a pendulous system, it is subject to acceleration and turning errors. The final stage in the development of a more reliable and accurate heading reference system was to integrate the heading information from the flux valve with the directional properties of a gyroscope, thus gaining the benefits of both and minimising the individual errors.

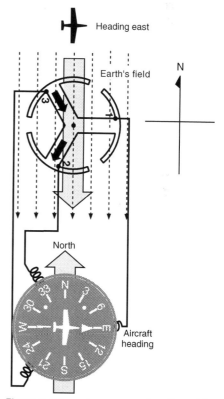

Figure 2-8 **Aeroplane on new heading with rotor realigned with field from flux valve**

Monitored Gyro-Heading System

Essentially, a monitored gyro system consists of a detector unit, a slaving amplifier, a directional gyro, and a heading indicator connected in a closed loop with control synchros to produce error signals that can be amplified and used to precess the directional gyro until it is aligned to the detector.

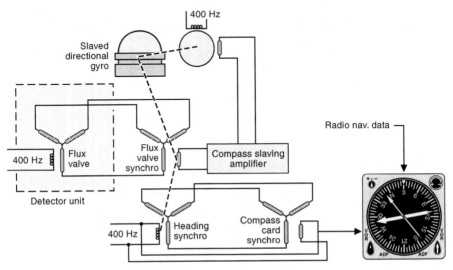

Figure 2-9 **Schematic of a monitored gyro system**

In early systems, the gyro was contained within the instrument case, while more modern systems have the gyro mounted remotely with a synchro system to transmit the data to the cockpit instrument.

The heading of the aircraft is normally shown by a card rotating below a fixed index, rather than a needle against a fixed card. It is also usual to input navigation data from NDB and VOR beacons, with the combined data displayed on the radio magnetic indicator (RMI).

Radio Magnetic Indicator

The radio magnetic indicator (RMI), shown at figure 2-10, receives heading data from its associated remotely mounted heading detector (flux valve), the compass card rotating to show current heading against the lubber line at the 12 o'clock position.

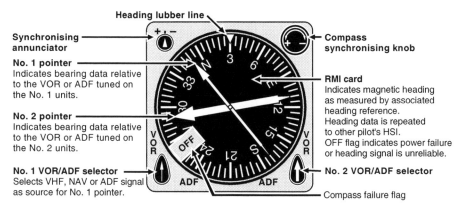

Heading lubber line

Synchronising annunciator

No. 1 pointer
Indicates bearing data relative to the VOR or ADF tuned on the No. 1 units.

No. 2 pointer
Indicates bearing data relative to the VOR or ADF tuned on the No. 2 units.

No. 1 VOR/ADF selector
Selects VHF, NAV or ADF signal as source for No. 1 pointer.

Compass synchronising knob

RMI card
Indicates magnetic heading as measured by associated heading reference. Heading data is repeated to other pilot's HSI. OFF flag indicates power failure or heading signal is unreliable.

No. 2 VOR/ADF selector

Compass failure flag

Figure 2-10 **Radio magnetic indicator**

The RMI heading value (i.e. compass card orientation) is relayed, or *bootstrapped*, to the other pilot's horizontal situation indicator (HSI), described below.

It is customary to wire the heading references and displays as shown in figure 2-11, where heading reference 1 drives the first officer's RMI, which then bootstraps the data to the captain's HSI. Similarly the captain's RMI receives heading data from reference 2, and bootstraps this to the first officer's HSI. By doing this, each pilot is presented with two independent heading references.

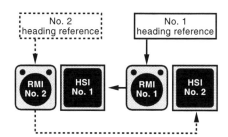

Figure 2-11 **Heading reference interface schematic**

In addition to heading, the RMI displays the magnetic bearing to VOR or NDB stations. The head of the bearing pointer, when read against the compass card, shows the direction to fly to reach the ground station, while the tail of the pointer shows the bearing, or the radial, of the aeroplane from the selected navigation aid. There are normally two VHF NAV and two ADF sets of equipment fitted – the single-bar pointer responding to VHF NAV1 and ADF1, while the double-bar pointer responds to VHF NAV2 and ADF2. By using the selector knobs, the pilot can interrogate each unit.

On initial power-up, the RMI may not be correctly aligned, and its synchronising mechanism is quite slow, so the RMI has a compass-synchronising knob that can be used manually to turn the compass card until it is correctly aligned indicated by the synchronising annunciator centring and by noting that the RMI heading agrees with the standby magnetic compass.

Note: As the synchronising knob is used to turn the RMI compass card, the associated HSI, on the other pilot's panel, will also turn.

Horizontal Situation Indicator

The horizontal situation indicator (HSI), depicted in figure 2-12, derives its name from the fact that its display represents a plan view of the aeroplane's situation with regard to magnetic heading, and its relationship to, and deviation from, a selected VOR/ILS course, track or radial. A display of DME distance is also provided.

The magnetic heading information is provided from a remote sensor, and boot-strapped by a synchro transmission from the other pilot's RMI. By positioning the selected heading bug to the desired heading, an error signal is generated, which commands the flight director and/or autopilot, when engaged, to acquire the selected heading.

The course setting knob (CSE) is used to position the course needle to the desired VOR/ILS course. There is also a digital readout of the selected course. The course deviation indicator (CDI) turns with the course needle, and shows any deviation of the aeroplane from the selected course.

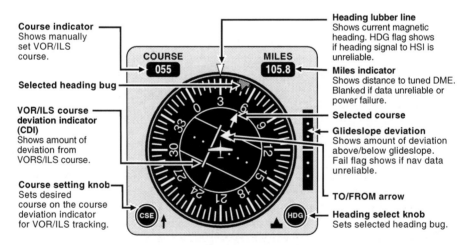

Figure 2-12 **A horizontal situation indicator**

In VOR tracking mode, a to/from arrow shows whether the aeroplane is flying towards or away from the VOR station.

In figure 2-12, the aircraft is heading 030°M, has a selected heading of 050°M, and the selected course of 055°M, which is displaced 1 dot to the left of the aircraft. As the course deviation reduces, the pilot should turn right onto the selected heading of 050°M to intercept the centreline (nil wind).

In the glideslope deviation indicator on the right of the instrument, the aircraft is represented by the centre index mark, and the relative position of the glideslope is shown by the moving pointer. In this case, the glideslope deviation indication shows the aircraft is 1½ dots below the glideslope.

Air Data Instruments

Mach/Airspeed Indicator (or ASI/Machmeter)

The Mach/airspeed indicator (MASI), shown at figure 2-13, combines the functions of both a conventional airspeed indicator and Machmeter. The instrument receives its information from its associated air data computer, and presents airspeed using a single needle, and both Mach number and airspeed in digital displays. The striped needle (barber's pole) shows the maximum permitted airspeed (V_{MO}).

The Mach display is normally blanked out at low Mach numbers, typically below M 0.4. The four bugs mounted on the external face of the instrument are manually positioned, and are used to remind the pilot of various significant speeds, such as V_1, V_2, or V_{REF}.

The command airspeed knob sets the airspeed bug to which the autothrottle will respond when engaged. This command airspeed is also fed to the air data computer, to govern the fast/slow display on the attitude indicator. If the ADC fails, the digital readouts of Mach no. and airspeed will be covered by a flag, and the airspeed pointer will read zero.

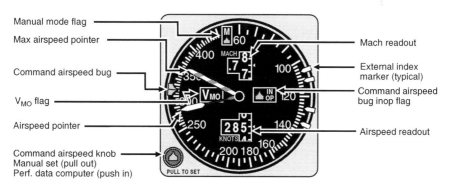

Figure 2-13 **Mach/airspeed indicator**

Altimeter

The electric servo altimeter is driven by its associated air data computer. The display has both a needle and a digital readout, the needle turning once per thousand feet, as shown in figure 2-14. The digital display is blanked if ADC information is unreliable, or if power is lost. Where the captain has an (electric) servo altimeter, then either the other pilot's altimeter must be an altimeter driven directly by static pressure, or a standby pressure altimeter must be provided.

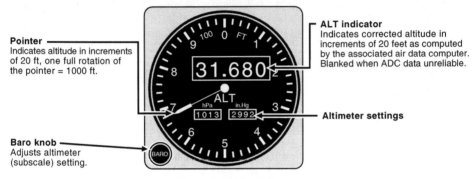

Pointer
Indicates altitude in increments of 20 ft, one full rotation of the pointer = 1000 ft.

ALT indicator
Indicates corrected altitude in increments of 20 feet as computed by the associated air data computer. Blanked when ADC data unreliable.

Altimeter settings

Baro knob
Adjusts altimeter (subscale) setting.

Figure 2-14 **The altimeter**

These pressure instruments are usually fitted with a motor-driven vibrator to reduce the effects of *hysteresis* (error due to lag) during rapid changes in height such as an emergency descent. Under these conditions the indicated altitude will lag behind the correct value, and the aircraft will be lower than the altimeter reading.

Vertical Speed Indicator

The vertical speed indicator (VSI) receives its information from its associated air data computer, and may show an off flag if the data is unreliable or if power is lost. Modern VSIs, called *instantaneous VSIs,* are fitted with a mechanism to improve response.

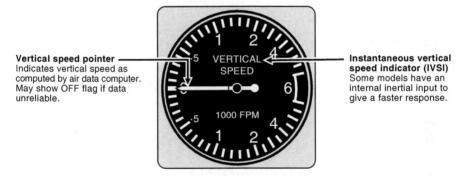

Vertical speed pointer
Indicates vertical speed as computed by air data computer. May show OFF flag if data unreliable.

Instantaneous vertical speed indicator (IVSI)
Some models have an internal inertial input to give a faster response.

Figure 2-15 **The vertical speed indicator**

Altitude Alerting System

Jet aircraft, with very high rates of climb and descent, gave rise to a number of altitude 'busts', where the pilot failed to anticipate level-out or forgot the assigned altitude. A simple reminder of desired altitude was introduced to the cockpit in the form of a manually set digital display. Later versions are linked by synchros to the air data system, and give audio and visual warning as the selected altitude is approached.

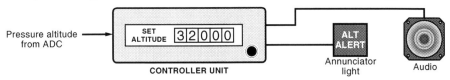

Figure 2-16 **Typical altitude alerting system**

The lead time on the warning may be a function of vertical speed. The latest systems also offer an alert if the aircraft deviates from the selected altitude. Most operators have crew procedures to enhance altitude awareness.

Altitude Alert

The altitude alert light (ALT ALERT), which is shown above the attitude indicator on the instrument panel in figure 2-5, is controlled by the altitude preselector. The light illuminates as the aeroplane approaches the selected altitude (typically within ±900 ft when climbing or descending), and goes out when within a predetermined limit, typically ±300 ft of the target altitude, as shown in figure 2-17.

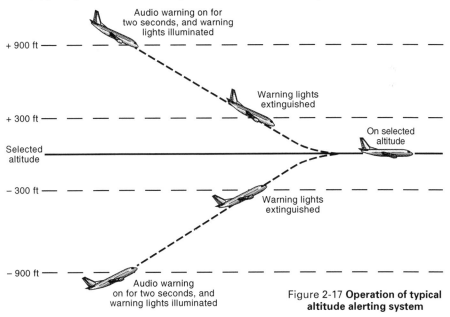

Figure 2-17 **Operation of typical altitude alerting system**

Once the selected altitude has been captured, the alert light will illuminate if there is an altitude deviation from the selected altitude, again typically ±300 ft, as shown in figure 2-18. The light may be accompanied by a warning tone.

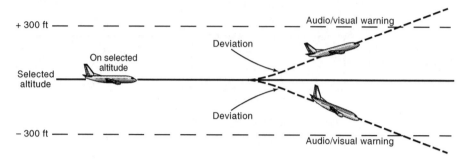

Figure 2-18 **Typical altitude alerting system showing aircraft deviating from the selected altitude**

Attitude Indicators

Electric Attitude Indicator

Further development of the attitude indicator led to the introduction of electric attitude indicators that, although still sensitive to earth's gravity, had reduced sensitivity to acceleration and turning errors. These used a gimbal system that offered 360° freedom in pitch and roll, together with pitch attitude presentation using a roller blind, usually suitably coloured to show blue sky (nose up) and brown earth (nose down). The pitch scale was greatly expanded, particularly in the pitch attitudes in the range ±20°. The roll attitude was shown against a bank angle scale, usually restricted to bank angles of 60° for transport aircraft.

> **Note:** In some presentations, the bank pointer is at the bottom of the display and may be called a ground pointer, which shows the angle and direction of bank. In presentations where the pointer is at the top of the scale, the sky pointer does not show the direction of the turn, only the amount of bank. The attitude indicator shown at figure 2-19 shows the aircraft in a left turn, with 15° of bank and about 6° nose down.

The instrument also has a fast-erect facility to assist with rapid alignment when power is first applied to the instrument. When the fast erect is used, usually by pulling the knob, the gimbal cage is mechanically forced into alignment with the airframe. Although intended for use on the ground, the fast-erect mode can be used in the air, but great care must be taken to ensure there is level unaccelerated flight at the time, or a false attitude will result. There is also a pitch-adjust knob to mechanically adjust the zero-pitch reference.

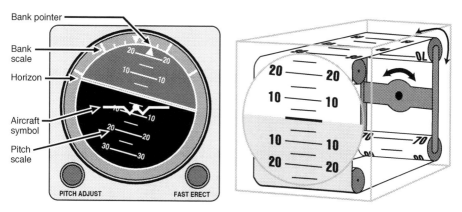

Bank pointer
Bank scale
Horizon
Aircraft symbol
Pitch scale
PITCH ADJUST   FAST ERECT

Figure 2-19 **Simple electric attitude indicator and roller blind schematic**

Remote Vertical Gyros

Similar to the remote heading reference systems, the attitude indicators in modern transport aircraft are driven by a number of remotely mounted vertical gyros (VGs), which use synchro systems to transmit attitude information to cockpit displays.

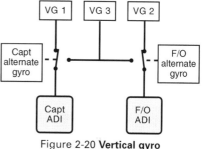

Figure 2-20 **Vertical gyro interface schematic**

The systems provide attitude data to both pilots, the flight director computer(s) and the autopilot computer(s). The remote vertical gyros are often positioned in an electronics bay, where sufficient cooling can be provided. A simplified arrangement is shown in figure 2-20.

To provide redundancy, each pilot's attitude director indicator (ADI) is driven by its associated VG, with an alternative attitude reference available to either pilot.

Normally, all VGs are powered up and running, and are able to supply attitude information immediately upon selection. Note that both pilots could switch to VG 3 at the same time, and normally this would result in a caution or warning that both pilots were showing the same source.

Attitude Director Indicator

The attitude director indicator (ADI), shown in figure 2-21 (page 68), receives its attitude information from its associated vertical gyro, or by switching to another VG.

Besides the basic attitude reference, the ADI displays additional information relating to localiser and glideslope deviation, and to airspeed deviation. It is important to note that in the glideslope and localiser deviation indicators, the aeroplane is indicated by the fixed central mark, and the relative positions of the glideslope and localiser are shown by the pointer. Thus in figure 2-21, the aeroplane is in a level 15° bank left turn, closing on the selected course from the right, and is slightly below the glideslope.

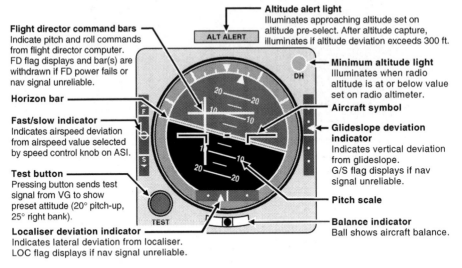

Altitude alert light
Illuminates approaching altitude set on altitude pre-select. After altitude capture, illuminates if altitude deviation exceeds 300 ft.

Flight director command bars
Indicate pitch and roll commands from flight director computer. FD flag displays and bar(s) are withdrawn if FD power fails or nav signal unreliable.

Horizon bar

Fast/slow indicator
Indicates airspeed deviation from airspeed value selected by speed control knob on ASI.

Test button
Pressing button sends test signal from VG to show preset attitude (20° pitch-up, 25° right bank).

Localiser deviation indicator
Indicates lateral deviation from localiser. LOC flag displays if nav signal unreliable.

Minimum altitude light
Illuminates when radio altitude is at or below value set on radio altimeter.

Aircraft symbol

Glideslope deviation indicator
Indicates vertical deviation from glideslope. G/S flag displays if nav signal unreliable.

Pitch scale

Balance indicator
Ball shows aircraft balance.

Figure 2-21 **Attitude director indicator**

Airspeed deviation from the value set on the ASI (fast/slow) is presented in a similar manner to glideslope, and in this case, the IAS is on target.

Modern ADIs have provision for the display of flight director (FD) information, hence the name of the instrument. This information can be either in the form of command bars as shown, or as V-bars. The use of the flight director is explained in the next section.

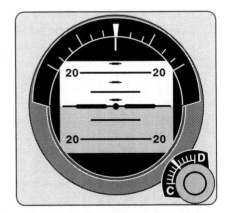

Figure 2-22 **Standby attitude indicator**

Standby Attitude Indicator

A standby attitude indicator (figure 2-22) is provided to give backup in case of a failure of the power supply or the transmission system between a VG and its associated ADI. This standby instrument is completely self-contained, with its internal gyro and lighting powered directly from the aircraft battery. No pilot action is required (or permitted) to make the standby reference available.

Miscellaneous Instruments

Radio Altimeter (Radar Altimeter)

Low-level operations – for instance, an ILS approach to 200 feet (a typical minimum for a Cat 1 approach) – require a radio altimeter (RADALT) to be fitted. There may be more than one – the B767 has three.

Modern radio altimeters transmit and receive in the super-high frequency band, i.e. between 4,200 MHz and 4,400 MHz (4.2 to 4.4 GHz). They show the height of the aircraft above the ground immediately below the aircraft, the radio altitude (RA). Radio altimeters normally operate in the range from zero to 2,500 ft AGL. They operate like a mini-radar bouncing a signal off the earth below. The display will blank if power fails or the data becomes unreliable, and when above 2,500 ft.

Radar altitude is not altitude.
It is the height above terrain (AGL).

Early radio altimeters used a circular display, but the latest versions have a vertical tape display, showing an expanded scale to enhance precision

The pilot can select the decision height (DH) for a precision approach, and this is displayed as a digital readout and by a bug against the tape as shown in figure 2-23.

When the radio altitude reaches the selected DH, the decision height light will illuminate, as will the decision height light on the ADI. These lights remain illuminated while the radio altitude is at or below the value set. Some systems also provide a warning tone to indicate that the radio altitude is approaching the selected value.

If the ground in the approach area is not level with the runway, some adjustment has to be made to the selected decision height, and this information is normally included in the instrument approach chart.

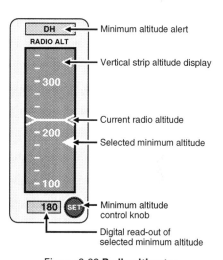

Figure 2-23 **Radio altimeter**

Large aircraft may have the sensing aerials embedded in the landing gear doors, or have a built-in correction to show the height of the main landing gear above the ground. The radio altimeter output is also made available to the ground proximity warning system (GPWS), described in chapter 5.

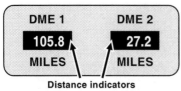

Distance indicators
Show distance to tuned DME stations.
Bars show loss of reliable signal.
Display blank if power fails.

Figure 2-24 **DME indicator readout**

Distance Measuring Equipment

There are normally two sets of distance measuring equipment (DME) fitted, the dual indicator showing the distance from the respective aid, as shown in figure 2-24. Loss of a reliable signal may be shown by light bars across the display; loss of power will cause the indicator to blank.

Instrument Comparator System

With so many of the instrument flight references being transmitted from remote duplicated sensors, an instrument comparator system is provided to compare the referenced information with the displayed information, and one pilot's references with the other pilot's. Two typical displays are shown at figure 2-25.

WARN
Illuminates in red to show a failure of one or more of the following: attitude; heading; radio altitude below 1,500 ft; NAV; or G/S after capture.

ATT
Illuminates to show a discrepancy between the two attitude indicator systems.

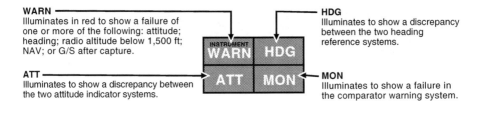

HDG
Illuminates to show a discrepancy between the two heading reference systems.

MON
Illuminates to show a failure in the comparator warning system.

Figure 2-25 **Typical instrument comparator annunciator panels**

The alerting system compares pitch and roll attitude, heading, localiser and glideslope indications. Discrepancies between references result in a caution light; the crew must then identify and isolate the offending system. There is also a failure light to show failure of power to the monitors.

Flight Director

In manual instrument flight, the pilot scans the basic flight instruments to see what the aircraft is doing, and assesses the deviation between the current situation and the desired flightpath. The pilot then adjusts the aircraft attitude and thrust to achieve a transition to the correct flightpath. The control inputs that the pilot uses vary, depending on the size of the deviation, and the speed with which that deviation is changing (the trend).

From experience, the pilot also knows that only small corrections are required when getting close to whatever instrument aid is in use. The multiple inputs and outputs chasing each other through the pilot's mind can be better handled by a computer which can easily compare data, and issue appropriate commands to the pilot.

Zero Reader

One of the very early applications of a computer resulted in an instrument called a *Zero Reader*, as shown in figure 2-26. The principle of the Zero Reader was that the pilot would program the system by selecting a mode, such as an ILS approach, and the computer would assess the difference between what the aircraft was doing and what the pilot wanted it to do, e.g. intercept (capture) the localiser and glidepath. The computer would then tell the pilot what to do in the form of pitch commands presented by a horizontal bar against a vertical scale, and roll commands by a vertical bar against a horizontal scale.

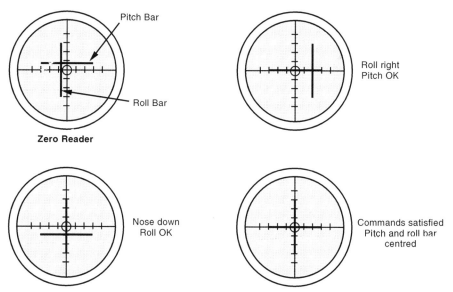

Figure 2-26 **Zero Reader presentation**

Pitch Command

A pitch command bar movement above the zero position in the centre of the scale meant that the aircraft nose had to be raised. As the pilot moved the flight controls in response to the pitch command, the command bar displacement from zero would reduce, until the command bar read zero when the pilot's control inputs and the aircraft response satisfied the computer. If the pilot's input, or the aircraft response, exceeded what the computer wanted, the command bar would move in the opposite direction, commanding a reduction in pitch attitude.

Roll Command

When the roll command bar moved to the left of the zero reference, this represented a command to roll to the left. The roll command bar would centre as the required bank angle satisfied the computer. Similarly, the roll command bar moving to the right meant that the pilot should roll to the right. Note that this does not mean turn right, only that the bank angle should be adjusted to the right, which could result in more right bank, or less left bank.

Summary

As the aircraft situation came to match the pilot's intentions, for instance, when closing on the centreline during a localiser intercept, the roll command bar would move to tell the pilot to apply bank to turn onto the centreline. As the course deviation reduced, the command bar would call for a bank reduction. In this way by flying the aircraft (represented by the small circle at the intersection of the scales of the Zero Reader) towards the intersection of the command bars – called *flying to the cross* – the pilot would achieve a rollout to wings-level when established on the localiser.

It should be noted that the Zero Reader did not show aircraft attitude, nor the actual deviation from a desired performance. It only indicated the control inputs needed to reduce the deviations to zero in order to achieve the flight pattern that the pilot had programmed into the Zero Reader. The pilot referred to other flight instruments to see what current deviations existed, and, in particular, what the aircraft attitude was.

Flight Director Operation

In a similar way to the Zero Reader, the flight director (FD) computer compares current aircraft performance with desired performance as selected by the pilot, and provides command guidance to the pilot to achieve a smooth transition to that performance. Pitch and roll guidance is presented on the attitude indicator in the form of command bars. These can either be a system of two separate bars at right angles (split cue), which present pitch and roll commands separately, or an inverted V-bar which presents combined pitch and roll commands (integrated cue). Both systems are shown in figure 2-27.

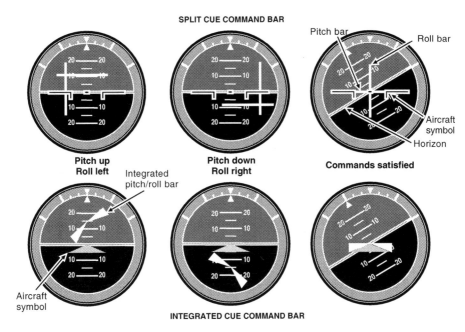

SPLIT CUE COMMAND BAR

Pitch up
Roll left   Integrated
pitch/roll bar

Pitch down
Roll right

Commands satisfied

Aircraft
symbol

INTEGRATED CUE COMMAND BAR

Figure 2-27 **Flight director presentations: top row shows split-cue command bar indications; bottom row shows integrated-cue command bar indications**

Command Bar Movement

There are no deviation scales for command bar movement in either system, but the further the command bar is from the centred, aligned position, the greater the correction must be; small command bar deviations from the aircraft symbol only require small corrections. As with the Zero Reader, the command bars will centre to the zero position as the computer becomes satisfied with the response.

Again note that the command bars do not show actual aircraft attitude, but only the required control inputs to change attitude. However, with the FD commands being shown superimposed on the ADI, aircraft attitude information is immediately available.

Usually, the FD pitch command is limited to +25°/−10° of pitch attitude, while the roll command is limited to about 30° of bank.

Note that the bars may be centred while the aircraft is not straight and level. For example, when turning to a selected heading, the roll command bar will centre when the correct bank angle is achieved, and remain centred during the turn. As the required heading is approached, the roll command bar will command a roll input in the opposite direction to reduce the bank angle until the wings are level, and the selected heading is achieved.

Split-Cue Command Bar Operation

To explain the operation of the roll command bar, consider a right turn to a preselected heading. The pitch command bar has been removed for clarity. Figure 2-28 shows the roll bar indication while maintaining present heading.

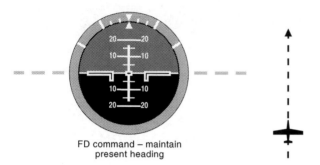

FD command – maintain
present heading

Figure 2-28 **Roll bar indication while maintaining present heading**

When the pilot selects the new heading, the roll command bar will move to the right, as shown in figure 2-29. For small heading changes, the computer will command a small bank angle; for larger heading changes, the roll command will call for more bank, usually up to a maximum of 30°.

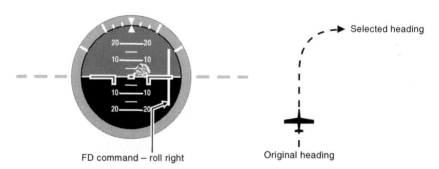

FD command – roll right   Original heading

Figure 2-29 **Roll bar indicating roll right upon selecting a new heading to the right**

As the pilot rolls to the right, the roll command bar will move towards the centre position. As the roll bar command reduces, so should the pilot reduce the roll control input, reducing to zero roll control input as the roll command bar centres when the flight director computer is satisfied with the bank angle, as in figure 2-30. The roll command bar will remain in the zero position while the steady state turn continues.

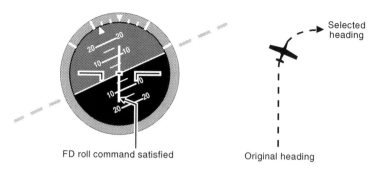

FD roll command satisfied   Original heading

Figure 2-30 **Roll command bar centred for steady turn state**

As the selected heading is approached, the roll bar moves to command a roll to the left, i.e. to reduce the bank angle (see figure 2-31).

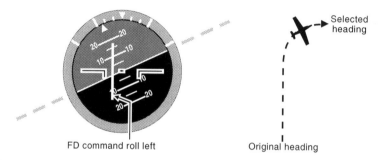

FD command roll left   Original heading

Figure 2-31 **Roll bar indicating to reduce angle of bank as new heading is approached**

As the pilot rolls left, reducing the bank angle, the roll command bar will centre. Following the guidance given by the roll command bar, the aircraft will roll out wings-level on the new heading (see figure 2-32).

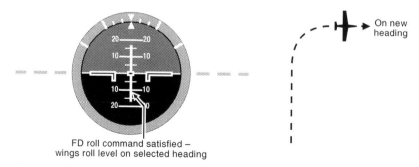

FD roll command satisfied –
wings roll level on selected heading

Figure 2-32 **Roll bar centres as aircraft rolls out on new heading**

The pitch bar responds in a similar manner to the roll bar, centring when the pitch command is satisfied. The pitch command bar is horizontal and moves vertically in relation to the aircraft symbol on the attitude director indicator.

A movement of the pitch command bar below the aircraft symbol calls for a nose-down attitude change, and a movement above the aircraft symbol calls for a nose-up attitude change. The operation of the pitch bar is illustrated in figure 2-33.

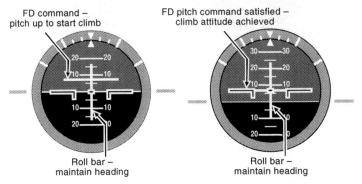

Figure 2-33 **Operation of the pitch command bar**

Integrated Cue Operation

With the integrated cue system, a movement of the V-bars above the aircraft symbol calls for a nose-up attitude change. A left roll movement of the V-bars relative to the aircraft symbol is commanding a left roll input. Note that the V-bars do not move from side to side, they can only roll left and right relative to the aircraft symbol. Flying the aircraft to tuck the aircraft symbol into the V-bars will satisfy the FD computer.

Summary of Command Bar Operation

By adjusting the aircraft attitude to keep the command bars satisfied (centred), the pilot can transition to, and maintain, the programmed performance mode that may be a combination of any of the following parameters:
- altitude;
- track;
- heading;
- speed;
- vertical speed;
- vertical profile;
- ILS localiser;
- ILS glidepath; and
- go-around attitude.

In manual flight, the FD provides flight attitude commands for the same modes as the autopilot, although the bank angles and lead computations may be slightly different. The FD command bars may be in view while the autopilot is engaged for easy transition from autoflight to manual flight.

Flight Director Control Panel

In some aircraft, a separate FD control panel (such as in figure 2-34) may be installed.

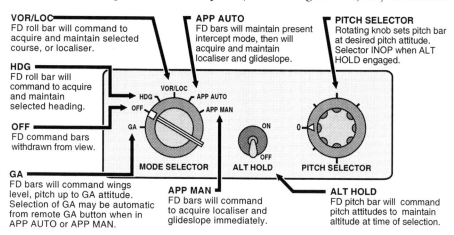

VOR/LOC
FD roll bar will command to acquire and maintain selected course, or localiser.

HDG
FD roll bar will command to acquire and maintain selected heading.

OFF
FD command bars withdrawn from view.

GA
FD bars will command wings level, pitch up to GA attitude. Selection of GA may be automatic from remote GA button when in APP AUTO or APP MAN.

APP AUTO
FD bars will maintain present intercept mode, then will acquire and maintain localiser and glideslope.

APP MAN
FD bars will command to acquire localiser and glideslope immediately.

PITCH SELECTOR
Rotating knob sets pitch bar at desired pitch attitude. Selector INOP when ALT HOLD engaged.

ALT HOLD
FD pitch bar will command pitch attitudes to maintain altitude at time of selection.

Figure 2-34 **Typical flight director control panel**

In addition to the three control switches, there are four flight director (FD) mode annunciator lights (adjacent to the autopilot annunciators), as shown in figure 2-35 (page 78). In this installation the conventional autopilot would be controlled through a separate control panel, as discussed in chapter 4.

Pitch Selector

The pitch selector allows the pilot to set the desired pitch attitude, usually between 10° nose down and 15° nose up by rotating the knob. Once selected, the bars will command the pitch attitude adjustments needed to achieve and maintain the desired pitch angle. The roll bar will command wings level until a navigation mode is selected.

Mode Selector

The functions of the various selections on the mode selector are described below.

OFF: The off position turns the flight director off and removes the command bars from view.

HDG: The heading mode is used to hold the selected heading set by the heading bug on the HSI. The command bars will command varying bank angles that are needed to acquire, and then maintain, the heading set on the HSI. The bank angles are normally limited to between 25° and 30°.

VOR/LOC: The VOR/LOC mode slaves the bank function of the command bars to the VOR radial set on a HSI, or to the localiser path of a tuned ILS localiser. In the depicted installation, only one VHF NAV receiver can be selected, although a separate switch may allow you to direct either of two VHF NAV receivers to this mode selection.

APP AUTO: Selection of approach automatic commands the roll function of the command bars to maintain the present intercept mode (heading or VOR radial tracking), and to capture and maintain the localiser course. The pitch function of the command bars will maintain the present pitch function (usually altitude hold), and is armed to capture and maintain the glideslope. In some aircraft, the system will not capture the glideslope unless the localiser has been captured first.

APP MAN: Selection of approach manual commands an immediate capture of localiser and glidepath, overriding any current roll or pitch modes, e.g. an aircraft below the glideslope will climb to capture the glideslope, and/or will turn with 25° bank to establish a 45° intercept of the localiser. In some equipment, this mode is called MAN G/S.

GA: When GA (go-around) is selected, typically when reaching instrument minima and electing to execute a missed approach, the FD will command a pre-programmed go-around pitch attitude, typically 15° nose up (or 13° nose up, engine out) with wings level. More modern systems normally have the GA function of the FD activated by pressing a button on one of the power levers, the selector being spring-loaded to move from APP AUTO, or APP MAN, to the GA mode.

Alt Hold Selector: When engaged, the altitude hold selector switch slaves the pitch function of the command bars to maintain the present altitude. Note that this is not necessarily the same altitude as the preselected altitude set on the altitude select control. If there is a significant vertical speed when ALT HOLD is selected, the FD will command a smooth transition which may overshoot the selected altitude, and then return to the desired altitude.

Flight Director Mode Annunciators

The flight director mode annunciator shown in figure 2-35 uses coloured lights to indicate the current status of the flight director; typically, all the lights will be illuminated at one time or another during the course of an ILS approach, as described below. For instance, HEADING illuminates in green to show that the flight director is in heading mode; GLIDESLOPE illuminates in amber to show that the FD is armed to capture the glideslope, and illuminates in green when the glideslope has been captured.

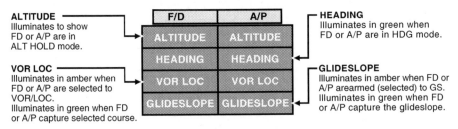

Figure 2-35 **Typical flight director and autopilot mode annunciators**

Typical Precision Instrument Approach

Now, let us run through a typical ILS approach to Runway 27 at airport X, using the flight director to give guidance during manual flight. The various stages (1–9) of the approach are illustrated in figure 2-36 and described on the following pages.

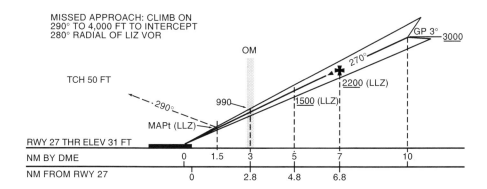

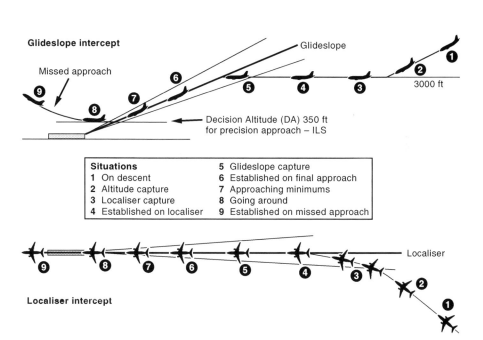

Figure 2-36 **Schematic of ILS profile – glideslope and localiser**

Stage 1

Let us assume that the aircraft has been cleared to descend to 3,000 ft, and maintain present heading to intercept the localiser. See figure 2-37. The crew selects 3,000 ft in the altitude preselect, and sets up an appropriate rate of descent. At the same time, the pilot flying selects the current heading on the HSI, and selects the FD HEADING mode. The FD HEADING mode annunciator will illuminate in green. The crew should tune and identify the ILS frequency, and set the inbound localiser course of 270° on the HSI as shown in figures 2-37 and 2-38

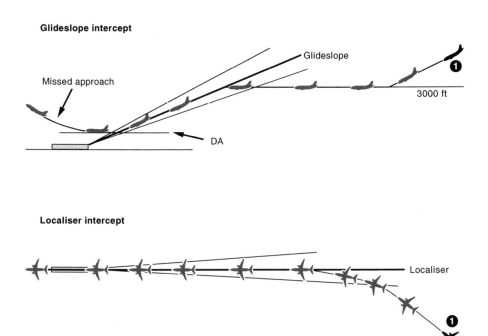

Figure 2-37 **Aircraft cleared for ILS approach, and intercept localiser.**

Green

1 Passing 5000 ft on descent at 3500 ft/min to 3000 ft, as set in Altitude Pre-select.
Heading - 330° on Heading Select; FD mode - HDG; FD annunciator - HEADING (green).
FD roll bar Centred, FD pitch bar commanding slight 'nose up'.
VHF NAV is tuned to ILS frequency 109.3, inbound course set to 270°.
CDI bar full scale right, G/S deviation full scale up.
Both ADF's tuned to locator NDB; ADF/ADF selected on RMI, NDB bearing 315°.

Figure 2-38 **Indication on preselecting new altitude and current heading.**

Stage 2

When the aircraft descends to approximately 3,300 ft, the altitude alert will sound, and the pilot must raise the nose to level off at 3,000 ft. (Note that this FD does not have an altitude capture capability.) The pilot can adjust the pitch selector to command a higher nose attitude. When level at 3,000 ft, the pilot should select ALT HOLD to on, the FD mode annunciator will show altitude hold in green, as shown in figures 2-39 and 2-40. The FD pitch commands will now assist the pilot to maintain altitude at 3,000 ft. When cleared by ATC to intercept the localiser, the pilot sets the FD mode selector to VOR LOC, thus arming the FD to intercept the inbound localiser course. The mode annunciator will now show VOR LOC in amber, indicating that the FD is armed to capture the localiser centreline.

Glideslope intercept

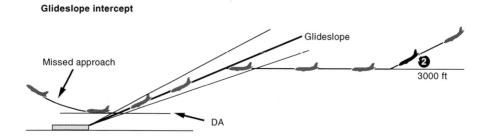

Localiser intercept

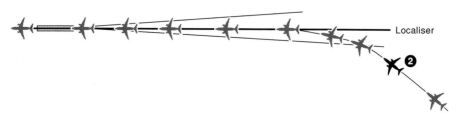

Figure 2-39 **Levelling off at 3,000 ft.**

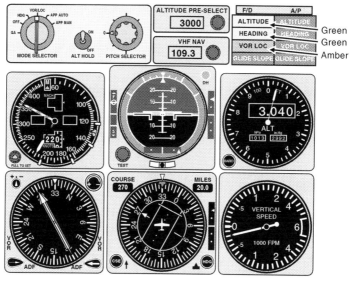

2 Approaching altitude capture passing 3040 ft.
FD pitch command bar commanding slight 'nose up'.
When level at 3000 ft - FD mode ALT HOLD - ON, pitch selector inoperative;
FD annunciator shows ALTITUDE (green).
ATC clearance to intercept the localiser - select FD mode to VOR/LOC;
FD annunciator shows VOR LOC (amber).
ADF Bearings 30° off nose, CDI bar full scale to right.
As IAS reduces, FD pitch command will call for slight 'nose up' change of attitude to maintain altitude.

Figure 2-40 **Altitude hold selected and VOR/LOC.**

Stage 3
As the aircraft closes on the centreline, the FD will capture the inbound course, and give commands to turn to intercept. The VOR/LOC mode annunciator will show green.

Glideslope intercept

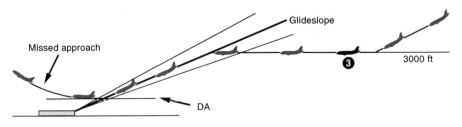

Localiser intercept

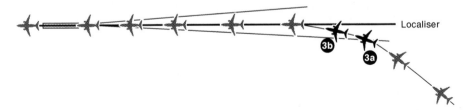

Figure 2-41 **Preparing to capture the localiser.**

Figure 2-42 **Opposite – indicating localiser captured and roll command to close on centreline, and indicating correct bank angle.**

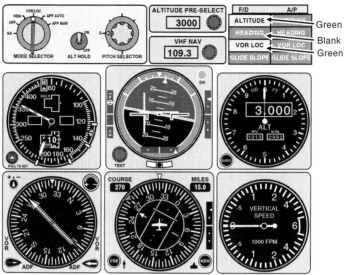

Green
Blank
Green

3a Localiser capture; FD annunciator VOR LOC turns green, HEADING annunciator blanks.
FD roll command to roll left, aircraft starting left turn, bank angle increasing towards 25°.
FD pitch command slight nose up to maintain level flight as IAS reduces.
CDI bar closing.
Heading Select bug set to inbound course 270°.
ADF bearing 275°.

3b Aircraft established in left turn, with 25° bank.
FD roll command is satisfied and roll bar is centred.
FD pitch command is in ALT HOLD.
Aircraft is closing on localiser, with the CDI bar one dot right.

Stage 4

When ATC gives *'clear to final'*, the pilot selects the FD mode selector APP AUTO, as shown in figures 2-43 and 2-44. The GLIDE SLOPE annunciator will illuminate in amber, indicating that the FD is armed for the glideslope intercept. Still in level flight, with ALT HOLD as the active pitch mode, the glideslope indicator on the HSI shows the glideslope above the aircraft, but gradually moving down.

Glideslope intercept

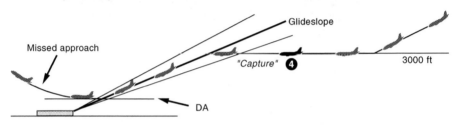

Localiser intercept

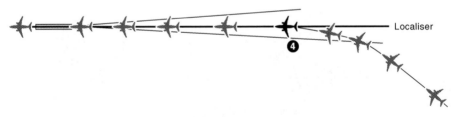

Figure 2-43 **Preparing to capture the glideslope**

FD "approach auto"

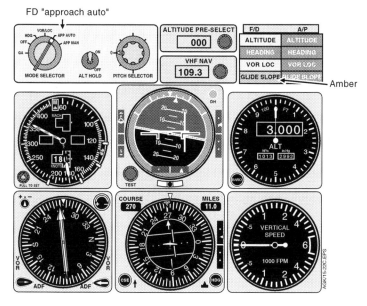

Amber

4 Aircraft very close to localiser, CDI bar 1/2 dot right.

FD roll command bar calling for a roll to the right, to reduce the bank angle to zero, as the aircraft becomes established on the centre line.

With ATC 'clear to final' FD mode selected to APP AUTO.

FD annunciator GLIDE SLOPE illuminated in amber.

FD roll command VOR LOC.

FD pitch command ALT HOLD.

Glideslope deviation indicator moving down scale.

ADF bearing 270°.

Figure 2-44 **APP AUTO selected, closing in on glideslope above aircraft and almost on localiser**

Stage 5

When the glideslope deviation indicator closes on the zero deviation mark, the FD will capture the glideslope, as shown in figures 2-45 and 2-46. The glideslope annunciator will turn green, and the FD pitch command will move to acquire a sufficient rate of descent to stay on the glidepath. The FD ALT HOLD switch will snap off, the altitude annunciator will go out, and the missed approach altitude can be set. The missed approach heading can now be set on the HSI. Note that most FD systems command smaller bank angles once the localiser has been captured.

Glideslope intercept

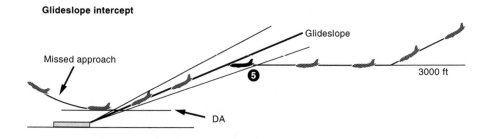

Established

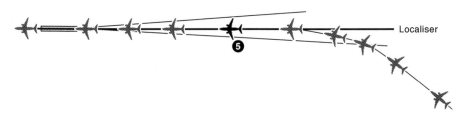

Figure 2-45 **Missed approach settings preselected, glideslope almost captured**

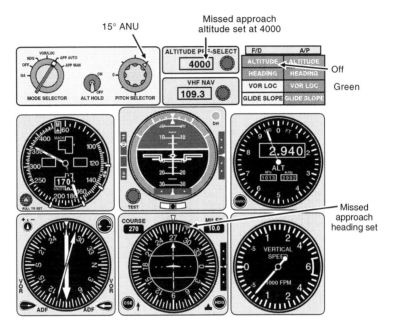

❺ As the glideslope deviation reduces to zero, the FD captures the glideslope, and the FD annunciator GLIDE SLOPE turns green.

FD mode ALT HOLD snaps OFF automatically; altitude annunciator goes out; FD pitch bar commands 'nose down' to follow the glideslope.

FD roll commands maintain the localiser centreline.

The altitude pre-select is set to the missed approach altitude, 4,000 ft.

The Heading Select bug is set to the missed approach heading, 290°.

One of the ADFs is tuned to a missed approach navaid; the other ADF is still tuned to locator beacon.

The pitch selector is set to 15°ANU for a possible missed approach attitude.

Figure 2-46 **Roll commands maintaining localiser centreline.**

Stage 6

The flight director will continue to give guidance to stay on the glideslope and the localiser, as shown in figures 2-47 and 2-48, where a crosswind has caused the aircraft to drift to the right of the centreline. The localiser deviation indicator on the flight director shifts to the left and the CDI is displaced 1 dot left on the HSI.

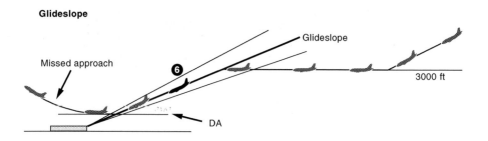

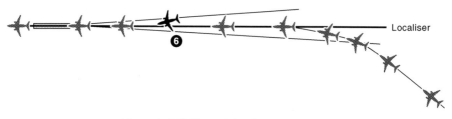

Figure 2-47 **Drifting right of the centreline**

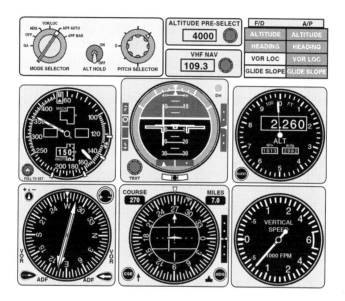

6 Established on final approach, drifting slightly right.
FD pitch commands satisfied, maintaining glideslope.
FD roll commands slight left turn, to maintain the localiser, correcting for crosswind.
IAS command bug set to 130 kt.

Figure 2-48 **Indicating a drift right of the localiser centreline.**

Stage 7
Passing the outer marker at 980 ft on QNH, check altitude 990 ft; no correction needed to decision altitude (DA).

Note: In most FD systems, the sensitivity of glideslope tracking is reduced at very low levels, typically below 300 ft, to avoid over-controlling as the glideslope beam becomes very narrow.

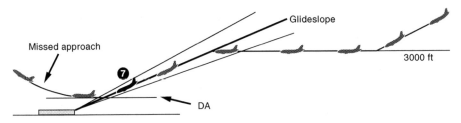

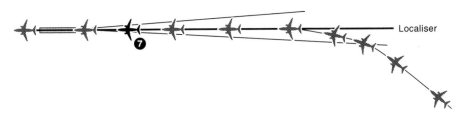

Figure 2-49 **Passing the outer marker**

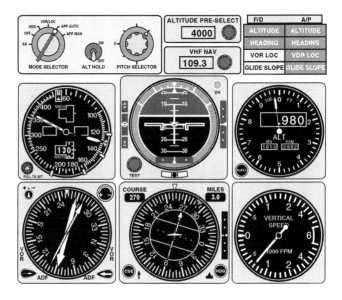

7 Approaching minima; glideslope tracking desensitised. IAS at bug.
Only very small corrections needed to keep command bars centred.

Figure 2-50 **Correct altitude indicated at outer marker**

Stage 8

Now at the decision altitude (DA) of 350 ft on QNH. The radio altimeter will indicate the decision height (DH) of 319 ft, and the DH warning light on the ADI will illuminate.

At this point on the approach, you have to satisfy yourself that you have sufficient visual cues to continue the approach visually to a landing; if not you must initiate the missed approach procedure.

Should you decide to make a missed approach, the FD can be switched to the go-around (GA) mode by pressing a switch either on the control column or on the throttle that will command a wings-level pitch up to a suitable angle, typically about 15° nose-up.

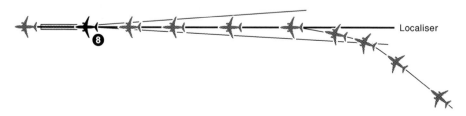

Missed approach

Missed approach

Glideslope

3000 ft

DA

Localiser

Localiser

Figure 2-51 **At decision altitude**

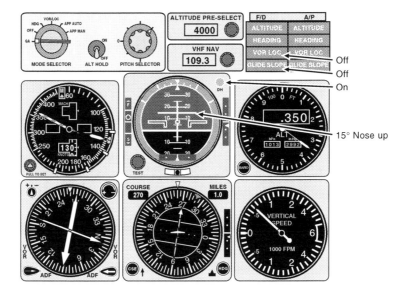

⑧ Going around!
Press the GA switch (on throttle or control column).
FD mode selector moves automatically to GA mode; GA annunciator (if fitted) turns green.
FD annunciators VOR LOC and GLIDE SLOPE extinguish.
FD pitch bar commands call for 'nose up' to about 15°.
FD roll bar commands wings level.

Figure 2-52 **At decision altitude. Initiating a missed approach.**

Stage 9

You decide to initiate the missed approach procedure.

If fitted, the flight director mode annunciator will show GA in green. The VOR LOC and glideslope annunciators will go out. When established in the missed approach, the relevant navigation aids can be tuned and identified.

Missed approach

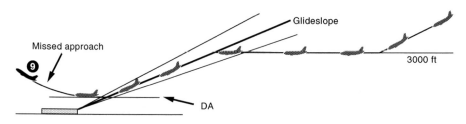

Localiser

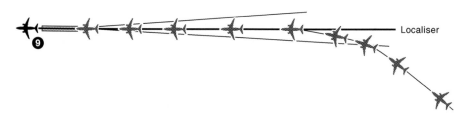

Figure 2-53 **Missed approach**

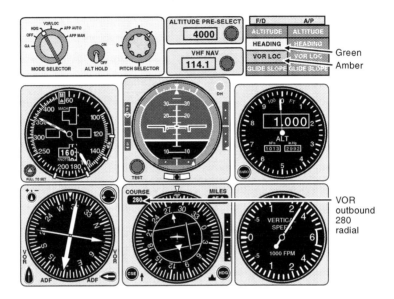

Green
Amber

VOR
outbound
280
radial

9 Established in the missed approach.

Missed approach instructions; *Heading 290° to intercept the 280° radial of the 114.1 VOR; climb to 4,000 ft.*

Heading select bug set to missed approach instructions 290°.

FD mode selector set to HDG, FD annunciator HEADING will illuminate in green, roll commands will acquire and maintain heading.

Set pitch selector to suitable 'nose up' attitude, FD pitch bar will command pitch attitude adjustments to maintain selected pitch attitude.

Retune navigation aids in accordance with missed approach procedure.

When navaids are tuned and identified, FD mode VOR/LOC is selected; FD roll mode will stay in HEADING Select; FD annunciators will show HEADING (green) and VOR LOC armed (amber) ready to capture the VOR outbound radial 280°.

Figure 2-54 **Missed approach**

Advanced Cockpit Systems

The further development of smaller computers, combined with reliable cathode ray tubes (CRT), offered a means of accessing more data, and displaying it to the flight crew. The displays were easier to understand, and could be controlled to present only relevant information, enabling the crew to manage the overall operation more efficiently. In addition, navigation systems were improved by using a type of gyro developed for missile systems, the laser gyro, usually working in multiple installations to provide redundancy. The combination of flight management data and the presentation of attitude and navigational information on a series of CRTs is commonly referred to as *glass cockpit technology*.

Data Transfer

In the most modern aircraft, such as the B757/767 and the B747–400, many of the systems are controlled and monitored by individual computers, numbering 240 or more. This requires a complex data transfer system.

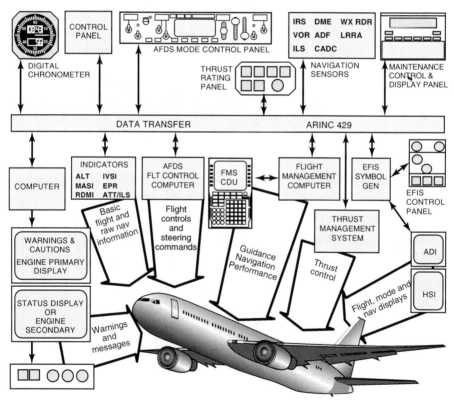

Figure 2-55 **ARINC 429 data transfer bus**

All transfer of information between systems used to be by direct wires *(hard wiring)*, resulting in very large and intricate wiring *looms.* Hard wiring is still used for the important links, such as between the autopilot control panel and the flight controls, but the bulk of data transfer is now by means of data transfer *buses.*

A data transfer bus is a pair of twisted wires, linking a number of digital computers together. There can be up to 20 units per bus, so that instead of many separate wires, data flows around the data bus in a *stream,* and user units pick off the information they require. In the B767 series, digital transfer buses of this type are made to an industry standard known as ARINC 429. (ARINC is the abbreviation for the American organisation Aeronautical Radio Incorporated.)

Electronic Flight Instrument Systems

A significant outcome of improved and smaller data processing units is their application to flight instrument displays. Rather than having numerous sensors driving an equal number of mechanical pointers, electronic information processing allows electronic display of information on cathode ray tubes (CRTs). This is the basis of the electronic flight instrument system (EFIS).

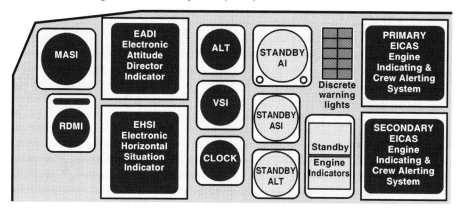

Figure 2-56 **Schematic of EFIS panel layout**

Note: Depending on customer option, the shape and arrangement of the CRT displays can vary from company to company. In some aircraft the EHSI screen is rectangular and in others it is square.

Principle of Electronic Flight Instrument Systems

The basic principle of EFIS is to take information from sources such as the pitot-static system, air data computer, attitude and heading references, and radio navigation receivers and process the data electronically. The result is then displayed on one or more CRTs, hence the term *glass cockpit.* More complex information, from sources such as the IRS and the flight management system (FMS), can also be processed and displayed.

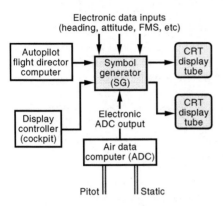

Electronic data inputs
(heading, attitude, FMS, etc)

Figure 2-57 **Schematic EFIS interface**

Symbol Generator

Figure 2-57 shows the basic layout of an EFIS display. Information from a sensor is provided electronically to the processing unit, commonly called the *symbol generator* (SG). This term is used because its main function is to provide an output of symbols that can be displayed on a CRT. One SG can provide information to more than one CRT, with two being the norm.

Some sensor information can be fed directly from the appropriate system to the symbol generator, provided that the system processes information in an appropriate electronic format. Examples of these types of input are remote sensing gyro systems for heading or attitude information, flight management systems and outputs of the autopilot flight director computers.

Some 'raw' sensor information must, however, be processed before being input to the symbol generator. An example of this is the pitot-static measurements for airspeed and Mach number which must be computed by the air data computer. The ADC then feeds the appropriate information to the SG, which generates the display.

The variety of information that is fed into the SG need not be displayed continuously. By appropriate selections on the display controller, the SG is instructed to display only that information required. In typical EFIS systems, the display tube is not 'smart', i.e. it has no processing capability, it merely displays the symbols. For this reason, one tube in a multi-tube system can be exchanged easily with other compatible tubes. The SG is the heart of the system.

Electronic Flight Instrument Systems Features

The main benefit of an EFIS system is the ability to show a huge range of information on a smaller number of instruments than was possible using older systems. Using EFIS, the pilot does not need to scan a large number of instruments to fly accurately. This feature is particularly important during times of high workload, such as an instrument approach. Any system that makes the task easier for the pilot should indirectly improve safety in certain situations, since the pilot should have spare capacity available. Hopefully, this will allow more efficient management of the additional tasks that can arise in emergency situations. The range of information available for display on modern EFIS systems is virtually unlimited and does not stop at the examples shown in this section. The ability to display full flight plan and track information at different range scales, and then integrate this with speed, altitude and time, has been a major development.

Electronic Flight Instrument Systems Interface

The EFIS interface layout in the B767 is shown in the schematic, in figure 2-58. As can be seen from the diagram, the left SG provides display information for the two screens located in front of the captain, and the right SG provides the same information in front of the co-pilot. A third, centre, SG is available to provide display information to either set of screens in case of failure.

The top display for each pilot is called an electronic attitude director indicator (EADI), and the lower display is an electronic horizontal situation indicator (EHSI).

These displays provide the basic information normally given by older electro-mechanical attitude indicators and horizontal situational indicators described earlier in this chapter, together with numerous additional features made possible by electronic symbol generation. There are two more screens in the centre of the instrument panel, and these display engine and system data as will be discussed later.

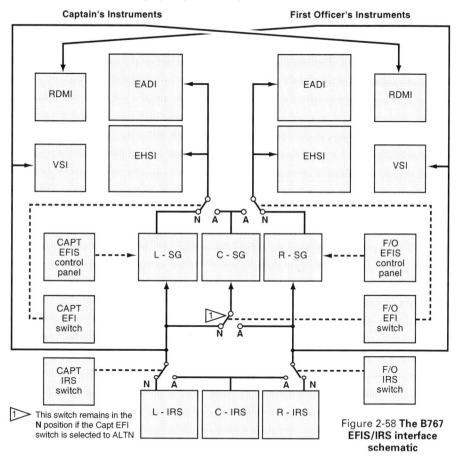

Figure 2-58 **The B767 EFIS/IRS interface schematic**

You will see from figure 2-58 that each pilot can switch to an alternative data source or to an alternative symbol generator. For example, in the system shown, a failure of the left-hand instruments caused by a failure of L–SG can be rectified by switching to C–SG. Similarly, the F/O can switch to C–SG, but note that only one pilot can use SG3 at any time in this arrangement.

Electronic Flight Instrument Systems Control Panel

A great benefit of the EFIS system is the ability to select information appropriate for the stage of flight. By simply making selections on the EFIS control panel, only the relevant information need be displayed, and, at the same time, unwanted display symbols are extinguished.

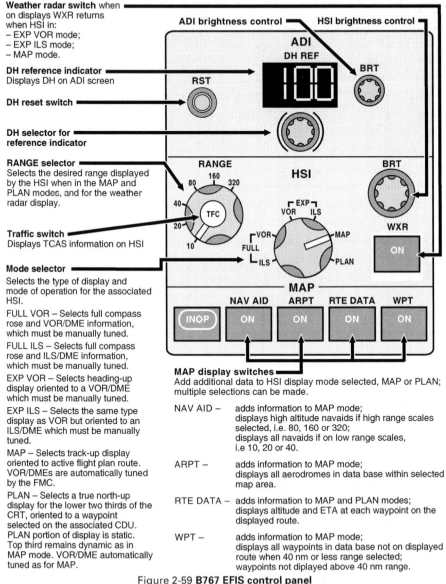

Weather radar switch when on displays WXR returns when HSI in:
– EXP VOR mode;
– EXP ILS mode;
– MAP mode.

DH reference indicator
Displays DH on ADI screen

DH reset switch

DH selector for reference indicator

RANGE selector
Selects the desired range displayed by the HSI when in the MAP and PLAN modes, and for the weather radar display.

Traffic switch
Displays TCAS information on HSI

Mode selector
Selects the type of display and mode of operation for the associated HSI.
FULL VOR – Selects full compass rose and VOR/DME information, which must be manually tuned.
FULL ILS – Selects full compass rose and ILS/DME information, which must be manually tuned.
EXP VOR – Selects heading-up display oriented to a VOR/DME which must be manually tuned.
EXP ILS – Selects the same type display as VOR but oriented to an ILS/DME which must be manually tuned.
MAP – Selects track-up display oriented to active flight plan route. VOR/DMEs are automatically tuned by the FMC.
PLAN – Selects a true north-up display for the lower two thirds of the CRT, oriented to a waypoint selected on the associated CDU. PLAN portion of display is static. Top third remains dynamic as in MAP mode. VOR/DME automatically tuned as for MAP.

MAP display switches
Add additional data to HSI display mode selected, MAP or PLAN; multiple selections can be made.

NAV AID –   adds information to MAP mode;
             displays high altitude navaids if high range scales
             selected, i.e. 80, 160 or 320;
             displays all navaids if on low range scales,
             i.e 10, 20 or 40.

ARPT –   adds information to MAP mode;
             displays all aerodromes in data base within selected
             map area.

RTE DATA –   adds information to MAP and PLAN modes;
             displays altitude and ETA at each waypoint on the
             displayed route.

WPT –   adds information to MAP mode;
             displays all waypoints in data base not on displayed
             route when 40 nm or less range selected;
             waypoints not diplayed above 40 nm range.

Figure 2-59 **B767 EFIS control panel**

Electronic Attitude Director Indicator

Figure 2-60 and figure 2-61 (page 104) show typical displays for an electronic attitude director indicator (EADI).

Command bars ━━
Provide steering and pitch commands to maintain or return to lateral and vertical profile. Removed from view when associated F/D switch is off. FD flag is visible when flight director fails.
In take-off mode, the pitch command bar indicates target rotation attitude until lift-off + 15 but not less than V_2 + 15.
If an engine fails while in take-off mode, the pitch command bar commands the speed existing at the time of engine failure up to a maximum of V_2 + 15 but not less than V_2.
The take-off pitch mode remains engaged until another pitch mode is selected, or until altitude capture. The roll bar provides wings level commands until lift-off, then commands to maintain track until another lateral mode is selected.

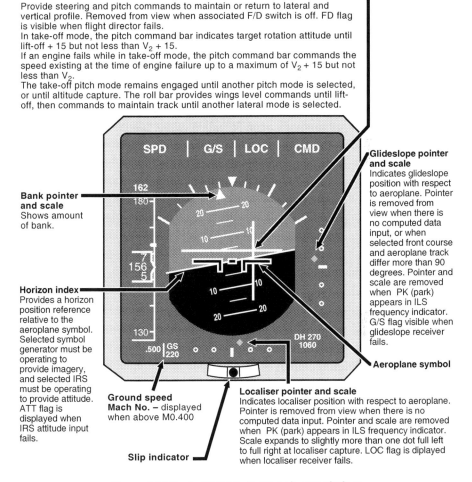

Bank pointer and scale
Shows amount of bank.

Horizon index ━━
Provides a horizon position reference relative to the aeroplane symbol. Selected symbol generator must be operating to provide imagery, and selected IRS must be operating to provide attitude. ATT flag is displayed when IRS attitude input fails.

Ground speed Mach No. – displayed when above M0.400

Slip indicator ━━

Glideslope pointer and scale
Indicates glideslope position with respect to aeroplane. Pointer is removed from view when there is no computed data input, or when selected front course and aeroplane track differ more than 90 degrees. Pointer and scale are removed when PK (park) appears in ILS frequency indicator. G/S flag visible when glideslope receiver fails.

Aeroplane symbol

Localiser pointer and scale
Indicates localiser position with respect to aeroplane. Pointer is removed from view when there is no computed data input. Pointer and scale are removed when PK (park) appears in ILS frequency indicator. Scale expands to slightly more than one dot full left to full right at localiser capture. LOC flag is diplayed when localiser receiver fails.

Figure 2-60 **Typical EADI indications/annunciations**

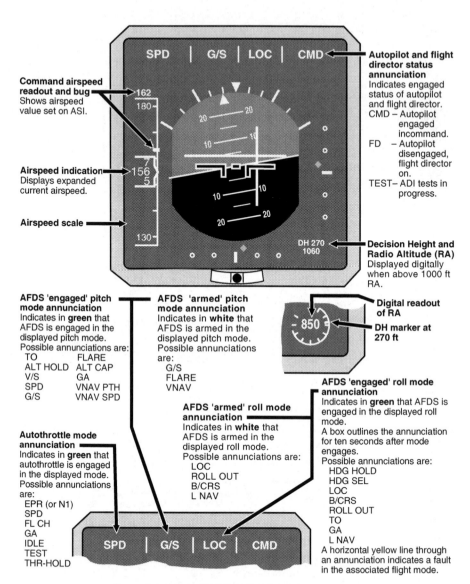

Command airspeed readout and bug
Shows airspeed value set on ASI.

Airspeed indication
Displays expanded current airspeed.

Airspeed scale

Autopilot and flight director status annunciation
Indicates engaged status of autopilot and flight director.
CMD – Autopilot engaged incommand.
FD – Autopilot disengaged, flight director on.
TEST– ADI tests in progress.

Decision Height and Radio Altitude (RA)
Displayed digitally when above 1000 ft RA.

Digital readout of RA

DH marker at 270 ft

AFDS 'engaged' pitch mode annunciation
Indicates in **green** that AFDS is engaged in the displayed pitch mode.
Possible annunciations are:
TO   FLARE
ALT HOLD ALT CAP
V/S   GA
SPD   VNAV PTH
G/S   VNAV SPD

AFDS 'armed' pitch mode annunciation
Indicates in **white** that AFDS is armed in the displayed pitch mode.
Possible annunciations are:
G/S
FLARE
VNAV

AFDS 'armed' roll mode annunciation
Indicates in **white** that AFDS is armed in the displayed roll mode.
Possible annunciations are:
LOC
ROLL OUT
B/CRS
L NAV

AFDS 'engaged' roll mode annunciation
Indicates in **green** that AFDS is engaged in the displayed roll mode.
A box outlines the annunciation for ten seconds after mode engages.
Possible annunciations are:
HDG HOLD
HDG SEL
LOC
B/CRS
ROLL OUT
TO
GA
L NAV
A horizontal yellow line through an annunciation indicates a fault in the associated flight mode.

Autothrottle mode annunciation
Indicates in **green** that autothrottle is engaged in the displayed mode.
Possible annunciations are:
EPR (or N1)
SPD
FL CH
GA
IDLE
TEST
THR-HOLD

Figure 2-61 **Typical EADI indications/annunciations**

The following information can be displayed:
- raw attitude information (pitch and bank);
- flight director command bars;
- indicated airspeed;
- command airspeed setting;
- decision height (DH) and radio altitude;
- ILS localiser and glidepath deviations; and
- autopilot and flight director systems status annunciators.

Note: The various mode abbreviations in the EADI are explained in chapter 4.

Attitude information is provided by the respective IRS as shown in figure 2-58 (page 101), with the centre IRS as an alternative source. Before the FD command bars can be displayed, the alignment of the IRS must have been completed.

The display in figure 2-61 shows an attitude of zero pitch and 10° right bank. Commanded airspeed has been set at 162 kt as shown on the digital display above the airspeed tape, and by the position of the command airspeed bug.

Despite the fact that the autothrottle has been engaged (as shown by the SPD annunciator) to hold that commanded airspeed, the actual speed is 156 kt. The aircraft is on an ILS final and the flight director has been engaged to hold localiser and glidepath (LOC, G/S and CMD annunciators showing). The command bars require a slight pitch-up and right bank, as the aircraft shows ½ dot below glideslope and ½ dot left of localiser. A DH of 270 ft has been set, and the height above ground as measured by the radio altimeter is shown as 1,060 ft.

In some installations, the display will change to a radial ring display when below 1,000 ft radio altitude, showing the RA readout digitally in the middle of the display. As the descent continues, segments of the ring erase, indicating the radio altitude. The DH is shown as a marker on the radial display.

Electronic Horizontal Situation Indicator

The following information can be displayed on the electronic horizontal situation indicator (EHSI):
- sector of compass arc;
- present track line and digital readout;
- heading bug and reference line;
- distance to and ETA for next waypoint;
- present aircraft heading;
- present aircraft position;
- planned track;
- location of VORs and waypoints;
- tuned ILS frequencies and VOR;
- vertical profile indicators;
- wind vector;
- range marks; and
- altitude range arc.

Electronic Horizontal Situation Indicator Modes

There are various modes which can be displayed on the EHSI, and these are described in the following paragraphs.

Full ILS/VOR

Although not generally used, both ILS and VOR data can be displayed against a full 360° compass rose as shown in figure 2-62. The display is the same as on non-EFIS horizontal situation indicators.

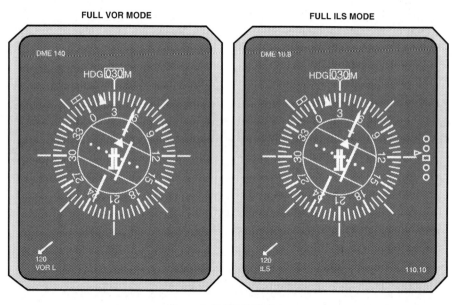

Figure 2-62 **EHSI display**

Expanded (EXP) ILS/VOR Mode

The EHSI display in the expanded ILS mode is shown in figure 2-63. Note that the ILS and the VOR displays are oriented heading up.

The aircraft is on heading of 262°M with a track of 246°M aiming to intercept the selected ILS localiser course of 280°. The aircraft is 1½ dots right of the centre-line and slightly below the glideslope.

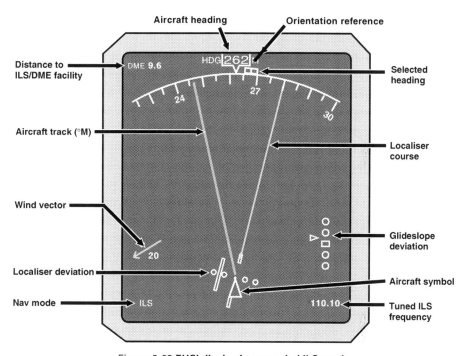

Figure 2-63 **EHSI display in expanded ILS mode**

In the VOR mode, the to and from indications are displayed next to the aeroplane symbol, and the glideslope deviation is removed as shown in figure 2-64. Weather radar information can be displayed in both ILS and VOR modes.

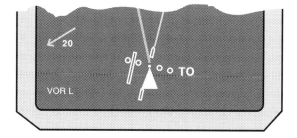

Figure 2-64 **EHSI display in expanded VOR mode**

Map Mode

Figures 2-65 and 2-66 show the EHSI in the map mode. The benefit of this mode is that it provides a map-type display that gives an easy presentation for orientation purposes. You will see from the diagram that the EHSI display is track up, i.e. the current track is shown at the 12 o'clock position, against the lubber line, with the current heading shown by an arrowhead against the compass arc.

One advantage of this type of display is that the pilot can turn the aircraft to position the track line over the desired waypoint or navaid symbol, and the aircraft will then fly accurately to that point regardless of wind effect.

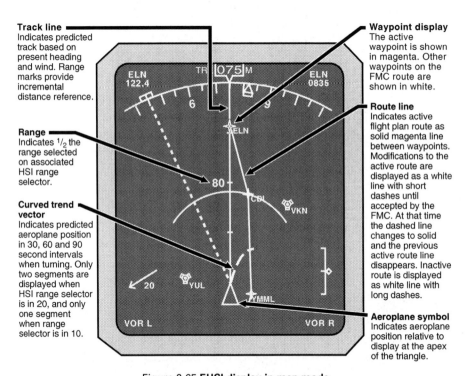

Track line
Indicates predicted track based on present heading and wind. Range marks provide incremental distance reference.

Range
Indicates ¹/₂ the range selected on associated HSI range selector.

Curved trend vector
Indicates predicted aeroplane position in 30, 60 and 90 second intervals when turning. Only two segments are displayed when HSI range selector is in 20, and only one segment when range selector is in 10.

Waypoint display
The active waypoint is shown in magenta. Other waypoints on the FMC route are shown in white.

Route line
Indicates active flight plan route as solid magenta line between waypoints. Modifications to the active route are displayed as a white line with short dashes until accepted by the FMC. At that time the dashed line changes to solid and the previous active route line disappears. Inactive route is displayed as white line with long dashes.

Aeroplane symbol
Indicates aeroplane position relative to display at the apex of the triangle.

Figure 2-65 **EHSI display in map mode**

Distance display
Indicates distance to
active waypoint in
MAP or PLAN modes.
Indicates distance to
tuned DME in ILS or
VOR modes.

Magnetic track/heading display
Indicates magnetic track (TRK-M) in MAP
or PLAN modes. Indicates magnetic
heading (HDG-M) in ILS or VOR modes.

Heading pointer
Indicates
aeroplane heading
in MAP or PLAN
modes.

**Selected heading
bug**
Indicates heading
selected with MCP
heading selector. A
dotted line extends
from aeroplane
symbol to the
relative bug position
when the selected
heading is outside
the visible compass
rose. The bug
automatically
moves to the
localiser course at
localiser capture.

ETA display
Indicates ETA to
next waypoint.

NAVAID display
Shows tuned
navaid in green.
Shows all navaids
within range when
MAP display is in
STAtion mode.

Altitude arc
Intersects track at
the point where
altitude set in MCP
altitude indicator
will be reached.

**Vertical deviation
indicator**
Indicates altitude
deviation from the
selected vertical
profile. Displayed
in the MAP mode
during descent
only. Scale
indicates ±400 ft
deviation. VTK
flag displayed
when vertical track
data has failed.

Wind display
Indicates wind
direction and
speed (in knots)
relative to map
display orientation.

VHF/NAV frequency display
Displays tuned VOR (L or R).

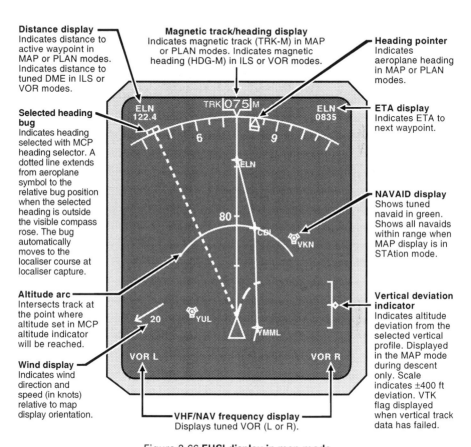

Figure 2-66 **EHSI display in map mode**

The annotations on these two diagrams explain some of the more common symbols that can be displayed on the EHSI screen. These symbols can be displayed in different colours, and the general presentation is as follows:

green	(G)	indicates engaged flight mode displays, dynamic conditions;
white	(W)	indicates present status situation, scales, and armed flight mode displays;
magenta (pink)	(M)	indicates command information, pointers, symbols, and fly-to condition;
cyan (blue)	(C)	indicates non-active and background information;
red	(R)	indicates warning;
amber	(A)	indicates cautionary information, faults, and flags;
black	(B)	indicates blank areas, off condition.

In the display shown in the diagrams, the crew had planned to track YMML–ELN, but the aircraft is left of track to the north-west of YMML, tracking 075°M direct to ELN, the active waypoint. However, with the aircraft turning right, passing through a heading of 083°, the aircraft track trend is back to the right as shown on the track trend indicator, and there is clearly a crosswind component from the right. The heading bug is set on 044°. The ELN waypoint is just over 120 nm away as shown by being slightly above the third 40 nm range mark (the second mark shows 80 nm, indicating that each mark is 40 nm value). The precise distance to go to ELN is shown as 122.4 nm with an ETA at ELN of 0835.

Planned cruising altitude should be reached at about 70 nm from present position as shown by the altitude range arc. The VORs are set to both left and right, as selected on the associated VOR/DME panel, and there is a crosswind component from the right with the wind arrow showing a wind from the south-east at 20 kt. Weather radar information can be superimposed on navigation information in the map mode (see chapter 5).

Plan Mode

In the plan mode shown in figure 2-67, track and heading information are still displayed at the top of the screen, but the lower part is oriented to magnetic north and the flight plan waypoints can be stepped through and matched with tracks and distances from flight planning data.

By using the range selector on the control panel, the route presentation can be expanded to show more detail; this is particularly useful in checking terminal area manoeuvring.

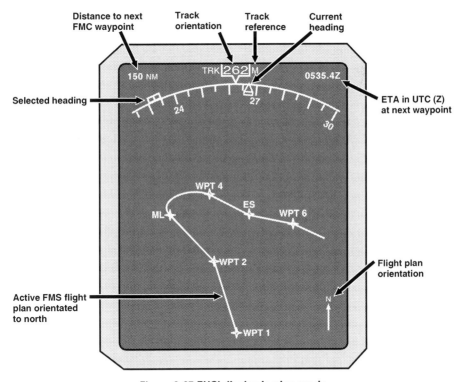

Figure 2-67 **EHSI display in plan mode**

Selection of Information

The use of EFIS requires careful thought and proper training. The ability to select information appropriate to the stage of flight is a great benefit because by simply making selections on the EFIS control panel (figure 2-59, page 102) you can display the relevant information needed. However, it is important to extinguish unwanted display symbols since the display tubes can easily be cluttered with excessive symbols. Unchecked, excessive symbology can create confusion, particularly in high-workload situations. In general terms, keep the displays as clean as possible.

Composite Displays

Because a typical symbol generator has the capability to generate displays on either the EADI or EHSI, it follows that it can vary the information given to either tube. The main benefit of this feature is the ability to generate a combined display on one tube if the other tube fails. Such a combined display is called a composite display. It shows attitude information, abbreviated track information and a variety of annunciators when needed.

Multi-Function Display

Smaller turbo-prop or light jet aircraft may only have EFIS displays in front of the captain's position, together with a separate central display for checklist, navigation and weather radar purposes. When fitted, this tube is called a multi-function display (MFD).

Figure 2-68 shows a typical composite display. Apart from basic attitude information, this display shows an integrated-cue (V-bar) command bar.

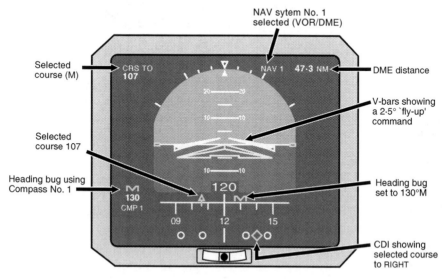

Figure 2-68 **EFIS composite display on an MFD**

This example shows:

- NAV 1 annunciator indicates that the active navigation display is using VOR No. 1.
- DME distance 47.3 nm from the co-located VOR/DME selected by NAV 1.
- The course annunciator at top left shows that a course of 107° TO is set on the CDI. This is confirmed on the bottom part of the instrument which shows a course of 107°M using the very small upward-pointing arrow on the top of the left-to-right compass numbers.
- The deviation from the selected course is shown by a small diamond rather than the normal CDI bar. In this case, the aeroplane is seen to be 1 dot to the right of the selected course of 107°M.
- The left-to-right compass display shows a heading of 120°M, and this is confirmed by the digital heading display immediately above it.
- The heading bug is set to 130°M, as shown on the compass display, and the digital display on the bottom left confirms this and shows that compass system No. 1 (CMP 1) is being used.
- A conventional coordination ball indicator is attached to the MFD.

An MFD can also be used for a composite EADI/EHSI display in the event of a failure of either of these two CRTs.

Electronic Flight Instrument System Failure Flags

Failure of various inputs will cause an appropriate warning flag to be displayed on the relevant EFIS display. Figure 2-69 shows typical warning flags for an EADI, and figure 2-70 (page 114) shows that for an EHSI.

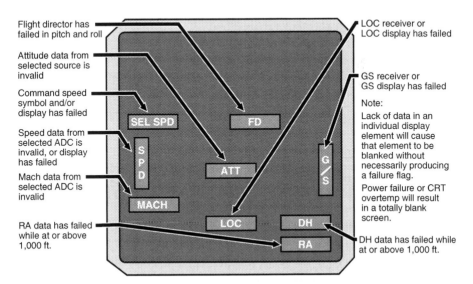

Figure 2-69 **EADI failure flags**

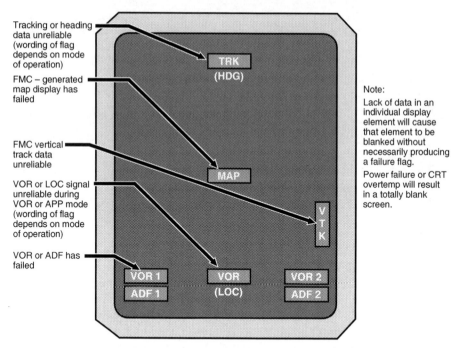

Tracking or heading data unreliable (wording of flag depends on mode of operation)

FMC – generated map display has failed

FMC vertical track data unreliable

VOR or LOC signal unreliable during VOR or APP mode (wording of flag depends on mode of operation)

VOR or ADF has failed

TRK (HDG)

MAP

V T K

VOR 1   VOR   VOR 2
ADF 1   (LOC)   ADF 2

Note:
Lack of data in an individual display element will cause that element to be blanked without necessarily producing a failure flag.
Power failure or CRT overtemp will result in a totally blank screen.

Figure 2-70 **EHSI failure flags**

Engine Indicating and Crew Alerting System

In the Boeing version of the glass cockpit, the engine parameters are displayed on CRT presentations like the two shown in figures 2-72. The upper display shows primary engine parameters, and the lower display shows secondary engine and systems data. The crew can also call up displays of flight control position and subsystem status on the secondary display. Ground engineers can access a range of information to assist rectification.

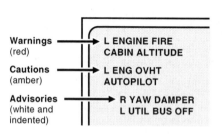

Warnings (red) ——→ L ENGINE FIRE
                     CABIN ALTITUDE

Cautions (amber) ——→ L ENG OVHT
                      AUTOPILOT

Advisories (white and indented) ——→ R YAW DAMPER
                                    L UTIL BUS OFF

Figure 2-71 **EICAS alert messages**

In addition to the engine and system status displays, crew alerting messages can be presented on the left side of the primary display, as shown in figure 2-71. Messages are presented in order of occurrence and in order of importance, the most vital messages being in red, with caution messages in amber. System malfunctions are automatically displayed, with the offending parameter in amber or red. During engine start and shutdown, inappropriate messages are inhibited.

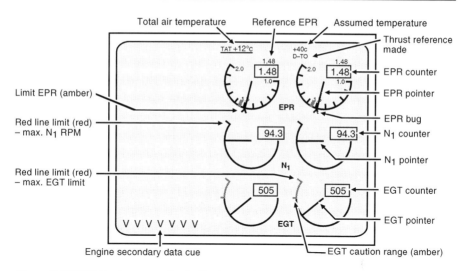

Figure 2-72 **EICAS primary engine indications (above); EICAS secondary display (below)**

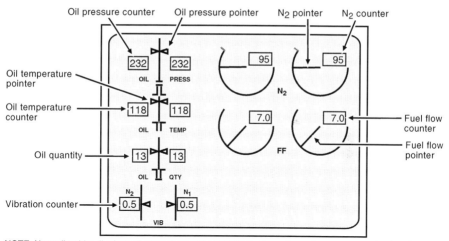

NOTE: Normally white displays change to amber or red if values reach cautionary or warning levels.

Non-EFIS Flight Instruments

Mach/Airspeed Indicator

The Mach/airspeed indicator (MASI) is essentially the same as found on the conventional instrument panel, and shown in figure 2-13 (page 63). The difference is that there is no manual setting control for the command airspeed bug. This function is performed manually by the IAS/Mach selector on the AFDS mode control panel (see chapter 4), or by the FMC.

Radio Distance Magnetic Indicator

The radio distance magnetic indicator (RDMI) (figure 2-73) is a standard RMI with the addition of dual DME readouts.

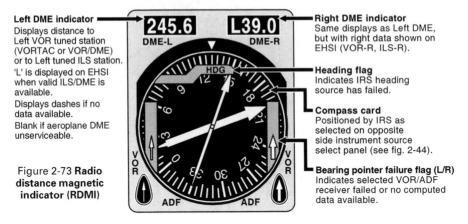

Left DME indicator
Displays distance to Left VOR tuned station (VORTAC or VOR/DME) or to Left tuned ILS station.
'L' is displayed on EHSI when valid ILS/DME is available.
Displays dashes if no data available.
Blank if aeroplane DME unserviceable.

Figure 2-73 **Radio distance magnetic indicator (RDMI)**

Right DME indicator
Same displays as Left DME, but with right data shown on EHSI (VOR-R, ILS-R).

Heading flag
Indicates IRS heading source has failed.

Compass card
Positioned by IRS as selected on opposite side instrument source select panel (see fig. 2-44).

Bearing pointer failure flag (L/R)
Indicates selected VOR/ADF receiver failed or no computed data available.

Other Instruments

The altimeter is the same as described previously, taking its displayed information from the air data computer. The VSI display is the same as before, but derives its display from the IRS vertical speed data.

Standby Instruments

Loss of electrical power in a modern transport aeroplane like the B767 is a very unlikely occurrence, but provision has to be made for the possible loss of all electronically derived instrument information. Standby flight instruments, similar to the conventional ones described earlier in this chapter, are installed.

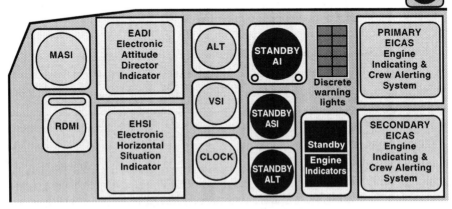

Figure 2-74 **Standby instruments**

Standby Engine Instruments

Should both EICAS displays be lost, engine primary data is presented in a digital display.

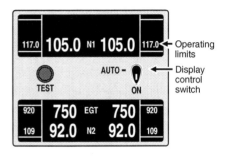

Figure 2-75 **Standby engine indicator**

Electronic Centralised Aircraft Monitoring

The electronic centralised aircraft monitoring (ECAM) system was introduced in the Airbus 310, and is similar in function to EICAS, with the addition of system displays in schematic and checklist form. In the Airbus the ECAM displays are mounted side by side, as shown in figure 2-76, with the left unit showing system status, failure warnings, and corrective actions in checklist format, while the right unit shows system schematics.

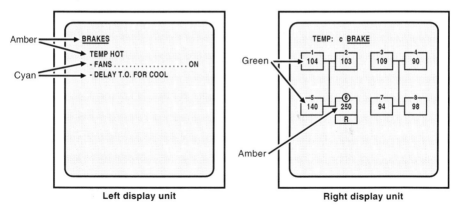

Left display unit   **Right display unit**

Figure 2-76 **ECAM typical failure display**

Attitude Heading Reference System

Although not used in aircraft fitted with full IRS such as the B767, many smaller aircraft in service today use an *attitude heading reference system* (AHRS).

The Honeywell AHZ-600 attitude heading reference system (AHRS) is an inertial sensor installation which provides aircraft attitude, heading, and flight dynamics information to cockpit displays, flight controls, weather radar antenna platform, and other aircraft systems and instruments. The AHZ–600 differs from conventional vertical and directional gyro systems in that the gyroscopic elements are rate gyros that are strapped down to the principal aircraft axes (like IRS). A digital computer mathematically integrates the rate data to obtain heading, pitch, and roll information. A flux valve and three accelerometers provide long-term references for the system. The strapdown mechanisation provides the aircraft dynamic information required by modern, high-performance flight control systems.

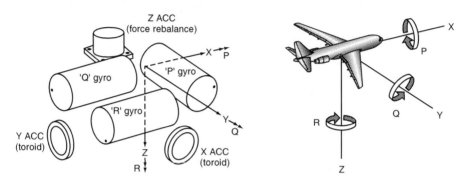

Figure 2-77 **Schematic of attitude heading reference system**

The AHRS installation consists of the flux valve, the compensator/controller, and the attitude and heading reference unit (AHRU), as shown in figure 2-78.

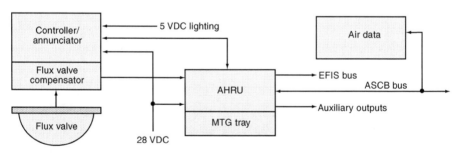

Figure 2-78 **AHRS system components**

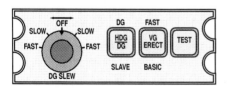

Figure 2-79 **AHRS controller**

The flux valve detects the relative bearing of the earth's magnetic field and is usually located in the wing or tail section away from disturbing magnetic fields. The compensator/controller is mounted in the cockpit (figure 2-79).

The AHRU is the major component of the system and comprises the following four major subsystems (see figure 2-80).

• The *inertial measurement unit* (IMU) senses the aircraft's body dynamics. It contains the rate gyros, accelerometers, and support electronics.

• The *central processor unit* (CPU) performs the numerical computations necessary to extract the attitude and heading information. It contains the microprocessor, arithmetic logic unit, program memory, and scratchpad memory. In addition to its computational activities, the CPU controls and monitors the operation of the entire system.

• The *input/output* (I/O) unit supervises the analog-to-digital and digital-to-analog conversions. The flux valve is connected to the I/O unit through the compensator using the current servo approach which provides increased accuracy over conventional open-loop connections.

• The power supply converter converts aircraft power to the regulated DC voltages and DC power signals required by the system.

The strapdown system offers several advantages over traditional vertical and directional gyros. In a conventional vertical gyro, automatic vertical erection is 'cut off' when the roll angle, or in some cases the pitch angle as well, exceeds a certain value, typically $5° - 10°$. This causes the gyro to produce a vertical error proportional to its free drift during extended large bank angle manoeuvres. A related problem concerns shallow bank angles just below 'cut-off'. In this case, the automatic erection loop causes the gyro to erect to the false vertical induced by the turning acceleration.

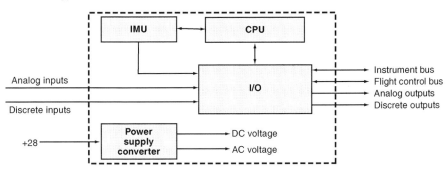

Figure 2-80 **AHRU simplified block diagram**

The AHZ-600 uses a velocity-damped, Schuler-tuned vertical erection loop proved in advanced strapdown systems. This mechanisation eliminates the need for small erection cut-off angles and maintains continuous erection to the true local vertical under all normal flight manoeuvres. Conventional gyros are also susceptible to 'gimbal lock' under certain conditions.

Modern flight control systems are able to make effective use of rate and acceleration feedback terms. These terms, which are not directly available from simple vertical or directional gyros, have had to be derived from position data or obtained from extra rate gyros and accelerometers. The AHZ-600 AHRS, however, provides direct measurements of these quantities and supplies all required data for the automatic flight control system (AFCS) in both earth-based and aircraft body axis coordinate reference frames. Angle of attack is computed for the flight control system as a function of true airspeed, pitch, attitude and rate.

Two modes are provided for routine operation – the normal mode in the attitude channel, and the slaved mode in the heading channel. The normal mode uses true airspeed from the air data computer to compensate for acceleration-induced attitude errors. The AHZ-600 also computes TAS as a monitor function to verify the reasonableness of the data received. The loss of TAS is recovered by using the computed value or, if available (as in the optional dual air data installation), the opposite side's TAS data. Use of other than the normal TAS channel is automatic and is not annunciated. The slaved mode uses the flux valve to align the heading outputs. To prevent errors due to the north-turning phenomenon, the flux valve slaving is cut off during manoeuvres that would induce such errors. Two reversionary modes are provided to maintain performance in the event of certain types of system failures: basic and DG.

The basic mode operates without TAS compensation and results in a simple first-order vertical-erection scheme similar to that of a conventional vertical gyro with roll cut-off. Since this kind of operation is susceptible to stand-off errors following certain types of manoeuvres, a fast-erect command input from the controller is provided. Entry into the basic mode is automatic and is annunciated on the controller. If all true airspeed data is invalid, but indicated airspeed remains valid, the AHZ-600 will use IAS for compensation and will annunciate the basic mode.

The DG mode is entered by a flight crew command on the controller and is provided to disable the automatic slaving of the heading outputs. Operation in this mode is similar to that of a conventional directional gyro and is annunciated on the controller. Although the DG mode may be entered at any time, the mode is usually reserved for operation in the event of a slaving loop failure. Such failures are indicated by the slaving error output or the SLAVE FAIL annunciator on the controller.

A two-speed manual slaving input switch is provided on the controller to manually slew the heading output while operating in the DG mode. Use of the slew control in the slaved mode is inhibited, and no single failure of the slew control inputs will result in a runaway heading output. The free drift of the internal AHRU heading reference is less than 24 degrees per hour while operating as a directional gyro. An additional feature of the AHZ-600 provides fast slaving when changing from the DG mode to the slaved mode. This reduces the time spent at the end of the runway should the system be inadvertently left in the DG mode prior to flight.

Several test modes are incorporated into the AHZ-600. The preflight test is performed automatically upon application of power to the AHRU or by flight crew command. These tests extend the normal AHRU self-monitoring activities. All flags are dropped upon entry into this mode to protect the aircraft from accidental activation during flight. In addition, the AHRS annunciates the test mode selection with a separate discrete output so that user equipment, such as the EFIS, may make appropriate use of the test data.

Chapter 3

Flight Management Systems

A *flight management system* (FMS) has the ability to monitor and direct both navigation and performance, and to supply corrections to the flightpath through an autopilot interface. Many less complex systems are capable of providing automatic navigation by interfacing a navigation computer to the autopilot, but these are more correctly called *navigation management systems.*

The functions performed by a flight management system will vary among aircraft types depending on their size and price range. An FMS fitted to a modern turboprop regional airliner is not as likely to cover as many geographic areas as the FMS fitted to a B767-300ER used on international operations. However, there are two functions common to all flight management systems:

* automatic navigation; and
* flightpath management.

The flight management system takes information from other systems, such as the clock, the inertial reference system, air data computers and ground-based navigation aids (VOR/DME), and integrates all of this information into a single system that can be used to control the flightpath of the aircraft, both directionally and vertically.

The flightpath over the earth is referred to as *lateral navigation* (LNAV), and the vertical profile is referred to as *vertical navigation* (VNAV).

The FMS provides LNAV and VNAV information that can be used as guidance when flying manually (by following the flight director) or that can be used to control the flightpath of the aircraft automatically via an autopilot (pitch and roll) and autothrottle (engine thrust).

FMS equipment is continually being improved with new functions and simpler operating procedures. What you see in an actual aircraft may differ slightly from the descriptions in this manual, but the general principles will be similar.

In the B767, the flight director and the autopilot both receive the same data from the FMS, so the flight director and the autopilot both do the same thing. This is not the case in all aircraft types where some autopilots perform independently of the flight director, as discussed in chapter 4.

Flight Management System Installation

To simplify the discussion about flight management systems, let us consider the FMS as fitted to the B767. This FMS comprises:

* the flight management computer (FMC);
* the inertial reference system (IRS) containing three inertial reference units (IRUs);

- the autopilot flight director system (AFDS);
- the thrust management system (TMS);
- the air data computers (ADC);
- the electronic flight instrument system (EFIS);
- the engine indication and crew alerting system (EICAS); and
- various navigation and system sensors.

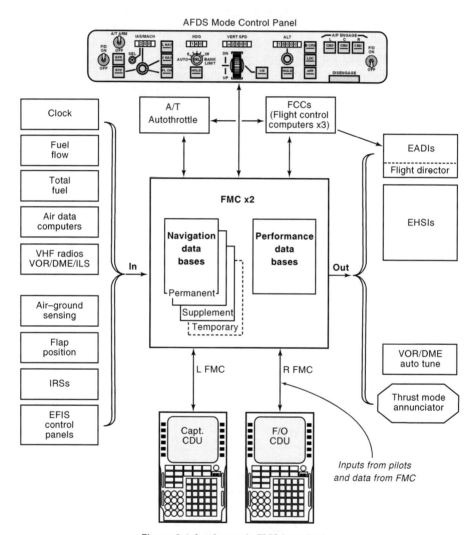

Figure 3-1 **A schematic FMS installation**

Flight Management Computer (FMC)

The nerve centre of the flight management system is the flight management computer (FMC), with its stored navigation and performance data. A typical FMS includes two flight management computers and their two associated control display units (CDUs). The CDUs allow the crew to communicate with the computers, and interface with the various avionics systems, digital computers and instruments which make up the total FMS. Each CDU is connected only to its associated FMC; however, the two FMCs are interconnected so that they normally operate as a single computer.

The two FMCs 'talk' to each other to compare data, but one FMC (usually the left one) will be the master, and will provide the LNAV and VNAV commands to the AFDS and the autothrottle. If the two sets of the data do not agree, the master FMC will resynchronise the slave FMC by automatically reloading the slave with data from the master. If the master FMC detects a fault within itself, however, then the slave FMC will reload the master FMC with the slave's data.

Resynchronising of an FMC may happen periodically whenever there is a significant mismatch, and the process may take some seconds, during which time the CDU will display a message such as 'RESYNCING OTHER FMC', or 'SINGLE FMC OPERATION'.

Either CDU or FMC can perform all the associated FMS functions in the event of a failure.

Inputs to the FMC come from:
- a very accurate clock;
- fuel sensors, for both total fuel and fuel flow;
- air data computers that provide airspeed, Mach no., temperature and altitude data;
- radio navigation aids for navigation source information – these aids can be auto-tuned by the FMC or manually tuned using the FMC, or by overriding the automatic mode of the VHF/NAV tuning head;
- air–ground sensing that records take-off and landing times, and switches various systems from ground to airborne mode, such as pressurisation/air conditioning, electrical channel isolation and FMC navigation mode;
- flap position that enables configuration information to be included when optimum profiles are computed during departures and approach;
- IRSs for position, attitude and heading source information;
- EFIS control panels, which enable the pilots to select the various navigation and performance modes for display on the EFIS screens; and
- autopilot flight director system (AFDS) where the FMS is hard-wired to the AFDS, and the specific type of FMS link desired is selected on the AFDS mode control panel, which could be altitude control, navigation track, heading, localiser, or glideslope, etc. Thus, when the autopilot is selected, the link between the FMC and the flight control computers (FCC) is utilised to achieve the required performance.

Outputs from the FMC go to the autoflight system, which comprises the following, and is discussed in detail in chapter 4:

- autopilot flight director system (AFDS);
- the flight control computers (FCC);
- the autothrottle;
- EFIS – various displays of navigation, flight attitude and radio navigation bearings can be selected on the EFIS display tubes; and
- various annunciators and indicators.

FMC Databases

The FMCs contain two databases, one for navigational data, and one for performance data. These databases contain all the information that the crew is likely to need in flight and, apart from normal cross-checking purposes, preclude any need to refer to documentation.

Navigation Database

The navigation database stores information about radio aids, airports, runways, company and ICAO route structures and departure/approach procedures. This database is updated every 28 days, in line with the regular navigation data review. The revised data package is inserted into FMC memory by groundstaff some time before it becomes valid, and the flight crew can activate the revised database at the appropriate time through the CDU. It is important that the flight crew check that they are using the correct revision of the navigation database, by checking validity on the initial reference page of the CDU (discussed later in this chapter). In some circumstances, the crew might even need to change over to the revised navigation data in flight, if they are airborne at the appropriate time.

A mathematical model of the earth's magnetic field is stored in the navigation database, but it applies only between latitudes 73°N and 60°S. Outside these limits, true heading from the IRS is supplied to the EHSI and RDMI.

Performance Database

The performance database stores all the data relating to the specific aircraft/engine configuration, and is updated by ground staff when necessary. The purpose of the performance database is to provide the FMC with the data required to calculate pitch and thrust commands. All reference data normally required can be displayed on the CDU.

The stored data includes aircraft drag, engine characteristics, maximum and optimum operating altitudes, and maximum and minimum speeds. Airline operational planning staff can refine the database for an individual aeroplane or fleet by entering factors for drag, fuel flow and most economical (ECON) operation.

Control Display Unit (CDU)

The CDU is the communication link between the pilots and the flight management computer (FMC). The CDU consists of a data keyboard with a small screen. Since communication between the crew and the FMC is so important, it is worthwhile examining CDU operation in some detail. Master it. Don't be intimidated.

Figures 3-2 and 3-3 describe aspects of a typical CDU as fitted to a B767.

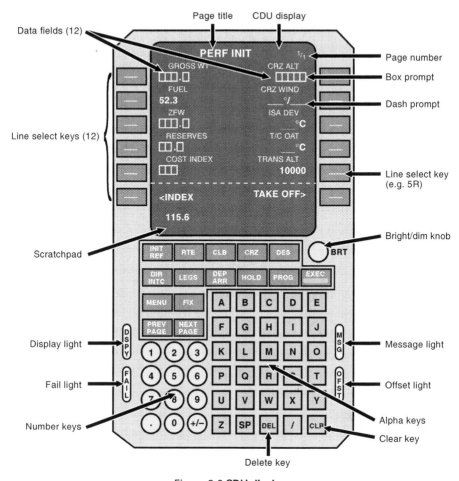

Figure 3-2 **CDU display**

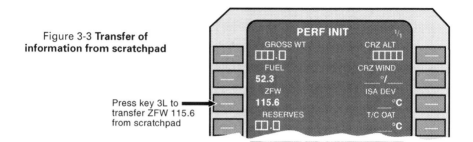

Figure 3-3 **Transfer of information from scratchpad**

Press key 3L to transfer ZFW 115.6 from scratchpad

At the top of the CDU screen is the page title and the page number. Down each side of the screen are six areas called *fields* that are used to display specific data appropriate to the title of that field. Each field has its own *line select key*, identified as line select key 1L, 2L, 5R etc. These line select keys control the flow of data between the field and the scratchpad. Data may come from the FMC, or may be entered by the flight crew. At the bottom of the CDU screen is the *scratchpad*. Data can be entered on the scratchpad by using the alphanumeric keys, and this information can be transferred to one of the data fields on the screen by pressing the associated line select key. Conversely, by pressing a line select key, the data on that line can be transferred from the data line to the scratchpad, provided the scratchpad is clear (use the CLR key to clear the scratchpad if necessary).

The scratchpad can also be used to carry information to another display page. Note that the FMC will not permit transfer of inappropriate data. In figure 3-2 (page 125), the zero fuel weight of 115.6 had been entered into the scratchpad, and this was transferred into the ZFW field by pressing line select key 3L, as shown in figure 3-3 (page 125).

CDU Messages

The scratchpad is also used by the FMC to present messages to the crew; if the FMC wants to show a message, and there is already something on the scratchpad, then a message light will illuminate on the CDU. Press the CLR button on the keyboard to clear the scratchpad, and display the message.

Entry of data into the FMCs is best done on one CDU at a time. The FMCs talk to each other on a data bus, and there may be a loss of data, or a refusal of the FMCs to accept data, if both pilots are trying to enter information at the same time.

By pressing one of the dedicated keys on the keyboard (e.g. LEGS or PROG), shown at figure 3-4, different data presentations can be selected, and paged through by pressing NEXT PAGE. Pressing LEGS will display LEGS page 1, then pressing NEXT PAGE will present LEGS page 2 and so on.

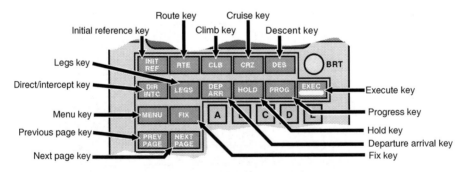

Figure 3-4 **CDU keyboard**

The EXECute key has a special function. When data such as a planned route is entered, it will appear first in an inactive mode, and the HSI presentation will show the planned route as a white dashed line. The EXEC key will illuminate, offering a reminder to both pilots to check the plan. When the crew are satisfied that this route is the one they want, pressing the EXEC key will activate the route, which will now appear as the active route (ACT RTE) in the page title, and as a magenta solid line on the HSI.

Information Displayed on CDU

Typical information that can be displayed on the CDU screen includes:

- current take-off and landing V-speeds and engine settings;
- landing V_{REF};
- climb profile, speed and altitude predictions;
- optimum cruise parameters, including best engine-out settings;
- TAS;
- groundspeed;
- heading (°M or °T);
- track (°M or °T);
- wind velocity;
- headwind/tailwind component;
- cross-track error;
- present position (latitude and longitude);
- distance to next waypoint;
- OAT and ISA temperature deviation;
- stored flight plans;
- present flight plan;
- current and predicted weight statements;
- fuel on board;
- estimated fuel remaining at waypoints and at destination;
- navigation source details;
- VOR/DME/ILS frequencies and positions;
- optimum engine-out parameters; and
- cost index, a balance between flight time and fuel economy.

Failures

Failure of an FMC or its associated CDU will be shown by the illumination of the FAIL light on the CDU (figure 3-2, page 125). Only one FMC and CDU is needed to provide full control of the AFDS and the autothrottle, and to provide data to the symbol generators for the EFIS displays.

FMS Interface

The primary cockpit control and displays in the B767 are the autopilot flight director system mode control panel (MCP), two control display units (CDU) and two

EFIS control panels with their associated electronic ADI and HSI. A schematic of the FMS interface is shown in figure 3-5.

Note: The abbreviations ADI and HSI (rather than EADI and EHSI) will be used throughout the remaining text.

The crew use the CDU to enter the lateral and vertical flight plan into the flight management computer, which combines the flight plan data with data from memory. The FMC calculates the present position of the aircraft, and generates the pitch, bank and thrust commands required to fly the optimum profile. The FMC sends commands to the autopilot, autothrottle and flight director, and provides information to the HSI. The crew use the HSI control panel to select the desired information on their displays (see chapter 2), and use the MCP to select the operating modes for the autopilot, the autothrottle and the flight director, as discussed in chapter 4.

In automatic flight, the pilot programs the FMC, which tells the flight control computers (FCC) and the autopilot what to do. In manual flight, the pilot makes the commanded attitude adjustments by following the movement of the flight director command bars on the ADI. This interface of the FMS with the autopilot flight director system is an essential element of the fully integrated FMS, and, for this reason, the AFDS is normally considered part of the flight management system.

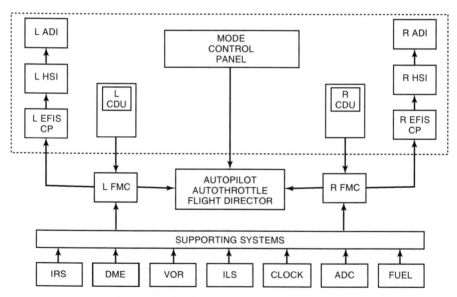

Figure 3-5 **Schematic of flight management system interface**

Inertial Reference System (IRS)

The IRS comprises three inertial reference units (IRUs). The IRU is an all-attitude, Schuler-tuned, strapdown inertial reference using laser gyros. The IRUs are controlled by a single inertial reference mode panel (IRMP) as illustrated in figure 3-6.

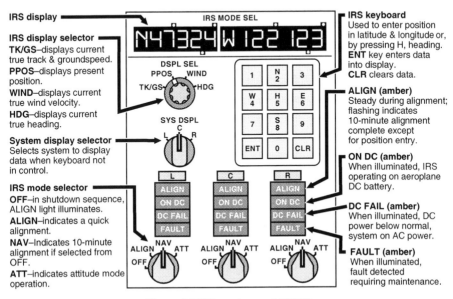

Figure 3-6 **IRS mode panel (IRMP)**

IRS Facilities

The IRS provides a wide variety of essential flight information as follows:

- primary attitude – pitch and roll;
- heading – true and magnetic;
- linear accelerations – lateral, longitudinal and normal axis;
- angular rates – pitch, roll and yaw;
- inertial velocities – north/south, east/west, groundspeed, track angle, vertical rate;
- position – latitude and longitude (lateral navigation), and inertial altitude (vertical navigation);
- wind data – windspeed, wind angle and drift angle; and
- calculated data – flightpath angle and acceleration, along and across track acceleration, inertial pitch and roll rate, vertical acceleration, and potential vertical speed.

The IRS requires inputs of latitude and longitude (present position) for initialisation, and air data computer altitude and true airspeed.

Note: The IRS provides a true heading output. The magnetic heading, which is required for normal use by the flight crew, is derived by applying the local magnetic variation obtained from a worldwide magnetic field model stored in the FMC database.

IRS Interface

Figure 3-7 shows how the various outputs from the IRS are interfaced with the various components of the overall flight management system. It also shows the necessary inputs to the IRS. The initial position required for alignment of the IRS can be provided from either the mode panel (IRMP) or from the flight management computer via the CDU.

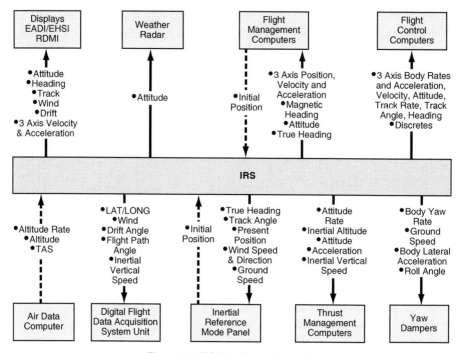

Figure 3-7 **IRS interface schematic**

IRS Alignment

For accurate IRS alignment, the aeroplane must be on the ground and stationary. Normal passenger loading and wind gusts will not affect proper alignment. During alignment, the IRS determines the local vertical and the direction of true north. The gyros in the IRU sense the angular rate of the aeroplane, and since the aeroplane is stationary, the angular rate is entirely due to earth rotation. The IRU computer uses this rate to determine the direction of true north. Since the magnitude of rotation depends on latitude, the IRU computer can also estimate the latitude of the present position.

Alignment is started by moving the IRS mode selector to NAV (see figure 3-6, page 129). The system then goes through an initial 10-second test, before starting the alignment processes. Depending on the latitude, the total alignment takes about ten minutes. During alignment, the present position in latitude and longitude must be entered. This is normally done on the CDU, and this position becomes the starting point for navigation calculation. Present position can also be entered using the IRMP. Once the alignment is completed, the ALIGN light extinguishes and, with the IRS mode selector to NAV, the system enters the navigation mode.

FMS Navigation Functions

The primary function of the FMS is to provide automatic navigation, both along the planned route (LNAV) and on the optimum flight profile (VNAV). The FMS will also provide automatic fuel monitoring, to ensure that reserve fuel is not compromised. In LNAV, the FMS will use more than one navigation source, such as an inertial reference supplemented with ground-based navigation aids.

Position Determination on the Ground

While the aircraft is on the ground, the FMC uses position data from the inertial reference system only, and requires at least one inertial reference unit to be aligned to update its present position. Because inertial systems accumulate position error as a function of time, the position information used by the FMC is also slowly accumulating errors. If these errors are large enough, they can be detected by observing the position of the aircraft symbol on the HSI in MAP mode, using the largest scale, or by comparing the FMS position with known parking bay coordinates. If a significant error is noticed, the correct position should be entered, and the IRS realigned. The aircraft must be stationary while this repositioning is completed.

Position Determination in Flight

When airborne, the FMC receives latitude and longitude data from all three IRUs, and resolves this information into an averaged position. Normally each FMC will use its own IRU data, i.e. the left FMC uses the left IRU, but in case of IRU failure, that FMC will transfer to the centre IRU. In addition to the IRS navigation source, the B767 flight management system is equipped with an automatic system that interrogates conventional navigation beacons, i.e. VOR and DME. When the HSIs are in the MAP or PLAN modes, the FMCs will automatically scan the navigation database to select and tune suitable pairs of DME stations, or a paired VOR/DME station, within 200 nm. The FMC order of priority is:

* IRS/DME/DME – IRS position plus an updated position from 2 DME stations that have a suitable cut at the aircraft;
* IRS/VOR/DME – IRS position plus an updated position from a (co-located) VOR/ DME; and lastly
* IRS only – with no updates from ground-based aids.

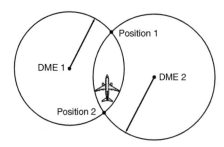

Figure 3-8 **DME/DME ambiguity**

DME/DME Updates

DME beacons are ground based, and will provide accurate circular position lines, and two suitably located DMEs will provide an accurate fix. With circular position lines, there is a possibility of ambiguity, as the circular position lines will meet at two positions, as shown in figure 3-8. The FMC resolves this ambiguity by choosing the intersection closest to the aircraft. This method is reliable unless the two positions are close together, and in that case the FMC cannot resolve the ambiguity, and will discard that DME pairing, until the aircraft has moved on to a position where the ambiguity can again be resolved.

Any pair of DME stations chosen for a DME/DME update must have a satisfactory intercept angle at the aircraft. The fundamental geometry used by the FMC in selecting station pairs for auto tuning is that the lines drawn to the aircraft from each station must intersect at an angle of between 30° and 150°, as shown in figure 3-9. However, unless the angle subtended at the aircraft is between 45° and 135°, the FMC will not use the signals for position updating. No pilot input is needed to switch from source to source, i.e. continual autotuning of ground-based navigation aids occurs.

VOR/DME Updates

When DME/DME updating is not available, the FMS will calculate a radio position using a radial and range from a single VOR/DME beacon. The VOR bearing element is not very accurate, so normally the FMS will only use VOR/DME when close to the aid. Usually VOR/DME updating will only occur in short bursts, and is given up as the aircraft approaches overhead the beacon.

IRS Only

When flying over wide expanses in countries like Africa, or outback Australia, or over the open ocean, where navigation aids may be few and far between, the FMC will use the IRS as the sole source of data, and the pilots will be given an 'IRS ONLY' message on the CDU. The IRUs may drift within the permitted tolerances, up to a value of (3+3t) nm, where t is the time in hours since the last alignment, and the FMC will continue to show calculated position on the map display on the HSI. After 3 hours of IRS only navigation, the map shift error could be as much as 10-12 nm, and in these circumstances it would be unwise to base a descent below LSALT using the position shown on the map display.

Other Radio Sources

When the aircraft is approaching to land and has captured the localiser, the FMS will use the deviation from the localiser to produce one position line to update its position. If the landing runway has an ILS/DME, then the FMS can compute an accurate position.

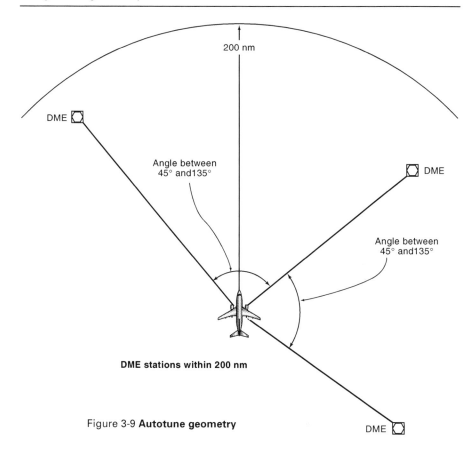

DME stations within 200 nm

Figure 3-9 **Autotune geometry**

Blacklisting

The flight crew can *blacklist* a VOR/DME that has been notified by NOTAM as unreliable. VOR/DME stations under test may radiate signals that are insufficiently accurate for navigation. The FMC cannot differentiate between good signals and test transmissions, nor can the FMC read the NOTAMS, so it is up to the crew to monitor which aids are being selected.

Note: The system uses navaids up to 200 nm away, so the serviceability of distant aids is significant.

Manual Tuning

While the FMC will endeavour to tune the best possible station pair, the pilots can tune stations manually, and if the FMC can use the signals, it will do so, as mentioned above. In any case, the tuned frequencies and station identifications are displayed on the HSI.

Lateral Navigation (LNAV)

On the ground, the pilot can load a flight plan route into the FMC by using the CDU to enter a sequence of waypoints or a pre-programmed company route. Waypoints may be entered as one of the following:

- published waypoint identifier (waypoint name);
- navaid identifier;
- published identifier (waypoint, airport or navaid), plus a bearing and distance;
- destination runway airport identifier (airport reference point); or
- course intersection latitude and longitude.

Some waypoints are called *conditional* (USA) or *pseudo* (UK) waypoints, and do not have an accurate position. Typically, conditional waypoints are associated with vertical constraints, such as a standard instrument departure (SID) requirement to maintain runway heading to 3,000 ft.

The FMS will calculate great circle tracks connecting successive waypoints, and presents this track and distance data as a series of legs on the CDU. In flight, the FMC refines its present position by calculations based on inputs from the three IRUs, and DME, VOR, or ILS. The FMC then uses its calculated present position to generate steering commands to achieve the great circle track along the active leg to the active waypoint. As a waypoint is passed, a leg switch occurs, and all waypoints scroll up one position on the active legs page. HSI map mode presentation and leg switching will continue during excursions from the flight plan.

While airborne, the FMCs do not update the IRS position. The (averaged) IRS position is only used when DME/DME or VOR/DME is not available. When this happens, and only IRS information is available, a message, IRS NAV ONLY, will appear on the FMS CDU scratchpad, and the HSI display will shift to whatever extent the (averaged) IRS position differs from the FMC computed position.

Multi-Sensor Inputs

Besides using IRS, DME and VOR to compute present position, some FMCs can also use additional sensors such as global positioning system (GPS).

The FMCs will continue to automatically scan the various navigation sources, assess their accuracy, and reject them if needed. The FMC will search through its database for suitable VOR/DME stations within 200 nm, and while no pilot input is needed to switch from source to source, the crew should be aware of which stations are in use, as displayed on the HSI and the CDU, and should cross-check the aircraft position from any other available radio aids, such as NDBs. A position update after a period of IRS only navigation will produce a lateral shift in position, i.e. a turn towards the corrected position.

Area Navigation Compliance

In the B767, the FMC with CDU meets regulatory requirements for an area navigation (RNAV) system when used with radio updating. With two FMCs, two CDUs and two or more IRSs, the systems may be used as the sole means of navigation in areas without radio coverage.

Holding Patterns

The FMC will compute holding patterns with constant-radius turns based on the current wind and the commanded airspeed. The pattern displayed on the HSI MAP is limited to remain within the ICAO tolerances. In LNAV mode, the AFDS tracks the displayed holding pattern using up to 30° bank angle, but if airspeed or wind-speed are in excess of the ICAO assumed speeds, the aircraft may leave the pro-tected airspace, as shown by the aircraft symbol or the trend vector outside the displayed pattern, and the crew may have to use the heading select mode to return to within the pattern.

Heading Hold Submode

A submode of heading hold will maintain current heading during the following conditions:

- when flying into a route discontinuity;
- when flying past the end of a lateral offset;
- when flying past the last route waypoint; and
- when executing a direct/intercept (DIR INTC) procedure, while the aircraft is outside the LNAV capture band of the active leg.

The CDU will display appropriate messages to alert the crew that corrective action may be required.

Vertical Navigation (VNAV)

Features of the standard FMS include integrated operation and control of several systems to provide automatic vertical navigation (VNAV) for optimum flight pro-files and performance management, together with automatic fuel monitoring, to ensure that reserve fuel is not compromised. The FMS performance database elim-inates the need for the crew to refer to performance manuals during flight; it pro-vides the data required to calculate pitch and thrust commands, and to ensure that speed restrictions or altitude constraints are observed. Reference data can be dis-played on the CDU, including aircraft drag and engine characteristics, maximum and optimum altitudes, and maximum and minimum airspeeds.

The data can be refined for individual aircraft by entering correction factors. The crew is warned if an altitude requirement cannot be met on present performance, so that corrective action can be taken. For instance, a steeper climb or descent can be commanded by the crew to meet an altitude constraint. Engine-out data, such as the optimum engine-out speed and the optimum engine-out drift down altitude, is also available.

After take-off, and above 400 ft RA (radio altitude), VNAV mode can be engaged if the altitude selected on the AFDS mode control panel is above the air-craft. VNAV mode will disengage if the MCP altitude is reached before reaching the FMC cruise altitude.

The VNAV profile that the FMC commands, if not modified by the crew, i.e. the default mode, is a climb at climb thrust at the airspeed limit associated with the departure airfield or airspace, say, 250 kt until above the limit altitude, then a climb at economy (ECON) speed to the cruise level entered on the CDU. Thrust is limited to maximum cruise thrust. Note that ECON operation refers to a speed schedule that is calculated to minimise the operating cost of the aircraft.

Climb/Cruise

Figure 3-10 shows a typical VNAV climb and cruise profile containing waypoint altitude constraints, and a speed transition with a limiting speed of 250 kt until above 10,000 ft. Mode annunciations that appear on the EADI are also shown.

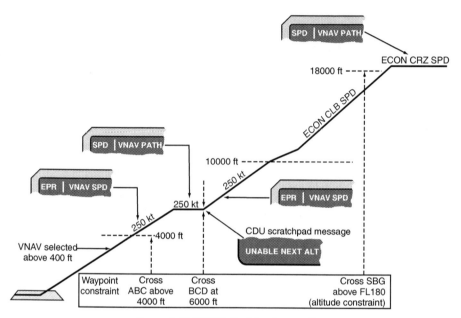

Figure 3-10 **VNAV climb/cruise profile**

The inability to reach FL180 before position SBG will be signalled by a message (UNABLE NEXT ALT) on the CDU scratchpad; the crew can then adjust the climb profile to meet the requirement, usually by selecting a different speed on the MCP that provides a steeper climb. Note that the IAS for the best climb angle can be found on the CDU climb page. VNAV will establish the aircraft in the cruise at the flight level entered on the CDU, and will adjust the autothrottle to achieve the ECON cruise speed.

Descent

Figure 3-11 shows a typical VNAV descent profile, with a *DRAG REQUIRED* message, shown on the CDU scratchpad, as the aircraft gets above the profile, a situation often caused by the effect of a tailwind on the planned descent – the crew would normally extend the speed-brakes to increase drag. Note that the descent profile also contains a missed approach segment after the landing runway threshold.

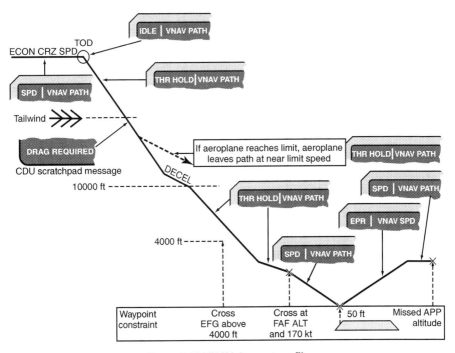

Figure 3-11 **VNAV descent profile**

Other FMS Functions

The main benefit of the FMS is its ability to automatically interface with other systems and components. This has resulted in the other systems being considered as integral parts of the full flight management system.

- Autopilot flight director system (AFDS) enables the FMC to control the aircraft in automatic flight by providing a link to the control surfaces.
- Autothrottle provides automatic thrust control from the start of take-off through climb, cruise, descent, approach and missed approach or landing.
- Electronic flight instrument system (EFIS) is an interface between the FMS and the EFIS allowing full presentation of navigation information, and advising the crew which automatic modes are engaged, armed or off (the AFDS and auto-throttle will be discussed in detail in chapter 4).

Typical CDU Operation

To explain the use of the CDU let us consider a typical flight from Melbourne to Sydney using the flight management system. Route details and other appropriate data are shown in figure 3-12. The coordinates of Melbourne Airport (YMML) are S37° 40.4 E144° 50.6, and your aeroplane is parked at Gate D4, S37° 40.2 E144° 50.7.

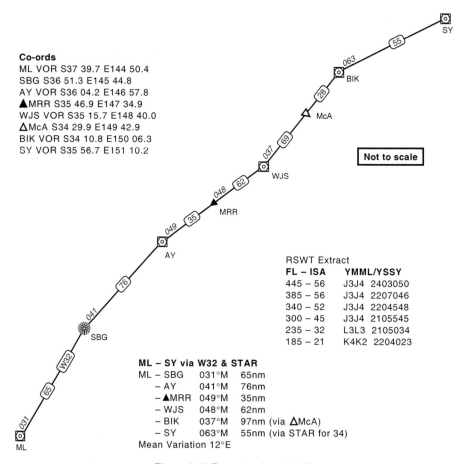

Co-ords
ML VOR S37 39.7 E144 50.4
SBG S36 51.3 E145 44.8
AY VOR S36 04.2 E146 57.8
▲MRR S35 46.9 E147 34.9
WJS VOR S35 15.7 E148 40.0
△McA S34 29.9 E149 42.9
BIK VOR S34 10.8 E150 06.3
SY VOR S35 56.7 E151 10.2

Not to scale

RSWT Extract

FL – ISA	YMML/YSSY
445 – 56	J3J4 2403050
385 – 56	J3J4 2207046
340 – 52	J3J4 2204548
300 – 45	J3J4 2105545
235 – 32	L3L3 2105034
185 – 21	K4K2 2204023

ML – SY via W32 & STAR

ML – SBG	031°M	65nm
– AY	041°M	76nm
– ▲MRR	049°M	35nm
– WJS	048°M	62nm
– BIK	037°M	97nm (via △McA)
– SY	063°M	55nm (via STAR for 34)

Mean Variation 12°E

Figure 3-12 **En route chart detail**

Identification

This is the first step in a start-of-flight sequence, and checking the IDENT page (figure 3-13) enables the crew to confirm that the correct database is installed. When power is first applied to the FMC, the IDENT page will be displayed on the CDU. If a different page is presented, selection of INIT REF on the CDU keypad will offer an INDEX cue, at line 6L. Selecting INDEX will display a list of reference pages, from which the appropriate page, in this case INIT REF, can then be selected.

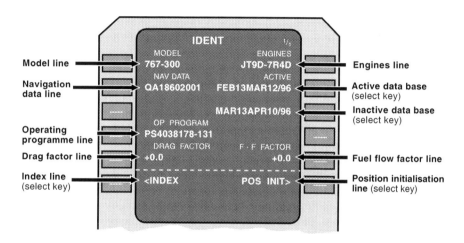

Figure 3-13 **Identification (IDENT) page**

During preflight cockpit preparation, the crew should check the information displayed on the IDENT page, particularly the validity of the database.

Let us assume that the date of the flight (in UTC) is March 13 and therefore the active navigation database for the 28-day period February 13 to March 12/96, shown at line 2R, is now out of date. The inactive database shown at line 3R has the appropriate range of effective dates, and is the database required.

To move the required database of March 13 to April 10/96 (currently shown as inactive) to the active date line, press line select key 3R. This will transfer the database to the scratchpad. If we now press line select key 2R, this database will be transferred from the scratchpad to the active date line position at line 2R. The old database of February 13 to March 12 will now show up in the inactive date line at line 3R.

In general, the next page in the preflight sequence will be offered at line 6R, but any page can be selected via the INDEX page cue at line 6L.

Position Initialisation

The next stage is to select the POS INIT (position initialisation) page by pressing the key at line 6R. This will then display the POS INIT page 1/2 (i.e. 1 of 2), as shown in figure 3-14. The last position (LAST POS at line 1R) coordinates that the FMC/IRS position retained in memory on shutdown at the end of the previous flight will be displayed, as will the GMT (UTC) time. The time will be synchronised to the time on the Captain's clock on the instrument panel. The boxes at the set IRS position line are displayed when the IRS is in ALIGN mode.

IRS Alignment

At this time, alignment of the IRS will be taking place. The present position needs to be supplied to the IRS, and this could be LAST POS, REF AIRPORT or GATE. However, the IRS needs to have the most accurate position for alignment, and this is the latitude and longitude of the gate at which the aeroplane is parked.

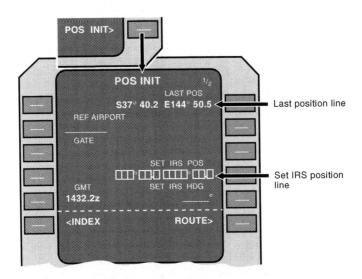

Figure 3-14 **POS INIT page 1/2 (i.e. page 1 of a total of 2 pages)**

The easiest way to tell the FMC and IRS of their present position is to enter the four-letter ICAO identifier for the airport (YMML for Melbourne) into the scratchpad using the keypad on the CDU. See figure 3-15.

Now press key at line 2L to transfer data from the scratchpad. Provided the airport information is in the navigation database, YMML and its coordinates will now appear at 2L/2R. If the coordinates of the airport are not in the database, then the crew can extract the present position data from navigation or instrument charts. This data can then be inserted into the scratchpad using the CDU keypad, and proceeding as above. Note that if an attempt is made to load an airport identifier (or waypoint) which is not stored in the database, the CDU message *'NOT IN DATABASE'* will be displayed.

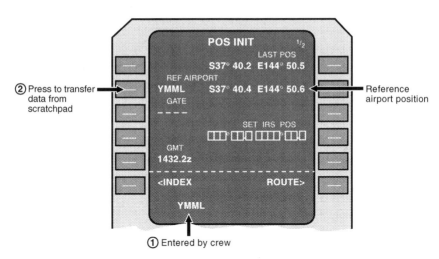

Figure 3-15 **Reference airport position entry**

The airport position could now be transferred via the scratchpad to line 4R, and used in IRS alignment. However, the most accurate present position is at the current location, in this case Gate D4 at Melbourne, and we can now proceed as before to load the coordinates of this gate.

Since IRS alignment is taking place, transfer Gate D4 position to the scratchpad by pressing key 3R, and then load this position into the IRS position line using key 4R.

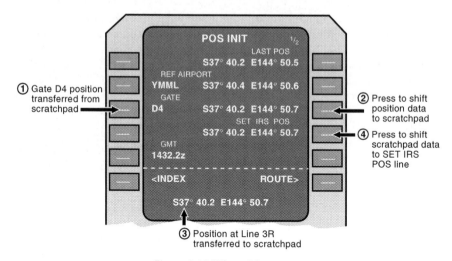

Figure 3-16 **IRS position entry**

Once the crew have entered the current position, they must cross-check the accuracy of the data entry. When the present position (in this case Gate D4) has been entered to the IRS SET POS line, this data is automatically transmitted to all three inertial reference units.

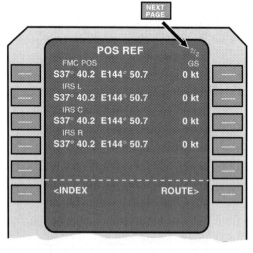

Figure 3-17 **FMS/IRS position**

By pressing NEXT PAGE on the CDU, page POS REF 2/2, position coordinates of the FMC and each IRS can be displayed and confirmed. The GS lines show the groundspeed as calculated by the FMC and IRS. Whilst stationary at the Gate, they will read 0 kt (figure 3-17). If the ALIGN light on the inertial mode panel is out, alignment of the three IRUs is complete, and they can function in the navigation mode.

Route and Departure Details

Now select ROUTE 1 (RTE 1) page by pressing line 6R key (figure 3-17) and fill in the flight plan details, as in figure 3-18. Major operators will usually have company route details in the database, which will automatically enter all the relevant waypoints in order; this company route may be identified by the three-letter code that you see on baggage tags (e.g. MEL for Melbourne, SYD for Sydney).

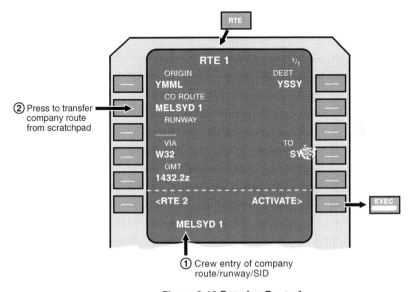

Figure 3-18 **Entering Route 1**

The most common route between Melbourne and Sydney would probably be called No. 1, and would be entered as MELSYD1. (An alternative route could be MELSYD2, which could be entered on Route 2, but for simplicity, only Route 1 will be considered.)

The particular route chosen will usually be specified on the paper flight plan used by the crew, or the crew may wish to modify the route, using waypoint identifiers from ERSA, such as ML, SY. *To avoid confusion, all NDB identifiers are entered as XXXNB, e.g. Strathbogie NDB would be loaded as SBGNB.* After transferring MELSYD1 to the company route at line 2L, all the waypoints on Route 1 will be loaded in the correct order.

Since the choice of runways at MEL will vary, the crew must load the departure details for the particular runway and SID. Runway and approach data for SY can also be loaded if known at this stage, but would normally be left until later in the flight.

SID Entry

Departure runway and SID details can be entered from the departures page, by selecting DEP/ARR on the keyboard (figure 3-19) and selecting the relevant data, e.g. Runway 34 and SID SBG3. Note that, once the runway has been selected, only the SIDs appropriate to that runway are offered. The selected runway and associated SID are now transferred in turn to the scratchpad, using keys 4L and 3R respectively.

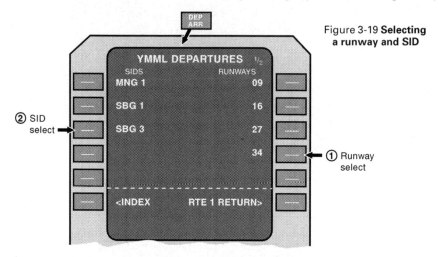

Figure 3-19 **Selecting a runway and SID**

Using key 6R, we select RTE 1 page 1/2, and transfer the RWY using key 3L, and the SID using key 4L, as shown in figure 3-20. To activate this data, press key 6R and the EXEC 4L key on the CDU keyboard will illuminate.

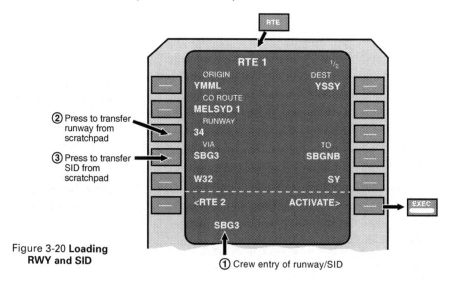

Figure 3-20 **Loading RWY and SID**

Confirming Route Details

The crew can now check that the correct route has been chosen, by reference to the CDU ROUTE and LEGS page(s), and by using the PLAN mode of the HSI, where the as yet inactive route will be displayed as a white dashed line between the waypoints, as shown in figure 3-21.

Note that the HSI PLAN display presents the route in the lower half of the display, with north up, (i.e. looking like a chart), while the visible portion of the compass rose is still TRACK up. In MAP mode, the whole display is TRACK up.

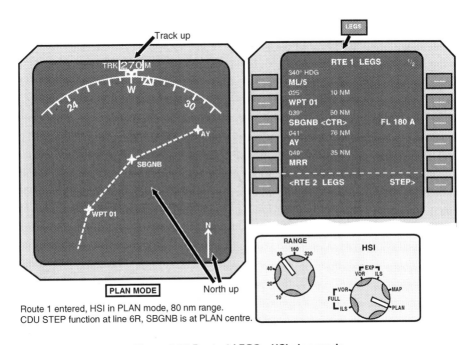

Route 1 entered, HSI in PLAN mode, 80 nm range.
CDU STEP function at line 6R, SBGNB is at PLAN centre.

Figure 3-21 **Route 1 LEGS – HSI plan mode**

The CDU shows that the waypoint in the centre of the plan display is SBGNB; the central waypoint can be stepped forward by using the STEP function at line 6R. By varying the range selected on the HSI control panel, the route can be expanded and compared with the navigation chart.

Route Activation

By returning to the map mode of the HSI, the CDU display on the Route 1 page
will show an ACTIVATE cue at line 6R, see figure 3-22.

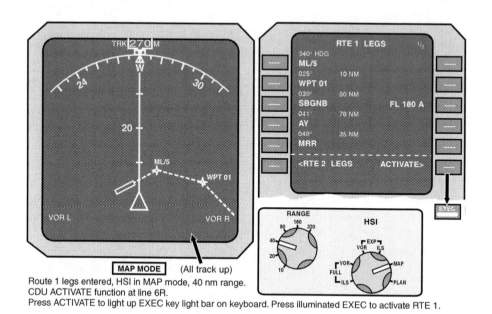

MAP MODE   (All track up)
Route 1 legs entered, HSI in MAP mode, 40 nm range.
CDU ACTIVATE function at line 6R.
Press ACTIVATE to light up EXEC key light bar on keyboard. Press illuminated EXEC to activate RTE 1.

Figure 3-22 **RTE 1 LEGS not yet active**

To activate the chosen route, select the ACTIVATE cue; the EXECute key will
illuminate. Press the EXEC key and activate the route. *Company procedures may
require both pilots to agree about the entered route, before the EXEC key is pushed.* Note
that the page title will change to show ACT RTE 1 (figure 3-23) and, on the HSI,
the active route will be displayed as a solid magenta line through the waypoints, in
either MAP or PLAN modes.

The active waypoint, ML/5, the one shown at line 1L on the CDU LEGS page
(figure 3-24), will be displayed on the HSI (map) as a bright magenta star. Subsequent waypoints are shown in white.

On the LEGS page, figure 3-24, note the altitude constraint, FL180A, a requirement to cross the SBG NB *above* FL180; FL180B would mean cross the position
below FL180. A requirement to cross the waypoint *between* two limits is shown as
FL180A FL200B.

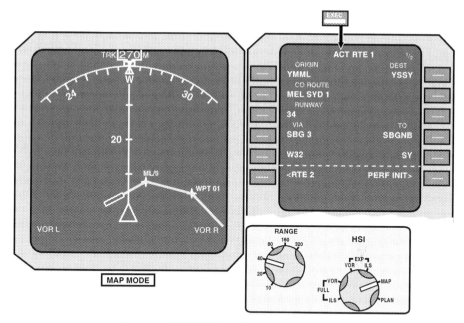

Figure 3-23 **ACT RTE 1 – HSI map 40 nm range**

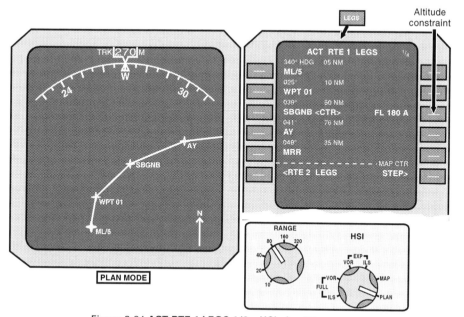

Figure 3-24 **ACT RTE 1 LEGS 1/2 – HSI plan 80 nm range**

Figure 3-25 shows the HSI range scale at 20 nm, with runway and initial departure detail.

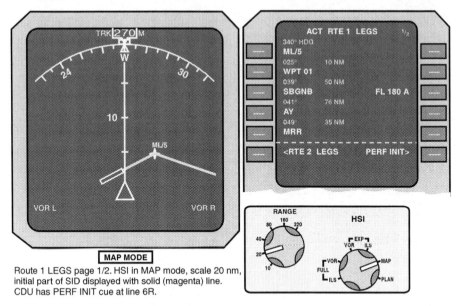

Route 1 LEGS page 1/2. HSI in MAP mode, scale 20 nm, initial part of SID displayed with solid (magenta) line. CDU has PERF INIT cue at line 6R.

Figure 3-25 **ACT RTE 1 LEGS, HSI map 20 nm range**

Performance Initialisation

Next, press key 6R (figure 3-25) to bring up the PERF INIT page, and enter information from the flight plan and load sheet into the relevant boxes as shown in figure. 3-26.

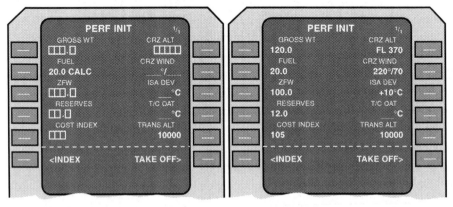

Figure 3-26 **PERF INIT page 1/1**   **Performance data entered**

Remember: the boxes must be filled. The information requested by the dashed line entries is not essential, but is used to fine-tune performance.

Normally, the data would be loaded in the order:
* cost index (airline specification);
* reserves at destination (flight plan fuel reserves);
* ZFW (zero fuel weight from loadsheet);
* CRZ ALT (flight plan cruise altitude); and
* any 'dashed' information that it is convenient to insert.

Take-Off Data Entry

The next selection, TAKE OFF, line 6R (figure 3-26), presents the TAKE OFF REF page shown in figure 3-27, that permits crew entry of:
* assumed temperature, if planning a reduced-thrust take-off;
* the thrust setting to be used for take-off (EPR) from the thrust management computer, using the assumed temperature;
* V_1, V_R, and V_2, as reminder items (later versions of the FMS may have automatic entry of this data, which can then be displayed on the speed scale in the ADI);
* a PERF INIT cue at line 5L, if PERF INIT data is not complete; and
* DEPARTURE page selection at line 5R, for crew selection of the appropriate departure procedure, including any vertical constraints, if not already selected.

Note that, for some engines, the N1 value, rather than EPR, may be displayed. Company procedures may still require the crew to refer to the flight manual and Jeppesen charts for confirmation of the computer-derived data.

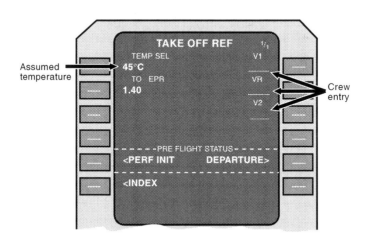

Figure 3-27 **TAKE OFF REF page 1/1**

Departure

As the aircraft lines up for take-off on Runway 34 at Melbourne, the runway centre-line will be hidden under the track line, and the active route in magenta shows a turn at 5 DME to track 025M to intercept the FTH VOR 039 radial, labelled as WPT01 a *conditional* waypoint. Both navaids are tuned to the ML VOR (figure 3-28).

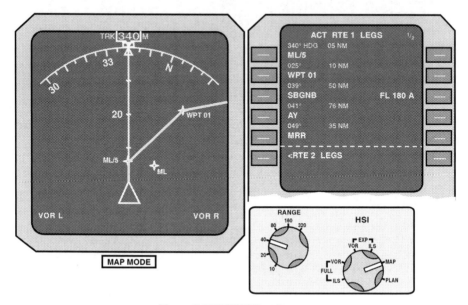

Figure 3-28 **HSI/CDU at line up**

After take-off, the flight director may be switched from take-off (TO) mode to LNAV and VNAV modes, and once above a predetermined RA, the autopilot can be engaged in the same modes, with the EFIS displays showing progress along the route (figure 3-29). The turn vector (curved, dotted) is indicating a right turn, and the pilot has moved the selected heading marker to 025°M (straight, dotted). Way-point ML/5 is being passed, and has become inactive. WPT01 is the active way-point, shown in magenta on the HSI, and at line 1L on the CDU. The CDU can be interrogated on various pages to present any stored data.

Figure 3-30 shows an ECON climb page, climbing at 320 kt into M = 0.74, to FL370, with a requirement to cross SBGNB above FL180. The altitude constraint can be procedural, or crew entered as an ATC requirement. The airspeed for max-imum angle of climb (V_X) is shown as 245 kt, and there is access to engine-out data.

The CLB DIR (Climb Direct) cue, at line 6R, would be used by the crew to eliminate any altitude or airspeed constraints removed by a revised ATC clearance.

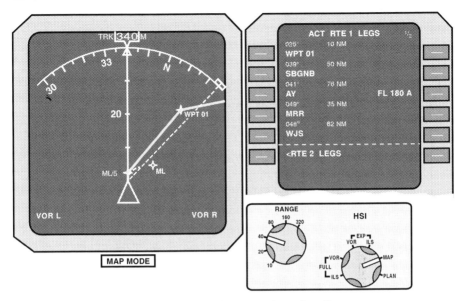

Figure 3-29 **HSI/CDU just after take-off**

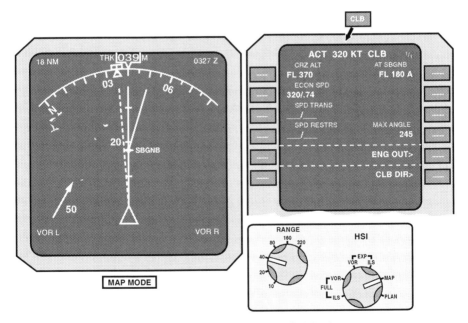

Figure 3-30 **Climb page (press CLB key)**

Route Modification – Direct/Intercept

At any point the crew can be instructed by ATC to track direct to a specified position. By pressing the DIR INTC (direct/intercept) key, a page like figure 3-31 is presented.

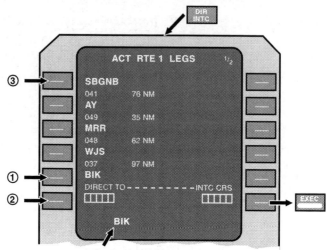

1. Crew entry of BIK in scratchpad, or line select line 5L
2. Line select line 6L to put BIK into the Direct To Box
3. BIK will become the active waypoint at line 1L,
   followed by the remainder of the flight plan waypoints
4. Press EXEC to activate modified route

Figure 3-31 **Direct/Intercept page 1/2**

This page is one of the LEGS family of pages, and shows the current active route, with a DIRECT TO box at line 6L, and an INTC CRS (intercept) box at line 6R. Let us suppose that ATC have cleared the aircraft direct to BIK, shown at line 5L. Line select 5L to put BIK in the scratchpad, then line select 6L to put BIK into the DIRECT TO boxes; the screen will then look like figure 3-32, a MODified route, which also shows on the HSI as a white dashed line, as in figure 3-32. This page is one of the LEGS family of pages, and shows the current active route, with a DIRECT TO box at line 6L, and an INTC CRS (intercept) box at line 6R. Let us suppose that ATC have cleared the aircraft direct to BIK, shown at line 5L. Line select 5L to put BIK in the scratchpad, then line select 6L to put BIK into the DIRECT TO boxes; the screen will then look like figure 3-32, a MODified route, which also shows on the HSI as a white dashed line, as in figure 3-32. If the crew is satisfied with the route modification, this route can be made the active route by pressing the (illuminated) EXEC key; the page title will change to ACT RTE 1 LEGS, and the HSI will show the direct track to BIK in magenta as shown in figure 3-33.

If the ATC requirement was to intercept a specified radial of the BIK VOR, inbound (say the 230° radial inbound to BIK), then selecting BIK into line 6R would bring up INTC CRS boxes at line 6R; enter 050°, i.e. the inbound course on the 230 radial.

The crew must ensure that the aircraft is on a suitable heading to intercept the desired inbound course, and this is easily discernible on the EHSI. Failing that, the CDU will bring up the message, *NOT ON INTERCEPT HEADING*.

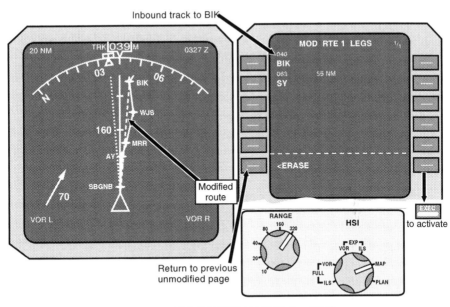

Figure 3-32 **MOD ROUTE 1 LEGS direct BIK**

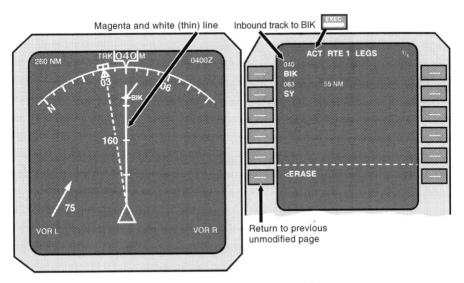

Figure 3-33 **Revised ACT RTE 1 LEGS**

Route Discontinuity

Occasionally a route page will appear with a route discontinuity between the legs, particularly if a route modification has been made, and the new route is not linked to the previous route. In figure 3-34, Sydney Control has diverted the flight, for separation purposes, from MRR to the NDB at Rugby, and thence to BIK and SY.

The crew have used the DIR/INTC page to make RUGNB the active waypoint, but have not told the FMS what to do after reaching RUGNB. There is therefore a gap between RUGNB and the next waypoint at BIK. This is shown as a *black hole* on the HSI, and as a route discontinuity message on the CDU.

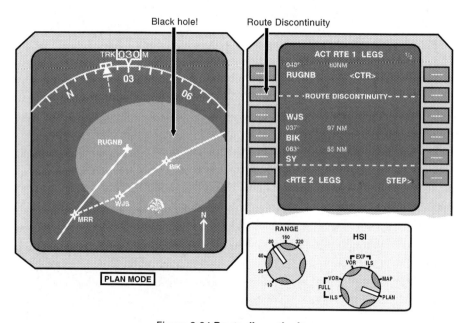

Figure 3-34 **Route discontinuity**

By bringing the waypoint BIK via the scratchpad to line 2L, the modified route will be linked to the original route, and the discontinuity and the black hole will disappear.

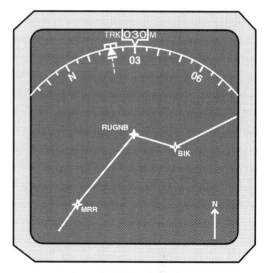

Figure 3-35 **Modified Route**

Progress

Press the PROG key on the CDU to display the PROGRESS page 1/2, shown at figure 3-36. This records that the aircraft crossed SBGNB at FL230 at 0326Z, and shows the distance to go (DTG), the ETA and fuel state at the next two waypoints and the destination. The distance and time to the descent is also shown.

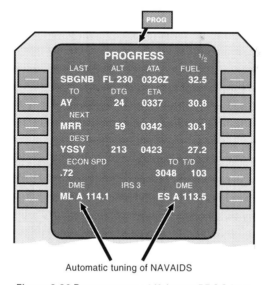

Automatic tuning of NAVAIDS

Figure 3-36 **Progress page 1/2 (press PROG key)**

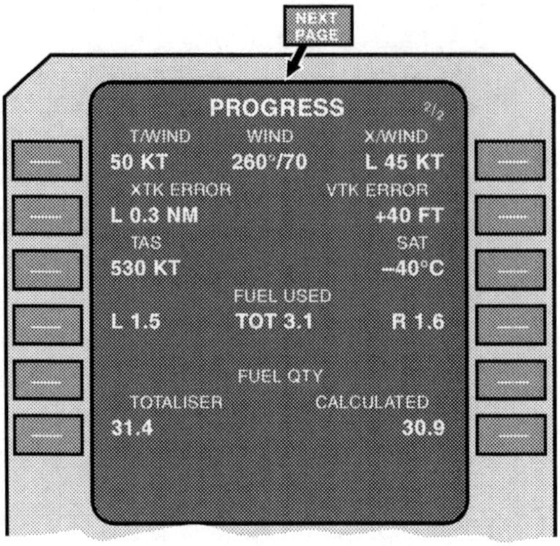

Figure 3-37 **Progress page 2/2 (press NEXT PAGE)**

Press NEXT PAGE to display progress page 2/2, figure 3-37, which shows details of the wind effect, track error, TAS, and fuel status.

Cruise

Press the CRZ key to bring up the active ECON cruise page, shown in figure 3-38. A step climb to FL390 is offered together with the resulting fuel saving. Access to engine-out data and long-range cruise data is also available.

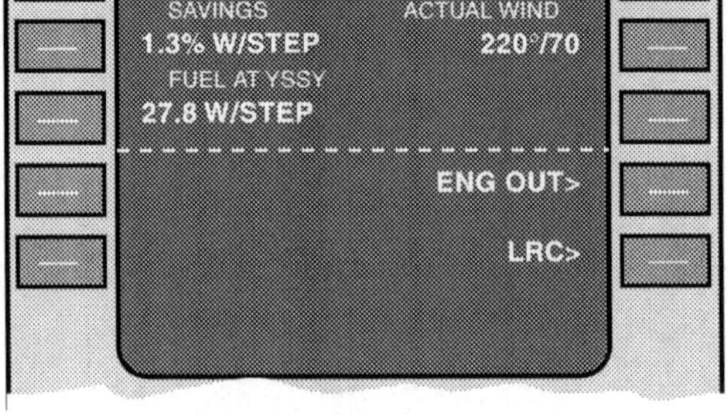

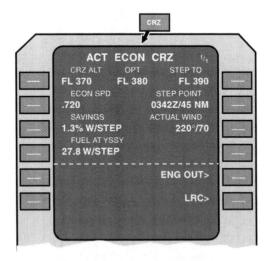

Figure 3-38 **Economy cruise (ECON CRZ) page**

Fix

Press the FIX key to bring up the FIX INFO page shown in figure 3-39. The fix ABC has been inserted via the scratchpad and the CDU displays that the aircraft is on a bearing of 180° from ABC at a range of 35 nm.

Pressing line 5L, the ABM cue, shows that the aircraft track will pass abeam ABC on a bearing of 130° at 20 nm from ABC.

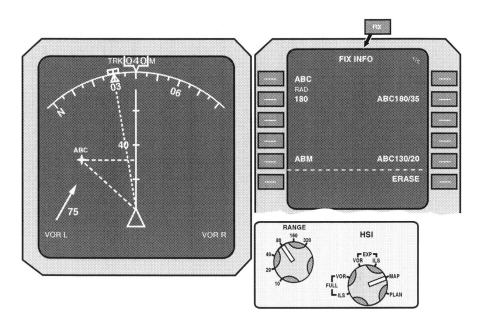

Figure 3-39 **Fix page 1/2**

A fix position can also be called up by line selection from another page, and selected radials can be entered, and the display will then show the distances along the flightpath to the intersection with the selected radial. Each of these intersections will be displayed on the HSI, and can be used to establish new waypoints, by line selection to the ACT RTE LEGS page. A second fix can be loaded on FIX page 2/2.

Holding

If there is a requirement to enter a holding pattern, pressing the HOLD key will bring up a page like figure 3-40, another of the LEGS family.

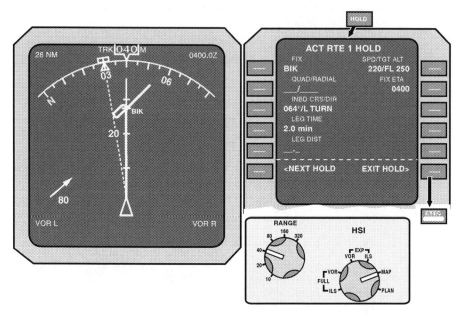

Figure 3-40 **HOLD page, holding pattern entry HSI/CDU**

Holding pattern details may be stored in the database, or the crew may enter appropriate data. Entry of a holding pattern is a route modification, so the EXEC key must be pressed to activate the route modification, and the FMC will be *armed to capture* the holding pattern, which will also be displayed on the HSI.

The diameter of holding pattern turns, i.e. the distance between the outbound and inbound legs, is a function of the groundspeed at the time of crossing the holding fix.

To take account of increases in TAS with increasing altitude at a fixed IAS, the length of the outbound leg above FL140 is based on 1.5 minutes or the time/distance limit specified for the holding pattern shown on the chart.

When holding at altitude, say at Bindook on the route into Sydney, with a fairly high TAS and a substantial tailwind, it is advisable to reduce airspeed well before arriving at Bindook to avoid a very large pattern being commanded by the FMC. It may be necessary to override LNAV, and perhaps use HDG SELECT.

To leave the holding pattern, press key 6R, EXIT HOLD; the aircraft will immediately turn towards the holding fix, and resume tracking to the next waypoint.

Arrival

Page selection of DEP/ARR will present possible approach paths (STARS) to the selected runway, which will include holding patterns and missed approach procedures (figure 3-41). In this case, ATC has cleared the aircraft via Oakdale 2 STAR to the Runway 07 ILS. The relevant detail is shown on the EFIS display. There may be a change to the descent profile depending on how much manoeuvring is planned.

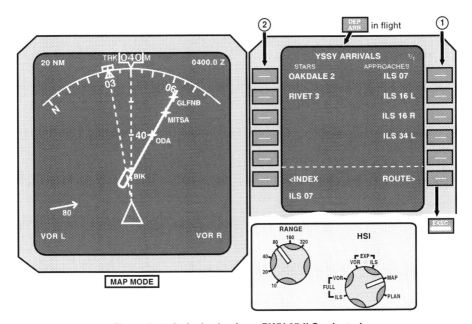

Figure 3-41 **Arrival selection – RWY 07 ILS selected**

This route amendment for RWY 07 ILS has been made active by pressing the EXEC key, and will now be shown on the CDU on ACT RTE 1 LEGS pages 1/2 and 2/2.

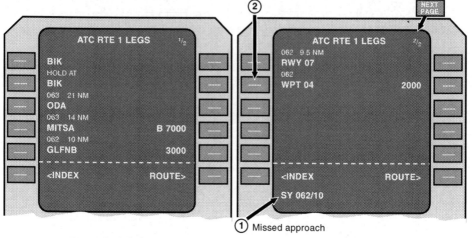

Figure 3-42 **Oakdale transition to RWY 07 ILS and missed approach**

Non-STAR Procedure

When there is no STAR procedure available, the crew may construct an approach by inserting appropriate waypoints, as shown in figure 3-43.

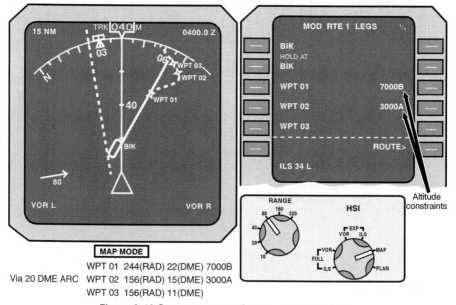

Figure 3-43 **Crew constructed approach to RWY 34L**

In this case, the intention is to turn right off the RWY 07 ILS track at 22 nm DME (SY), acquire the 20 nm DME arc, and follow this arc anticlockwise to intercept RWY 34L ILS. The waypoints inserted are:
*   WPT 01 – 244° (RAD) 22 (DME) (SY);
*   WPT 02 – 156° (RAD) 15 (DME) (SY); and
*   WPT 03 – 156° (RAD) 11 (DME) (SY).

Altitude constraints are:
*   Below 7,000 ft at WPT01.
*   Above 3,000 ft at WPT02.

The normal procedure to fly this DME arc path would be using HDG SEL, until just before the left turn to track to WPT 02, which is at SY156/15, a convenient point on the RWY 34L localiser. At this stage, the ILS approach could be armed.

Figure 3-44 shows the modified route in PLAN mode on the HSI and page 2/2 of the MOD RTE 1 LEGS, with RWY 34L ILS selected on the scratchpad from the YSSY arrivals page (line select key 4R on figure 3-41, page 159), and transferred from the scratchpad at line select key 1L.

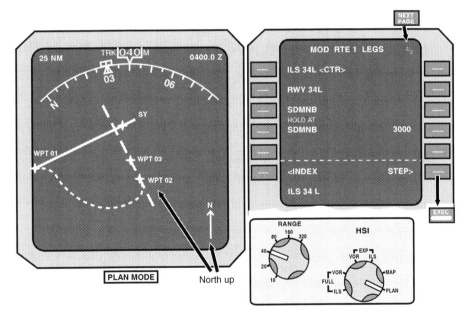

Figure 3-44 **Route modification – 20 DME arc approach**

Descent

Selection of the DEScent key will display a page like figure 3-45 that allows evaluation or revision of the VNAV descent phase of the flight. (See VNAV profile figure 3-11, page 137). The 300 kt DES page shows a descent at a selected speed of 300 kt to an end descent (E/D) point at the RWY 07 threshold, at 300 ft, crossing MITSA at 3,000 ft and 170 kt. An ECON descent can be set up using the ECON cue at line 5L. A speed reduction to 240 kt is required at 10,000 ft. Selection of the Oakdale transition to the 07ILS has imposed an altitude constraint to cross Mitsa below 7,000 ft (this constraint appears on the MOD RTE 1 LEGS page shown at figure 3-43, page 160).

The descent path error is shown as 350 ft above the profile, on the HSI, and CDU, producing a potential level off at 3,000 ft, 2 nm beyond Mitsa. Time to increase descent rate? The aircraft is left of the active route 063°M from the BIK VOR, heading 077°M and tracking 070°M, to intercept the 063 radial about 15 nm ahead. The active waypoint is ODA.

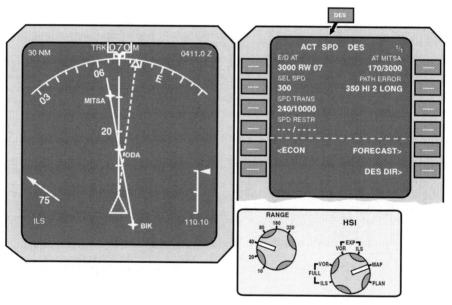

Figure 3-45 **Descent page**

Approach

At any convenient time in flight, selection of the INIT REF key will bring up an APPROACH REFerence page, as shown at figure 3-46, which displays:

- gross weight;
- appropriate VREF speeds for various flap settings;
- runway length;
- ILS frequency and ident; and
- ILS course.

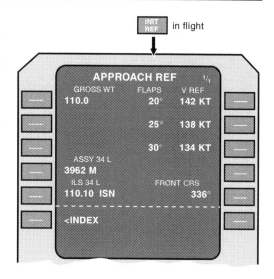

Figure 3-46 **APP REF page**

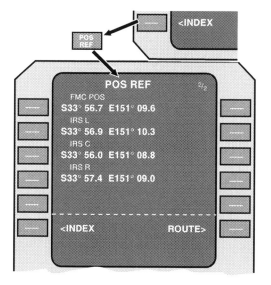

Figure 3-47 **Parking ramp position**

Shutdown

When the aircraft is parked, the crew can cross-check navigational discrepancies for the total system and each IRU, by comparing present (last) position with the known position on the ramp, as in figure 3-47. There is an acceptable tolerance. Greater errors should be notified to maintenance.

Summary of FMS

The flight management system provides the crew with the capacity to control virtually every facet of the aircraft's flightpath and profile. It embraces navigation, aircraft performance and automatic flight from take-off to touchdown.

However, because it is such a powerful tool, the crew must avoid the temptation to be complacent and believe that, *'nothing can go wrong ... go wrong ... go wrong ...'*

The crew are still responsible for the safety of the flight and should take full advantage of the facilities offered by the FMS to achieve a smooth, safe and, hopefully, uneventful flight.

For these reasons, a thorough understanding of how the FMS operates and its capabilities – and limitations – is essential. In this chapter we have aimed to give the reader an insight into the fundamentals of the FMS so that, when the time comes to undergo specific type training, it will be more easily understood.

Chapter 4

Automatic Flight Control Systems

The *automatic flight control system* (AFCS) is one of the most (if not the most) important systems associated with the control of the aircraft. It has the ability to interface with navigation systems and allow automatic navigation on a pre-programmed track and flight profile. These features contribute considerably to the overall safety of flight operations, provided that the crew maintain situational awareness.

The AFCS may consist of only the autopilot and the flight director, and provide an interface with other autoflight systems such as the yaw damper and autothrottle. However, in many aircraft these other systems are fully integrated in an autopilot flight director system (AFDS).

For convenience, these systems will be discussed in the following order:
• autopilot systems;
• yaw damper;
• autopilot flight director systems; and
• autothrottle.

The Autopilot

When aircraft first travelled significant distances, pilot workload was high because of heavy manual controls and the need to maintain straight and level flight for long periods. This was made difficult because of the continuous control corrections required as the aircraft attempted to diverge from its flightpath.

As a consequence, simple autopilots were developed to assist the pilot during long flights. The first autopilots were devices which kept the wings level by correcting deviations that were detected by a gyroscopic sensor. These were quickly upgraded to autopilots which maintained wings level whilst, at the same time, holding a set pitch attitude. Thus, by engaging the autopilot when the aircraft was established in the cruise, the pilot could use the autopilot to hold heading and altitude for significant periods. If a heading change was required, or when aircraft weight changed enough to require an adjustment to pitch attitude, the pilot could disconnect the autopilot, adjust the aircraft attitude and trim as needed, and then re-engage the autopilot.

From these early systems, it was a logical development to provide the autopilot with a range of data from other sensors, so that it could maintain the required flight conditions such as altitude, heading or track.

This principle is known as *coupling*, where the autopilot is coupled to a sensor to maintain a specific parameter.

Note: The autopilot is 'live' as long as electrical power is available, and it shadows aircraft behaviour so that when the pilot engages the autopilot, the transition to automatic flight is smooth (i.e. in trim).

Today, coupling the autopilot to a navigation system or a flight management system can provide automatic flight from after take-off to touchdown and even rollout in aircraft equipped for autolanding. However, most transport aircraft are equipped only for coupled autoflight from just after take-off to Category 1 ILS minima – normally about 200 ft decision height (DH).

Classification of Autopilot Systems

Although all modern transport aircraft are fitted with autopilots that provide full control of the aircraft in all three axes, systems fitted to smaller aircraft may give less control. Description of the different classes of autopilot follow.

Single-Axis Autopilot

This type of autopilot provides control of the aircraft about only one axis, the longitudinal axis. Consequently, it only provides roll control by automatically operating the ailerons.

In its simplest form, a single-axis autopilot is only a wing-leveller; however, in most systems, there is input from the directional gyro or compass system to maintain a set heading. The pilot may also operate the automatic bank control by providing commands through a small control wheel on the automatic pilot controller. In this way the pilot can achieve a heading change without disconnecting the autopilot.

Two-Axis Autopilot

In a two-axis system, control is provided about the lateral and longitudinal axes by the elevators and ailerons respectively. These systems normally have the capability to capture and hold a heading or VOR navigation track and a preset cruising altitude. Two-axis systems are common in lighter aircraft approved for IFR flight.

Three-Axis Autopilot

This is the full autopilot found in modern transport aircraft and provides full control and stability about all three axes (longitudinal, lateral and normal).

These systems also have significantly more operating modes, such as:
- heading capture and hold;
- altitude capture and hold;
- vertical speed hold;
- IAS hold in climb and descent;
- coupling to VOR, localiser and glidepath;
- coupling to FMS flight plan track;
- climb and descent profile (vertical navigation); and, for some aircraft,
- autoland.

Autopilot Components

The basic concept of an autopilot system is shown below in figure 4-1.

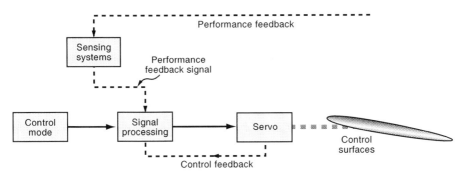

Figure 4-1 **Typical autopilot system**

Depending on the complexity of a particular system, components may have slightly different functions. General functions, however, are as described as follows.

Autopilot Control

The control function allows the pilot to engage and disengage the autopilot, and instruct it to follow selected paths such as navigation tracks, climbs/descents, and specified altitudes. These paths are normally referred to as *modes*.

The engage/disengage function may be located on the same panel as that used for selecting autopilot modes, or may be on a separate panel. When the autopilot is not engaged, selecting various modes will normally activate the flight director to give pitch and roll commands to allow the required mode to be achieved.

Signal Processing

The autopilot can command virtually any flightpath, provided it is within the performance capability of the aircraft.

To satisfy various altitude and speed requirements, the signal processing function must be capable of varying the demanded control deflection to suit the situation. Control inputs needed to hold an ILS glidepath at low speed will be different from those needed to maintain altitude and heading whilst in the cruise at a high Mach number. (This control response is called *gain*.) To meet these demands, the signal processing function of the AFCS must be suitably programmed, and in addition to providing an output signal to the controls to satisfy a selected mode (e.g. hold a selected altitude), the processor must constantly analyse inputs to see if the required values are being achieved.

Sensors must provide inputs about deviations from the selected value. Also, the processor must receive feedback from the control servos to ensure that the commanded control movements have been achieved.

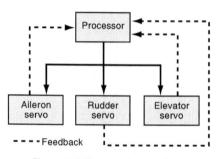

Figure 4-2 **Three-axis autopilot, controlling three servos**

Servos

Electrical signals from the processor command the flight control system to move as needed. Since a modern three-axis autopilot controls the aircraft in all directions, the processor must provide command inputs to three separate servo systems, as shown in figure 4-2.

The servos are normally hydraulic actuators that mechanically operate the control surface. As mentioned earlier, a feedback signal must also be provided. To achieve this, the servo responds to feedback that reduces the input signal and thus reduces the control applied.

Consequently, the feedback element produces a signal which cancels *(washes out)* the input signal, thereby limiting servomotor operation until it stops with the control surface in the required position. In the case of the rudder, command signals are provided by the yaw damper (which responds to a rate gyro).

Flight Control Surfaces

Because modern aircraft are very large and may have split control surfaces on each axis (e.g. inboard and outboard ailerons), a number of servomotors may be required for each axis. In addition to ailerons, lateral control may be achieved or assisted by spoilers.

Sensing Systems

Once the control surface has moved, an alteration to aircraft flightpath will occur. This alteration will then be detected by the appropriate system (e.g. air data computer for a change in speed), which will provide a performance feedback signal to the autopilot processor. In this way, command signals can be varied to ensure that the correct performance is achieved.

Performance feedback signals are typically provided by:
• air data computer (speed and Mach);
• encoding altimeter (altitude);
• gyro compass or inertial reference (heading);
• FMS (navigation track); and
• rate gyro (yaw damping).

Disengagement Warning

Autopilots feature a unique aural warning and a flashing light triggered if the autopilot disengages, either by the pilot selecting the system off, or by a failure. Either way, the pilot has to push a cancel button in order to silence the aural warning and extinguish the flashing light. The warning feature is particularly important for guarding against subtle disengagement which otherwise might go undetected.

Autopilot Control Systems

Autopilot Control Panel

Figure 4-3 shows a typical autopilot control panel for many earlier aircraft, such as those introduced into service up to the mid-1980s.

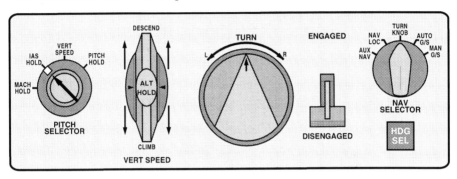

Figure 4-3 **Typical autopilot control panel**

The panel shown includes the engage/disengage function together with the various mode selections. On some installations, mode selector switches may be located on a separate mode selection panel. The controls displayed in figure 4-3 have the following functions.

Engage/Disengage Switch

This switch (figure 4-4) engages or disengages the autopilot. The autopilot cannot be engaged if the turn knob is out of the centre detent position. The switch is electrically held in the engage position, and loss of electrical power, or a signal from the autopilot disconnect on the control column, will cause the switch to spring back to disengage.

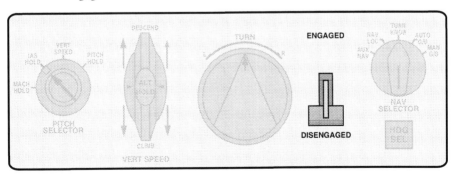

Figure 4-4 **Engage/disengage switch**

Pitch Selector

The pitch (mode) selector (figure 4-5) determines which vertical mode is engaged from the options shown on the selector:

- Mach hold;
- IAS hold;
- vertical speed; and
- pitch hold.

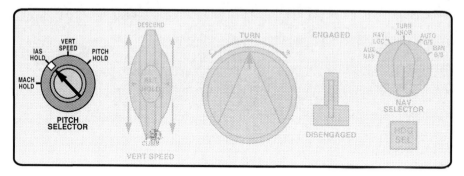

Figure 4-5 **Pitch selector**

When selecting either Mach, IAS, vertical speed, or pitch, the autopilot will hold the value existing when that mode is engaged. For example, if the autopilot was engaged in the IAS hold mode when the IAS was 230 kt, the autopilot would maintain that speed by adjusting pitch attitude. If engine thrust is reduced whilst in IAS hold, then clearly the autopilot will pitch the aircraft nose down, and vice versa.

Similarly, if the pitch hold mode is engaged, and engine thrust is reduced, the autopilot will maintain the pitch attitude and allow the airspeed to reduce. To adjust the Mach, IAS or pitch value being held, the pilot can rotate the vertical speed wheel in the appropriate direction to adjust the vertical speed, until the desired value of Mach, IAS, or pitch is achieved, when Mach or IAS hold can be selected again.

The hold modes (Mach, IAS, or pitch) become inoperative, and the pitch mode selector reverts to the vertical speed position, when:

- the vertical speed wheel is moved;
- altitude hold is engaged; or
- an ILS glideslope is captured.

Vertical Speed Wheel

When vertical speed is selected on the pitch mode selector, the pitch attitude is controlled by the pilot rotating the vertical speed wheel (sometimes called the pitch wheel) in figure 4-6. Movement of this wheel forward will signal the autopilot to lower the nose of the aircraft, commanding a higher descent value or lesser climb value, depending on the value being held. Conversely, movement of the pitch wheel backward will raise the nose of the aircraft. This is the basic pitch mode of the autopilot.

The vertical speed wheel is indexed in 500 ft increments and rotates automatically to match current vertical speed when the pitch selector is in any mode other than vertical speed, whether the autopilot is engaged or not. This ensures smooth engagement of the autopilot. Any movement of the vertical speed wheel will cause a corresponding attitude change to achieve the selected rate of climb or descent, as indicated by the scale on the wheel. In pitch modes other than vertical speed, any pilot-induced movement of the pitch wheel will override the selected pitch mode, and the pitch mode selector will revert to vertical speed.

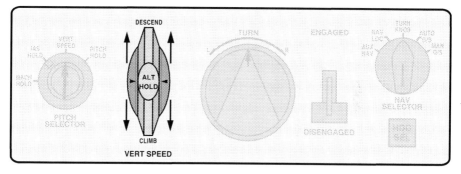

Figure 4-6 **Vertical speed wheel/altitude hold**

Vertical speed is INOP when:
- a glideslope is captured; or
- the autopilot is disengaged.

Altitude Hold

Altitude hold is a sub-mode of the vertical speed wheel. Positioning the pitch wheel in the central detent position, altitude hold, will command the autopilot to adjust the pitch attitude to hold the present altitude. On most autopilots any pre-selected altitude to be acquired on climb or descent is entered via a separate controller, and the autopilot vertical speed wheel will move to altitude hold as the selected altitude is captured.

Altitude hold will disengage if:
- go around is selected;
- the glideslope is captured in APP AUTO mode;
- APP MAN is selected;
- the vertical speed wheel is moved from centre detent position; or
- the autopilot is disengaged.

Navigation Mode Selector

In some installations the selector shown in figure 4-7 may be referred to as an azimuth or lateral mode selector. It allows the pilot to connect the autopilot to the required navigation system for automatic steering.

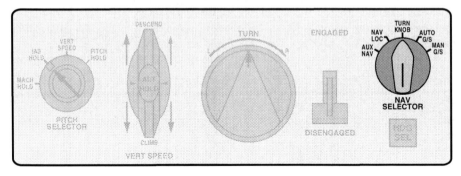

Figure 4-7 **Navigation (mode) selector**

Navigation modes available are:
- AUX NAV;
- NAV/LOC;
- TURN KNOB;
- AUTO G/S; and
- MAN G/S.

Selection of AUX NAV programs the autopilot to respond to signals from a secondary navigation receiver, such as INS or GPS.

The NAV/LOC selection programs the autopilot system to respond to signals from the primary VHF navigation system so that it will acquire and follow a selected VOR radial or localiser track.

The autopilot must be steered towards the selected course (until it is captured).

Positioning the navigation mode selector to TURN KNOB activates the turn knob; this is the manual steering mode of the autopilot.

AUTO G/S arms the autopilot system to maintain the current pitch and roll modes until the selected localiser track is intercepted, after which the autopilot will track the localiser. When the glideslope is captured, the pitch mode selector will revert to vertical speed, and the autopilot will control the aircraft to follow the glideslope and its associated glidepath. Some autopilots will not capture the glideslope unless the localiser has been captured first.

MAN G/S arms the autopilot to immediately intercept the localiser at a programmed intercept angle, usually 30°, and to climb or descend, as appropriate, to intercept and track the glideslope. Some autopilots will not respond to MAN G/S from above the glideslope, and in this case, the pilot must use the pitch wheel to institute a descent of sufficient magnitude to intercept the glideslope from below.

Turn Knob

The turn knob allows the pilot to steer the aircraft without disconnecting the autopilot.

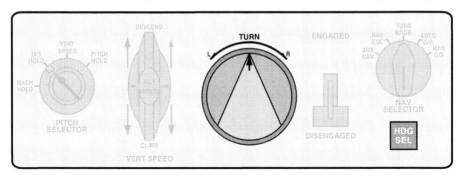

Figure 4-8 **The turn knob**

In the installation shown in figure 4-8, movement of the turn knob out of its detent will override any current navigation mode, and the navigation mode selector will revert to TURN KNOB mode. Once out of the detent position, the turn knob will remain at its displaced position, and the aircraft will continue to turn in the direction commanded by the turn knob. The further the turn knob is displaced, the greater the bank angle achieved, up to a maximum of about 30°. The knob must be centred manually to return to level flight. The turn knob must be in the detent position before another navigation mode can be selected (and for the autopilot to be engaged).

Heading Select Button

When selected, this button engages a heading function which commands the autopilot to follow the selected heading on the HSI. In other systems, the heading select mode may be engaged by another position on the NAV selector. However, by providing a specific button for this mode, as shown in this system, heading select (HDG SEL) can be selected quickly. Engaging HDG SEL will cancel other NAV modes.

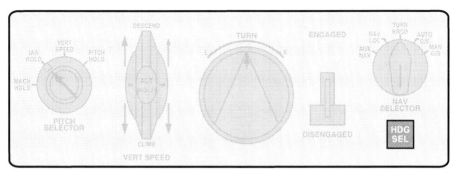

Figure 4-9 **Heading select**

Mode Annunciators

In all systems, some method of displaying the selected autopilot mode is provided. The system in figure 4-3 (page 169) uses a separate mode annunciator panel, in full view of the pilot, while the control panel can be located on the centre pedestal. Since the flight director can be engaged for the same modes as the autopilot, the system illustrated has the same annunciators for both systems (refer to chapter 2).

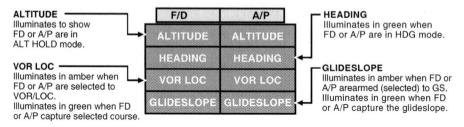

Figure 4-10 **Mode annuciators**

When armed or engaged, the appropriate annunciator is normally illuminated in amber for armed modes, and green for engaged modes. Thus if the autopilot is engaged for both altitude hold and heading hold, then the A/P annunciator together with the altitude and heading annunciators on the right will be illuminated.

On EFIS-equipped aircraft, autopilot and flight director modes are normally displayed on the ADI. For systems that use push buttons rather than the rotary selectors shown in figure 4-3, the mode annunciator may be part of each button.

Yaw Damper

You will be aware of the effects of reduced directional stability at high speed and altitude, and the interaction of lateral and directional stability which can lead to *Dutch roll*.

Depending on the inherent stability of an aircraft in a particular configuration, the Dutch roll oscillation may tend to gradually reduce, a process known as *damping*. Some aircraft have good damping characteristics and only mild levels of Dutch roll are experienced. However, in some swept-wing aircraft, the degree of Dutch roll can be significant, and requires active correction. Such a system is called a *yaw damper.*

Types of Yaw Damper

In a three-axis flight control system the rudder channel is used to balance turns initiated by the ailerons, and may also provide automatic yaw damping. This type of yaw damper is called a parallel type since the two functions of the rudder channel operate at the same time, i.e. in parallel. Alternatively, the yaw damping function may be independent of the autopilot rudder channel and may employ a separate control system to the rudder hydraulic power control unit. This type of yaw damper is called a series yaw damper since it is separate from the AFCS rudder channel. The yaw damper may utilise a separate small control surface (mini-rudder).

In some systems it is necessary to specifically engage the yaw damper if the aircraft is to be hand-flown. This can be done immediately after take-off, with the yaw damper remaining engaged for the entire flight. In systems that use the AFCS rudder channel for yaw damping, engaging the autopilot also engages the yaw damper if not already selected.

Irrespective of whether the yaw damper is a separate system or fully integrated with the AFCS, the method of operation is generally the same. The system in the B767 is illustrated in figure 4-11.

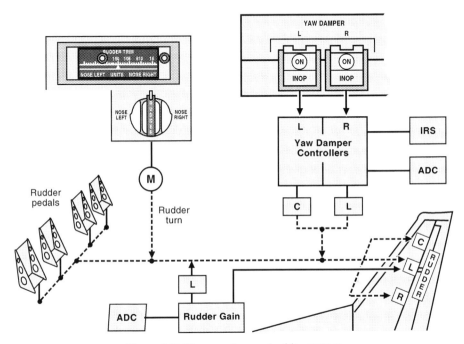

Figure 4-11 **The yaw damper/rudder system**

A rate gyro senses yaw and sends the appropriate signal to the yaw damping processor, which then commands the appropriate response from the control system. In the dual-channel yaw damper system, the yaw damper controller receives signals from the IRS and the ADC, and in turn signals the rudder servos to move the rudder. The yaw damper is integrated with the rudder control system. Parallel-type yaw dampers send the required signal direct to the rudder servomotors in the same way that other autopilot channels command the necessary control deflection from elevator and aileron servos. When both yaw damping and turn balance is required, the autopilot resolves the combined signals to determine the resultant rudder servo operation.

Airline aircraft which are certificated to require a serviceable yaw damper for dispatch will normally be fitted with two yaw damper systems to provide redundancy, with both systems operating independently. Loss of yaw damping may impose speed limits, particularly at high altitude.

When both yaw damping and turn balance control is required, autopilot processing resolves the combined signals to determine the resultant rudder servo operation. Yaw-damper-induced movements of the rudder are not transmitted to the rudder pedals.

Fly-By-Wire Systems (FBWS)

The use of computing techniques to control the aircraft's primary flight controls was an inevitable stage in the development of automatic flight control systems (AFCS). The original autopilots were simple systems that enabled hands-free piloting by automatically keeping the wings level and holding the pitch attitude set by the pilot.

To perform this function, the early autopilot needed some type of input to determine when the wings were not level, and an output which moved the primary flight controls via a suitable servomotor. Over the years the complexity of autopilot inputs increased by including such items as altitude, airspeed, compass heading and radio navigation track details. With modern processors, the list of possible inputs continues to increase so that now all the information handled by the navigation and performance computers can be controlled by the AFCS. At the same time, however, the method of AFCS output changed little. Larger aircraft required hydraulic actuators to operate the primary flight controls, and the AFCS simply provided another command link for these actuators, in addition to the pilot's control wheel. Until recently, some form of mechanical linkage was available between the pilot and the hydraulic actuator. The hydraulic actuator continued this mechanical link through to the flight control surface. This type of AFCS is shown in figure 4-12.

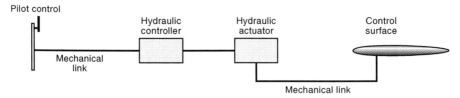

Figure 4-12 **Typical early type of AFCS**

Modern aircraft, such as the Airbus A320, operate to the best possible levels of efficiency. This has required flying the aircraft to very fine tolerances in the high subsonic region, where a small change in speed can incur significant drag penalties. These requirements, together with the need to reduce the weight penalties of heavy mechanical and hydraulic links, has inevitably led to increased use of electronics and computers in the modern AFCS. By replacing mechanical links with electric wires, the modern AFCS is now termed a fly-by-wire system (FBWS). Figure 4-13 illustrates the basic concept of a FBWS.

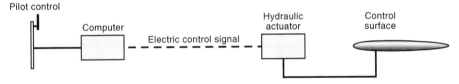

Figure 4-13 **Simple FBWS**

One of the first FBWS aircraft was Concorde, which required very fine flight control inputs in the transonic and supersonic speed bands. Transport aircraft that are equipped with FBWS are all configured with full flight envelope protection (cannot be overstressed, oversped, or angles of attack and altitude cannot be exceeded). Limiting parameters of speed, angle of attack and altitude are used so that the AFCS will not allow the flight controls to take the aircraft beyond those limits, regardless of pilot input!

Not all new transport aircraft are fitted with FBWS. An argument in favour of these systems is the higher level of automatic profile control and aircraft protection. Those in favour of FBWS contend a higher safety level, particularly when more than two automatic systems are available. On the other hand, some critics have argued that electronic screening of the computer systems may not be guaranteed and that uncommanded control inputs could occur. Such critics believe a manual reversion is essential to provide adequate levels of safety for airline operations. There was concern regarding lightning strikes. Despite these criticisms, improvements in computing performance, better screening methods, and the obvious savings of reduced weight make these systems inevitable for all jet transports in the next century.

Autopilot Flight Director Systems (AFDS)

The operating requirements of both the autopilot and flight director are very similar. The autopilot is programmed to maintain certain performance and navigation parameters, such as a constant cruise altitude and VOR track during a standard flight sector. When hand-flying the aeroplane, the flight director is programmed in the same way, to display and direct exactly the same values. Consequently, the command bars displayed on the ADI instruct the pilot to make the same attitude changes as would be made by the autopilot if it were engaged. This principle is followed in other flight modes, such as levelling out at a programmed altitude or maintaining ILS track and glidepath. It is logical, therefore, to integrate the two systems, the AFCS and the flight director, into a combined autopilot flight director system (AFDS) so that certain processing functions can be shared. In a modern system, it is normal for the AFDS to contain a separate FD computer that provides display instructions to the EFIS system, and the same instructions to the autopilot computer.

AFDS Mode Control Panel

Figure 4-14 shows a typical AFDS mode control panel (MCP) such as is found on the B767.

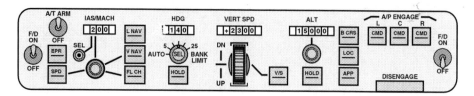

Figure 4-14 **Typical AFDS mode control panel**

This type of panel is generally located on or under the glareshield close to the central line of sight of both pilots. This allows the panel to include most flight director and autopilot mode selection and status annunciators. This panel also contains switches for engaging the autothrottle system and the flight director. The glareshield panel also contains EFIS and VHF-NAV controls (not shown here).

AFDS Mode Selectors

As shown, mode selectors of the push on/push off type are located at various positions on the panel. Each selector has a bar light incorporated in the switch face, to indicate the selection. Armed and engaged selections are displayed on the ADI, with armed selections usually shown in white or amber, and engaged modes in green. The functions of the various mode selectors are described below.

Flight Director

FD On/Off: A flight director (FD) switch, see figure 4-15, is provided for each pilot. When off, FD command bars are withdrawn. When first selected on, the command bars will be displayed, in the take-off mode (TO) if on the ground, or in current values of V/S (vertical speed) and HDG HOLD if airborne. In the TO mode, the command bars will show wings level and about 8°–10°ANU (nose-up attitude).

Autopilot

A/P Engage: In figure 4-16, the three autopilot engage switches are shown. The autopilot is normally engaged in the command (CMD) mode. Except during an ILS approach, only one autopilot can be engaged at a time; selection of another autopilot disconnects the first. Initial selection of an autopilot will provide the HDG HOLD and VS values existing at the time of selection, or the modes already selected with the flight director.

The disengage bar at the bottom of the panel must be up to allow the autopilots to be engaged. By moving the disengage bar down, all three autopilots are disconnected from the flight control servos.

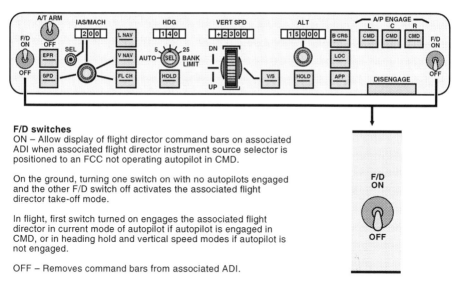

F/D switches
ON – Allow display of flight director command bars on associated
ADI when associated flight director instrument source selector is
positioned to an FCC not operating autopilot in CMD.

On the ground, turning one switch on with no autopilots engaged
and the other F/D switch off activates the associated flight
director take-off mode.

In flight, first switch turned on engages the associated flight
director in current mode of autopilot if autopilot is engaged in
CMD, or in heading hold and vertical speed modes if autopilot is
not engaged.

OFF – Removes command bars from associated ADI.

Figure 4-15 **Flight director control**

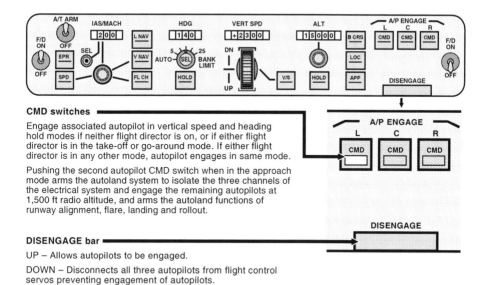

CMD switches
Engage associated autopilot in vertical speed and heading
hold modes if neither flight director is on, or if either flight
director is in the take-off or go-around mode. If either flight
director is in any other mode, autopilot engages in same mode.

Pushing the second autopilot CMD switch when in the approach
mode arms the autoland system to isolate the three channels of
the electrical system and engage the remaining autopilots at
1,500 ft radio altitude, and arms the autoland functions of
runway alignment, flare, landing and rollout.

DISENGAGE bar
UP – Allows autopilots to be engaged.

DOWN – Disconnects all three autopilots from flight control
servos preventing engagement of autopilots.

Red strip is exposed when bar is down.

Figure 4-16 **Autopilot engage switches**

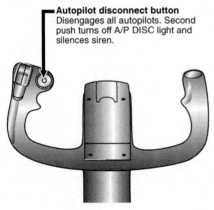

Autopilot disconnect button
Disengages all autopilots. Second push turns off A/P DISC light and silences siren.

When an engaged autopilot is disconnected – usually by pressing the disconnect button on the control column as shown in figure 4-17 – a warning siren also sounds, which can be cancelled by pressing the disconnect button a second time.

Figure 4-17 **Autopilot disconnect button**

A fault in an engaged autopilot may also cause a disconnect, in which case a warning siren sounds, and a warning light will illuminate, as shown in figure 4-18.

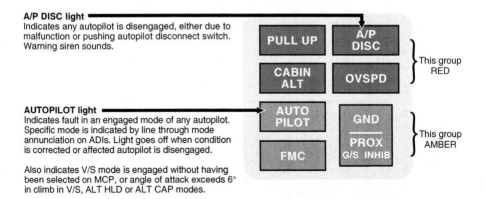

A/P DISC light
Indicates any autopilot is disengaged, either due to malfunction or pushing autopilot disconnect switch. Warning siren sounds.

AUTOPILOT light
Indicates fault in an engaged mode of any autopilot. Specific mode is indicated by line through mode annunciation on ADIs. Light goes off when condition is corrected or affected autopilot is disengaged.

Also indicates V/S mode is engaged without having been selected on MCP, or angle of attack exceeds 6° in climb in V/S, ALT HLD or ALT CAP modes.

Figure 4-18 **Autopilot warning lights**

With multiple autopilots engaged, when making an ILS approach with a planned autolanding, full rudder control becomes active, and the autopilot system can input the rudder control required to cope with an engine failure on the approach, and during the early stages of a missed approach.

Navigation Modes

LNAV: As shown in figure 4-19, the LNAV selector, when pushed, will arm the autopilot to capture and then track the lateral navigation track entered into the FMCS. Aircraft position sensing would normally be provided by an inertial reference, a GPS or a multi-sensor system. The aircraft must be steered towards the LNAV track to effect a capture. The ADI will show LNAV in white as the armed mode, and the LNAV in green as the active mode.

VNAV: As also shown in figure 4-19, the FMC of an advanced aircraft is capable of providing vertical navigation by computing a climb or descent profile to satisfy various requirements, such as maximum rate, optimum profile, maximum speed, or waypoint altitude restrictions. When the FMC has been programmed, and VNAV is selected, the autopilot will follow the required profile, with the engaged autothrottle system controlling the programmed speed. The ADI will show VNAV as the active pitch mode.

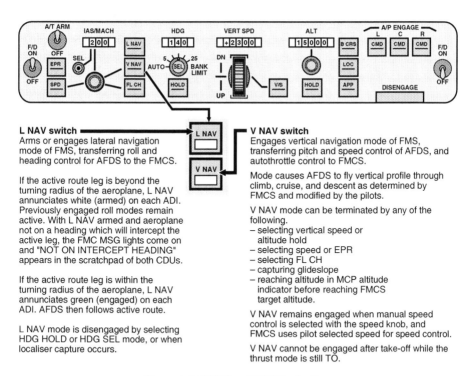

L NAV switch
Arms or engages lateral navigation mode of FMS, transferring roll and heading control for AFDS to the FMCS.

If the active route leg is beyond the turning radius of the aeroplane, L NAV annunciates white (armed) on each ADI. Previously engaged roll modes remain active. With L NAV armed and aeroplane not on a heading which will intercept the active leg, the FMC MSG lights come on and "NOT ON INTERCEPT HEADING" appears in the scratchpad of both CDUs.

If the active route leg is within the turning radius of the aeroplane, L NAV annunciates green (engaged) on each ADI. AFDS then follows active route.

L NAV mode is disengaged by selecting HDG HOLD or HDG SEL mode, or when localiser capture occurs.

V NAV switch
Engages vertical navigation mode of FMS, transferring pitch and speed control of AFDS, and autothrottle control to FMCS.

Mode causes AFDS to fly vertical profile through climb, cruise, and descent as determined by FMCS and modified by the pilots.

V NAV mode can be terminated by any of the following.
– selecting vertical speed or altitude hold
– selecting speed or EPR
– selecting FL CH
– capturing glideslope
– reaching altitude in MCP altitude indicator before reaching FMCS target altitude.

V NAV remains engaged when manual speed control is selected with the speed knob, and FMCS uses pilot selected speed for speed control.

V NAV cannot be engaged after take-off while the thrust mode is still TO.

Figure 4-19 **LNAV and VNAV selection**

Heading Control

HOLD: The heading hold switch shown in figure 4-20, when pressed, commands the autopilot to maintain present heading. If the aircraft is turning when HDG HOLD is selected, the autopilot will level the wings and hold the heading achieved at wings level. The ADI will show HDG HOLD in the roll mode display.

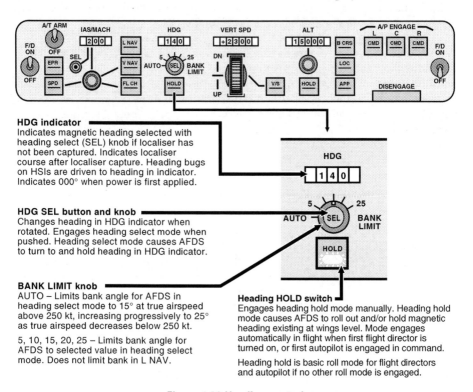

HDG indicator ■
Indicates magnetic heading selected with heading select (SEL) knob if localiser has not been captured. Indicates localiser course after localiser capture. Heading bugs on HSIs are driven to heading in indicator. Indicates 000° when power is first applied.

HDG SEL button and knob ■
Changes heading in HDG indicator when rotated. Engages heading select mode when pushed. Heading select mode causes AFDS to turn to and hold heading in HDG indicator.

BANK LIMIT knob ■
AUTO – Limits bank angle for AFDS in heading select mode to 15° at true airspeed above 250 kt, increasing progressively to 25° as true airspeed decreases below 250 kt.

5, 10, 15, 20, 25 – Limits bank angle for AFDS to selected value in heading select mode. Does not limit bank in L NAV.

Heading HOLD switch ■
Engages heading hold mode manually. Heading hold mode causes AFDS to roll out and/or hold magnetic heading existing at wings level. Mode engages automatically in flight when first flight director is turned on, or first autopilot is engaged in command.

Heading hold is basic roll mode for flight directors and autopilot if no other roll mode is engaged.

Figure 4-20 **Heading control**

HDG SEL: The HDG SEL selector is a push button located within the bank limit select knob. The HDG SEL knob rotates to set the desired heading in the digital display, and also positions the heading cursor on the HSI. Pressing the HDG SEL knob commands the autopilot to turn to and maintain the selected heading. With HDG SEL engaged, the aircraft can be steered by rotating the HDG SEL knob, to adjust the heading. Note that when turns of more than 180° are required, such as in holding patterns, the autopilot recognises the direction in which the HDG SEL knob has been turned and will turn the aircraft accordingly. The ADI will show HDG SEL in the roll mode display.

BANK LIMIT: Associated with the HDG SEL knob is an outer rotary selector which allows the pilot to limit bank angles available to the autopilot to improve passenger comfort. An AUTO position allows the autopilot to decide the amount of bank necessary, and is the most appropriate selection. During instrument approaches, the autopilot will use up to 25° of bank.

Altitude Control

ALT HOLD: The ALT HOLD button, shown in figure 4–21, when pressed, commands the autopilot to hold present altitude. If climbing or descending when ALT HOLD is selected, the autopilot will effect a smooth transition and recapture the altitude at which the selection was made. (Note that the altitude maintained by ALT HOLD is not necessarily the altitude displayed in the ALT SEL window.) The ADI will show ALT HOLD in the pitch mode display.

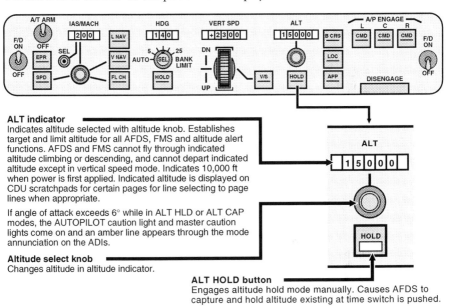

ALT indicator
Indicates altitude selected with altitude knob. Establishes target and limit altitude for all AFDS, FMS and altitude alert functions. AFDS and FMS cannot fly through indicated altitude climbing or descending, and cannot depart indicated altitude except in vertical speed mode. Indicates 10,000 ft when power is first applied. Indicated altitude is displayed on CDU scratchpads for certain pages for line selecting to page lines when appropriate.

If angle of attack exceeds 6° while in ALT HLD or ALT CAP modes, the AUTOPILOT caution light and master caution lights come on and an amber line appears through the mode annunciation on the ADIs.

Altitude select knob
Changes altitude in altitude indicator.

ALT HOLD button
Engages altitude hold mode manually. Causes AFDS to capture and hold altitude existing at time switch is pushed.

Figure 4-21 **Attitude control**

ALT SEL: The altitude select knob is turned to set the desired altitude in the ALT SEL window. The aircraft must be 'steered' towards the desired altitude by using flight level change (FL CH) or a vertical speed (V/S) mode. The ADI will show FL CH or V/S in the pitch mode display, until the altitude is captured, when the pitch mode will change to ALT CAP. This changeover may occur several hundred feet before the level-off, depending on the vertical speed at the time.

Once ALT is displayed, the pilot can vary the altitude selection on the MCP, but the aircraft will still level off at the original altitude programmed. Note that when ALT HOLD is displayed as the active pitch mode on the ADI, a new selection of FL CH or V/S must be made to continue climb or descent.

Vertical Speed Control

V/S: With vertical speed (V/S) selected, as shown in figure 4-22, the autopilot will maintain the vertical speed set in the V/S window. With V/S engaged, altitude hold and speed hold are disconnected since only one of the pitch modes can be operating at a time. The value shown in the window is adjusted by rotating the V/S wheel in the natural sense (up for nose down!). Think of it as a trim wheel. This mode is often used for intermediate descents when it is required to descend at a given rate for profile or ATC needs. If the autothrottle (A/T) is engaged in SPD mode when V/S is selected, the A/T will maintain the selected IAS. The ADI will show V/S as the active pitch mode. V/S can be used to fly the aircraft away from a captured MCP altitude. V/S is also the quickest way to initiate climbs or descents.

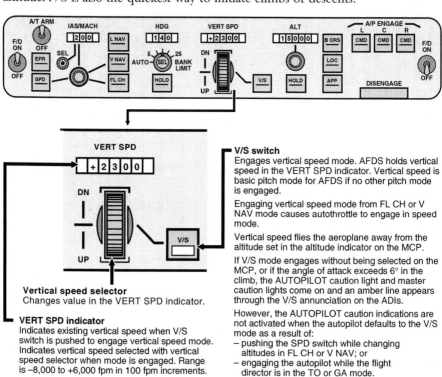

VERT SPD

V/S switch
Engages vertical speed mode. AFDS holds vertical speed in the VERT SPD indicator. Vertical speed is basic pitch mode for AFDS if no other pitch mode is engaged.

Engaging vertical speed mode from FL CH or V NAV mode causes autothrottle to engage in speed mode.

Vertical speed flies the aeroplane away from the altitude set in the altitude indicator on the MCP.

If V/S mode engages without being selected on the MCP, or if the angle of attack exceeds 6° in the climb, the AUTOPILOT caution light and master caution lights come on and an amber line appears through the V/S annunciation on the ADIs.

However, the AUTOPILOT caution indications are not activated when the autopilot defaults to the V/S mode as a result of:
– pushing the SPD switch while changing altitudes in FL CH or V NAV; or
– engaging the autopilot while the flight director is in the TO or GA mode.

Vertical speed selector
Changes value in the VERT SPD indicator.

VERT SPD indicator
Indicates existing vertical speed when V/S switch is pushed to engage vertical speed mode. Indicates vertical speed selected with vertical speed selector when mode is engaged. Range is –8,000 to +6,000 fpm in 100 fpm increments.

Figure 4-22 **Vertical speed control**

Speed Control

IAS/MACH: As shown in figure 4-23, selected autothrottle speed or Mach is set in the IAS/MACH window. With the A/T SPD mode button selected, and the autothrottle engaged, the system will hold the commanded IAS/Mach. The display is switched from IAS to MACH or back again by alternate presses of the IAS/MACH SEL button to the lower left of the IAS/Mach window. Changes in the displayed digits are achieved by rotating the two concentric speed control knobs. The outer knob changes the tens and hundreds digits whilst the inner knob adjusts the units. In this way any acceptable value of IAS or Mach can be selected.

FL CH: Selection of flight level change as shown in figure 4-23 commands the autopilot to initiate a climb or descent towards the altitude set in the ALT SEL window. The autothrottle will set climb power or flight idle as appropriate, with the autopilot controlling the airspeed in the pitch mode. As the selected altitude is approached, the autopilot mode will change to altitude capture (ALT CAP), and then to ALT HOLD as the autopilot levels the aircraft off, with the autothrottle maintaining the selected speed. The ADI will show FL CH as the active pitch mode, changing to ALT CAP and then ALT HOLD as the aircraft levels off at the selected altitude. Note that at high values of vertical speed, ALT CAP will occur several hundred feet before the selected altitude is reached.

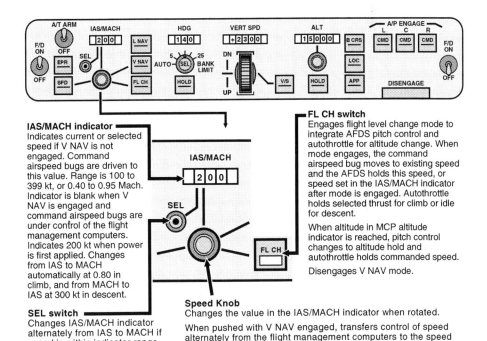

IAS/MACH indicator
Indicates current or selected speed if V NAV is not engaged. Command airspeed bugs are driven to this value. Range is 100 to 399 kt, or 0.40 to 0.95 Mach. Indicator is blank when V NAV is engaged and command airspeed bugs are under control of the flight management computers. Indicates 200 kt when power is first applied. Changes from IAS to MACH automatically at 0.80 in climb, and from MACH to IAS at 300 kt in descent.

SEL switch
Changes IAS/MACH indicator alternately from IAS to MACH if speed is within indicator range.

FL CH switch
Engages flight level change mode to integrate AFDS pitch control and autothrottle for altitude change. When mode engages, the command airspeed bug moves to existing speed and the AFDS holds this speed, or speed set in the IAS/MACH indicator after mode is engaged. Autothrottle holds selected thrust for climb or idle for descent.

When altitude in MCP altitude indicator is reached, pitch control changes to altitude hold and autothrottle holds commanded speed. Disengages V NAV mode.

Speed Knob
Changes the value in the IAS/MACH indicator when rotated.

When pushed with V NAV engaged, transfers control of speed alternately from the flight management computers to the speed knob or from the knob to the computers. IAS/MACH indicator indicates existing speed when knob is pushed to transfer speed control to the knob, and blanks when knob is pushed to transfer speed contol to the flight management computers. Selecting manual speed control does not disengage V NAV mode.

Figure 4-23 **Speed control**

ILS Switching

LOC (LLZ): Push-button selection of the localiser mode shown in figure 4-24 will arm the autopilot to capture and maintain the tuned localiser track towards the runway. The aircraft must be steered towards the localiser to effect capture. The ADI roll mode will show LOC armed, changing to LOC capture as the centreline is approached. Once LOC capture has been achieved, the other heading modes (HDG HOLD or HDG SEL) are cancelled. The missed approach heading can then be set in the HDG SEL window, without pressing the HDG SEL knob, in readiness for a possible missed approach.

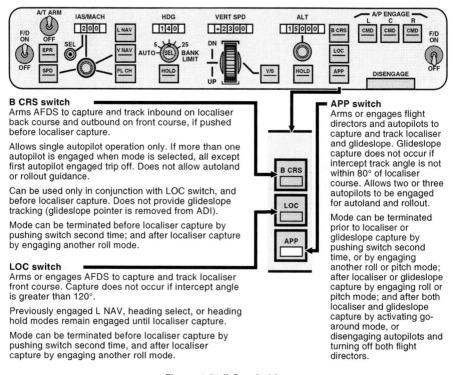

B CRS switch

Arms AFDS to capture and track inbound on localiser back course and outbound on front course, if pushed before localiser capture.

Allows single autopilot operation only. If more than one autopilot is engaged when mode is selected, all except first autopilot engaged trip off. Does not allow autoland or rollout guidance.

Can be used only in conjunction with LOC switch, and before localiser capture. Does not provide glideslope tracking (glideslope pointer is removed from ADI).

Mode can be terminated before localiser capture by pushing switch second time; and after localiser capture by engaging another roll mode.

LOC switch

Arms or engages AFDS to capture and track localiser front course. Capture does not occur if intercept angle is greater than 120°.

Previously engaged L NAV, heading select, or heading hold modes remain engaged until localiser capture.

Mode can be terminated before localiser capture by pushing switch second time, and after localiser capture by engaging another roll mode.

APP switch

Arms or engages flight directors and autopilots to capture and track localiser and glideslope. Glideslope capture does not occur if intercept track angle is not within 80° of localiser course. Allows two or three autopilots to be engaged for autoland and rollout.

Mode can be terminated prior to localiser or glideslope capture by pushing switch second time, or by engaging another roll or pitch mode; after localiser or glideslope capture by engaging roll or pitch mode; and after both localiser and glideslope capture by activating go-around mode, or disengaging autopilots and turning off both flight directors.

Figure 4-24 **ILS switching**

B CRS: The back course mode allows the autopilot to fly a reverse track along a localiser, away from the runway. The appropriate localiser frequency must be tuned, and the aircraft must be steered to enable BCRS capture. Back course tracking is used in some parts of the world to allow aircraft to track accurately away from an airport equipped with only a localiser, without the need to install a VOR or NDB.

APP: In aircraft with autoland capability, multiple autopilots are engaged to provide redundancy. Normally one autopilot will be active, with the others armed to become active with the aircraft established on localiser and glideslope, usually as the aircraft passes 1,500 ft radio altitude. When intending to fly an ILS approach, selection of the approach mode, as shown in figure 4-24, arms the autopilot(s) to capture both localiser and glideslope, whichever comes first. Because the aircraft should be established on the localiser before descending on a glideslope (GS), it is usual to select APP only after LOC capture (with ATC clearance to final).

The ADI will show LOC armed and then active in the roll mode display, with GS armed and then active in the pitch mode display. ALT HOLD will be cancelled at GS capture, and the ALT SEL window can be set to the missed approach altitude.

Go-Around Mode
GA: The go-around mode of the autopilot(s), and the autothrottle, is armed at GS capture and activated by pressing switches on the throttles. The autopilot(s) will command a pitch-up of about 15° with a heading hold submode that is not annunciated, but is that heading existing at the time GA was selected.

Because of the very high level of performance of modern aircraft in the all-engines go-around, the autothrottle will initially set maximum power, but then reduce power to maintain a climb of about 2,000 fpm at the airspeed existing at the time GA was selected.

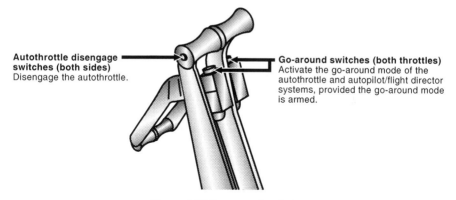

Autothrottle disengage switches (both sides)
Disengage the autothrottle.

Go-around switches (both throttles)
Activate the go-around mode of the autothrottle and autopilot/flight director systems, provided the go-around mode is armed.

Figure 4-25 **Go-around switches**

If multiple autopilots were engaged during the approach, they will remain engaged through the go-around until 400 ft RA is reached, when all other autopilots disengage (except the first autopilot selected).

Note: At this point, if the multiple autopilots have been coping with the rudder control inputs needed for asymmetric flight, this control input will not be available on single autopilot, and you may find you have an unexpected yaw/roll moment.

Autothrottle

Autothrottle (A/T) systems are normally only found on modern jet transport aircraft or large corporate jets. When fitted, they form part of a fully integrated autoflight system. As with other aspects of autoflight, an A/T is capable of providing very accurate adjustments to maintain selected flight parameters.

A typical A/T system provides automatic thrust control from the start of take-off through climb, cruise descent, approach and go-around or landing. In the B767 system, the performance management function of the flight management computer provides the A/T with appropriate engine settings at all stages of flight. Thus the A/T will hold modes directly commanded by the pilot e.g., IAS/Mach, or settings controlled through the CDU of the FMS, e.g. maximum rate of climb, ECON cruise, vertical navigation. The A/T system also ensures that the engines operate within the permitted engine limits.

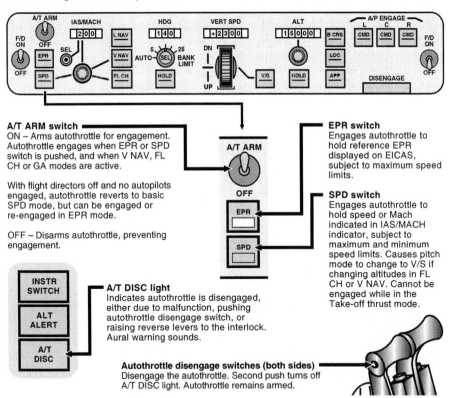

A/T ARM switch
ON – Arms autothrottle for engagement. Autothrottle engages when EPR or SPD switch is pushed, and when V NAV, FL CH or GA modes are active.

With flight directors off and no autopilots engaged, autothrottle reverts to basic SPD mode, but can be engaged or re-engaged in EPR mode.

OFF – Disarms autothrottle, preventing engagement.

A/T DISC light
Indicates autothrottle is disengaged, either due to malfunction, pushing autothrottle disengage switch, or raising reverse levers to the interlock. Aural warning sounds.

Autothrottle disengage switches (both sides)
Disengage the autothrottle. Second push turns off A/T DISC light. Autothrottle remains armed.

EPR switch
Engages autothrottle to hold reference EPR displayed on EICAS, subject to maximum speed limits.

SPD switch
Engages autothrottle to hold speed or Mach indicated in IAS/MACH indicator, subject to maximum and minimum speed limits. Causes pitch mode to change to V/S if changing altitudes in FL CH or V NAV. Cannot be engaged while in the Take-off thrust mode.

Figure 4-26 **Autothrottle control and disengage switches**

This A/T system has a number of operating modes that can be used, from brakes release through to landing. In this discussion, engine power settings will be quoted as engine pressure ratio (EPR), but N_1 settings (first stage compression rpm) would be equally valid. Typical A/T mode switches, arming switch, and performance data setting controls are shown below. In addition to these controls, a typical A/T system has A/T disengage switches and go-around modes.

Note: Depending on the engines installed in the aeroplane, engine indications will be either engine pressure ratio (EPR) or engine rpm (N_1).

Thrust Mode

Required EPR (or N_1) for the A/T EPR mode would be selected on a separate thrust mode control panel as shown in figure 4-27, normally located near the engine gauges on the EICAS display.

Climb thrust derate switches
Select either of two fixed percentage derate values for climb thrust computation. Switch 1 selects approximately 8% derate and switch 2 selects approximately 16%. When either switch is used to preselect climb derate, a '1' or '2' appears in white after the TO thrust mode annunciation on EICAS. When the climb mode becomes active, the digit changes to green.

Climb thrust derating can also be accomplished on the CDU.

With CLB 1 or CLB 2 mode displayed, a subsequent push of the active mode switch cancels 1 or 2. With CLB 2 mode displayed, pushing switch 1 selects CLB 1 mode.

Derate modes are inhibited above 12,500 ft.

Thrust mode select switches
Select the thrust mode to be used by the thrust management computer for reference EPR limit computation. Except when the take-off mode is active, the flight management computer automatically selects the thrust mode in V NAV operation. The active thrust mode and reference EPR are indicated on EICAS.

With V NAV engaged, manual selection of GA, CLB, and CON is inhibited. The reverse mode is activated automatically when the reverse levers are in the reverse range.

TO/GA – Selects TO (take-off) mode on the ground or GA (go-around) mode in flight. Cancels selected assumed temperature and preselected CLB 1 or CLB 2. Inhibited with GA mode displayed.

CLB – Selects CLB (climb) mode. Selects CLB 1 or CLB 2 if 1 or 2 preselected.

CON – Selects CON (max continuous) mode.

CRZ – Selects CRZ (cruise) mode.

TEMP SEL knob
Selects the assumed temperature for normal (derated) take-off thrust. Initial movement of the knob causes the flat rated temperature to be displayed on EICAS. Further rotation selects the desired temperature. The thrust management computer uses the higher of this temperature or the flat rated temperature to compute the take-off limit. If an assumed temperature is not selected, the computer uses the higher of TAT or flat rated temperature to compute the take-off limit.

The knob is active only in the take-off mode.

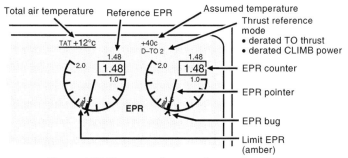

Figure 4-27 **Thrust mode control**

The available thrust modes are:

- take-off/go-around (TO/GA) – full power;
- climb power (CLB), plus two values of derated climb power;
- maximum continuous power (CON); and
- cruise power (CRZ).

Autothrottle Mode and Limit Annunciations

The mode in use and limiting parameter are displayed on the EADI annunciators.

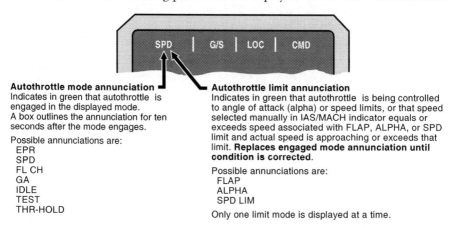

Autothrottle mode annunciation
Indicates in green that autothrottle is engaged in the displayed mode.
A box outlines the annunciation for ten seconds after the mode engages.

Possible annunciations are:
EPR
SPD
FL CH
GA
IDLE
TEST
THR-HOLD

Autothrottle limit annunciation
Indicates in green that autothrottle is being controlled to angle of attack (alpha) or speed limits, or that speed selected manually in IAS/MACH indicator equals or exceeds speed associated with FLAP, ALPHA, or SPD limit and actual speed is approaching or exceeds that limit. **Replaces engaged mode annunciation until condition is corrected.**

Possible annunciations are:
FLAP
ALPHA
SPD LIM

Only one limit mode is displayed at a time.

Figure 4-28 **Autothrottle mode annunciators**

Operation of a Typical Autothrottle System

The modes of the autothrottle are used as follows.

Reduced Thrust

Particularly with the higher-powered engines on the wide-body jets, engine instal-lations have various levels of reduced (derated) thrust settings available to reduce wear and tear. In fact, the engine life may be predicated on the use of reduced thrust whenever possible. In the B767, such reduced-thrust take-offs are classified as *nor-mal*. The values of reduced thrust will depend on the amount of surplus perfor-mance available using a particular runway, in particular ambient conditions. Specific weight and temperature limits, various limitations relating to tailwind, runway con-tamination, and aircraft serviceability are all factored to ensure that the performance of the aircraft will continue to meet runway and obstacle clearance requirements, with an adequate safety margin. The reduced-thrust value is implemented by telling the fuel control computer that it is much hotter outside than the fuel control com-puter thinks it is; this is the *assumed temperature* method, which is discussed in greater detail in our companion volume *Aeroplane Performance, Planning and Loading for the Air Transport Pilot*.

Normal Take-Off

In this case, where an assumed temperature is selected, the autothrottle is engaged by pressing the EPR switch on the glareshield panel, see figure 4-26 (page 188). With the aircraft on the ground, the autothrottle will engage in the take-off mode and the throttles will be advanced until reduced take-off thrust (assumed temperature) is achieved. Below 80 kt groundspeed, as sensed by the IRS, the throttles are adjusted continuously to sustain this EPR; if the pilot pulls the throttles back, they will move forward again! Should the pilot abandon the take-off, the autothrottle must be disconnected so that the throttles remain at idle. Above 80 kt groundspeed, electrical power to the throttle drive motor(s) is withdrawn, and the autothrottle mode changes to thrust hold (THR HOLD). Any adjustment now made by the pilot will not be countered by the autothrottle but maintained. After take-off, the autothrottle can be re-engaged in an active mode by pressing the EPR button on the glareshield panel, when the selected climb EPR will be maintained.

Full-Power Take-Off Mode

When conditions do not permit the use of reduced thrust, or if the pilot decides to use maximum thrust, this take-off mode can be engaged by pressing the TO/GA button illustrated in figure 4-27 (page 189). This selection overrides any assumed temperature inputs, and the engine is accelerated to the limiting EPR for the ambient conditions. THR HOLD mode and re-engagement of an active mode remain the same.

Climb Mode

The thrust mode control panel offers three values of climb power – (full) climb power, derate 1 climb power, and derate 2 climb power – enabling the pilot to select the derated thrust most suitable to the conditions of the day. Derate 1 is a reduction of about 8%, while derate 2 reduces climb power by about 16%. Derates are phased out at 10,000 ft.

Speed Mode

This mode is engaged by selecting an appropriate IAS or Mach in the AFDS speed setting window and pressing the speed mode control button, as shown in figure 4-23 (page 185). Once set, the A/T will move the power levers to maintain the desired speed – within the boundaries of allowed engine limits. Speed mode is normally used during climb, cruise, some phases of descent, and when established on final, to ensure the reference speed (V_{REF}) is achieved.

Flight Level Change Mode

When the FL CH mode is engaged, the autothrottle will set climb power or flight idle as required, depending on whether the selected altitude is above or below the aircraft.

Go-Around Mode

In most systems the go-around mode is armed as a standard procedure whilst on final approach; in the system described, GA is armed automatically when flap is selected or on capturing the ILS glideslope. When required, the go-around button on the throttle lever is pressed, commanding the A/T to set go-around thrust, until a satisfactory rate of climb, about 2,000 fpm, is achieved; the autothrottle will then reduce power, to maintain 2,000 fpm at that current airspeed. This same initial operation of the go-around button sets the FD command bars, and/or the autopilot to the go-around pitch attitude setting, and commands wings level. In installations that use an initial derated go-around thrust setting, a second press of the same switch commands full go-around thrust only limited by the FMC.

Autothrottle Limits

In conjunction with the pitch channel of the autopilot, the A/T system provides pitch and thrust commands to prevent the following typical limits from being exceeded:
- V_{MO}/M_{MO};
- flap limit speeds;
- undercarriage limit speeds; and
- minimum speed, or alpha floor (normally $1.3 V_S$).

Automatic Pitch Trim

In addition to the servo operation of primary flight control surfaces by the autopilot, it is also necessary to provide methods of automatically trimming the aircraft. In normal manual flight, trimming of the aircraft may be needed about all three axes using the aileron, rudder and elevator trim controls.

However, in autoflight, pitch control is generally confined to changes in pitch trim that are required by changing speed, configuration and weight. Such automatic trim systems usually employ a separate pitch trim servomotor which operates in parallel with the autopilot pitch control servo.

Automatic (autopilot) pitch trim is usually limited to about half the rate used when manual trimming. In aircraft that are trimmed using a variable incidence tailplane, a separate trim servomotor may be used to move the tailplane.

Modern aircraft have a number of methods of controlling the pitch trim, as described above, and appropriate isolation switches for each pitch servo or trim motor must be provided. In the event of autopilot pitch trim malfunction, the autopilot can be immediately disconnected by pressing the autopilot disconnect button on each control wheel, or by operating the pitch trim switch also located on the control wheel, as shown in figure 4-29.

The autopilot will also disengage if the pilot manually overrides the (runaway) change of trim. Another cut-out switch for the autopilot pitch trim system may also be provided on a specific trim control panel, as was shown in figure 4-29.

Other pitch motors/servos, such as the one used for automatic pitch trim, can normally be isolated by operation of a cut-out switch. The installation shown in figure 4-29 uses movement of the elevators to provide both autopilot control and automatic pitch trim.

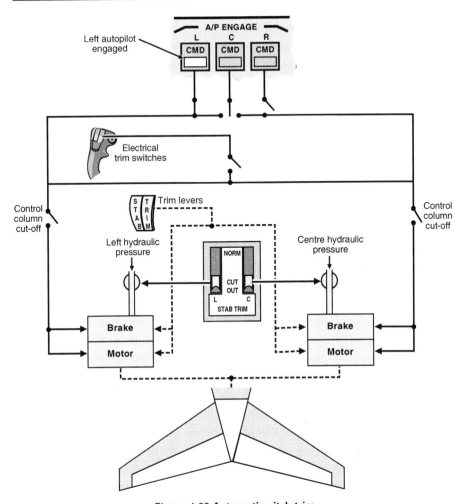

Figure 4-29 **Automatic pitch trim**

The diagram shows that stabiliser movement is controlled by a 'stab trim' mechanism which can be operated by two brake/motor installations. With an autopilot engaged, only one brake/motor installation is used, whereas the pilot's trim switch operates both brake/motor installations. This specific STAB TRIM panel provides the ability to isolate both left and centre hydraulic systems using the cut-out position of the two switches. Such protection is necessary to ensure motor malfunctions can be quickly isolated.

Autoflight Operations

Operations of modern jet transport aircraft rely heavily on the use of autoflight systems for the majority of airborne time. Although all qualified pilots should be capable of performing to similar standards as an autopilot, the use of automated systems ensures that required levels of accuracy are achieved consistently over prolonged periods. The other significant benefit of routinely using these systems is that the pilots have more time and reduced workload to monitor the flight. Consequently, they should be able to detect abnormalities or failures more readily.

The downside to using autosystems extensively is that certain piloting skills are not able to be exercised as often as desired to maintain very high standards. Although both knowledge and experience are very important factors in ensuring high piloting standards, the majority of piloting exercises rely heavily on motor skill.

Motor skills require regular practice to maintain a high performance standard. Whilst requiring the use of autopilots for most operations, a pilot needs regular access to at least a full flight simulator to maintain these important skills.

As described earlier, the A/T and autopilot can be operated throughout most of the flight, and on certain aircraft down to touchdown using autoland systems. During take-off and initial climb the A/T is used extensively to hold required engine thrust until climb speeds are achieved. Whilst climbing to cruise altitude the autopilot is normally operated in the speed hold mode for a constant IAS/Mach, whilst the A/T maintains engine power at scheduled settings.

At the top-of-climb, the autopilot automatically captures cruise altitude whilst the A/T regulates engine thrust to achieve desired cruise Mach. At the same time, and subsequently during the remainder of the flight, the autopilot can be coupled to hold a set heading or a VOR track, but is normally programmed to maintain the track of a selected flight plan using the FMC. In this mode, the autopilot initiates any track changes that are needed at turning points on command from the FMC.

The performance computing capabilities of the FMC allow the autopilot and A/T to initiate descent and maintain an optimum descent profile. The systems are capable of operating in the speed hold or vertical speed hold modes. When in the terminal area of a major airport, the systems can be coupled to an ILS localiser track and glidepath, whilst at the same time achieving a stable speed prior to landing.

In the autoland mode such systems can automatically initiate a flare in response to radar altimeter information, and at the same time reduce engine thrust during the flare, finally controlling the rollout, and using autobrake to bring the aircraft to a virtual standstill right in the centre of the runway.

Although considered as a separate system for many years, the AFDS is now commonly grouped with the processors that control the EFIS system and FMC functions in a fully integrated autoflight and automatic navigation system.

Autoflight Protection

As mentioned earlier, modern systems on large transport aircraft have all-important limitations programmed into the controlling processor. This prevents the aircraft from exceeding major limits such as V_{MO}/M_{MO}, and protects gear and flaps from overspeed. At the lower end of the speed range, the autopilot makes appropriate pitch and power adjustments to ensure that the maximum angle of attack *(alpha floor)* is not exceeded. In each case, an appropriate message is displayed on the various mode annunciators, typically accompanied by an aural caution alert.

Autoland

In the case of an autoland operation, some aspects of the AFCS are inhibited or reduced in sensitivity and response rate. Glideslope sensitivity is reduced below about 300 ft radio altitude. In aircraft with autoland capability, at about 200 ft RA, the longitudinal axis is aligned with the centreline of the ILS runway, with rudder and aileron input used to keep the aircraft tracking the centreline; at about 100 ft RA, the angle of attack protection is inhibited, otherwise the autoland system could not flare the aircraft for landing. The pitch trim may be wound well back out of trim, to give the elevator sufficient power for the flare. At this point, if the pilot decides to disconnect the autopilot and fly manually, a forward force of some forty pounds may be required to counter the trim. Similarly, the go-around mode is inhibited at about 5 ft RA.

Autoland Status

Autoland status annunciators, like the one shown at figure 4-30 are provided so that pilots can monitor the progress of the autoland manoeuvre, along with other AFDS mode annunciations.

AUTOLAND STATUS annunciators
UPPER INDICATOR – Indicates LAND 3 when three autopilot systems and required aeroplane system inputs are operable in approach mode. Indicates LAND 2 when only two autopilot systems and required aeroplane system inputs are operable in approach mode. Blank until approach mode is selected and above requirements are satisfied.

LOWER INDICATOR – Indicates NO LAND 3 when only two autopilots are operable for autoland. Can appear whenever electrical power is available. Indicates NO AUTOLAND when autoland capability does not exist.

Annunciators cannot change below 200 ft except to indicate NO AUTOLAND. If NO AUTOLAND is annunciated on landing, it remains annunciated until autopilots are disengaged.

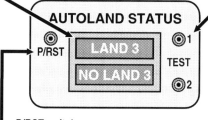

TEST switches
Test operation of associated autoland status annunciator.

1 – Causes LAND 3 and NO LAND 3 to appear in upper and lower indicators respectively.

2 – Causes LAND 2 and NO AUTOLAND to appear in upper and lower indicators respectively.

P/RST switch
Resets both pilots' autoland status annunciators as follows:

– Before approach mode is selected, changes NO AUTOLAND or NO LAND 3 indications to blank when pushed. Indication returns when released if condition causing indication still exists.

– After approach mode is selected, changes NO LAND 3 indication to blank when pushed. Remains blank until after landing and autopilots are disengaged. If NO AUTOLAND is displayed, indication remains until autopilots are disengaged.

Figure 4-30 **Autoland status annunciators**

A typical sequence of annunciations will advise the crew that the autoland systems are in the 'green', following a system self-test at 1,500 ft RA. The electrical system channels are isolated, and the autoland functions of runway alignment (drift correction), flare, landing and rollout are armed; these submodes are not shown as armed, but are only presented as the active mode at the appropriate time.

Malfunctions

In the event of servomotor malfunction, most autopilots are designed to disengage if excessive torque is applied to the servo system. For aircraft equipped for autolanding, the significantly reduced margin for error means that disconnection of the autopilot due to excessive servo torque could itself result in an accident. Consequently, autoland systems should:

* not disturb the flightpath following an active failure (that is a failure that actively operates a component in an unsafe manner, such as a runaway servo);
* warn of a passive failure (that is a failure that just stops some component working so that it cannot make subsequent adjustments or indications); and
* be able to maintain a steady controlled flightpath following either a passive or active failure.

To satisfy these requirements, there are basically two types of autoland systems and logic used:

* fail operational; and
* fail passive.

Fail Operational. A fail operational system has the capability to tolerate a failure of a component, and still remain coupled to complete an autoland manoeuvre (including rollout, in the case of the more refined systems). This capability is available because three autopilots are employed. All three are coupled and each is centrally monitored and compared for performance.

In the event of a failure of a component in one autopilot system, that system is automatically disconnected and the other two continue to operate in a fail passive mode. Because of this level of redundancy, fail operational systems can be authorised for very low visibility landing operations.

Fail Passive. Fail passive systems consist normally of two autopilot systems. Again, their performance is monitored and compared. In the event that either of them exceed pre-set operating limits, both systems disengage automatically with appropriate warnings. However, it is a certification requirement that the aircraft will remain in a steady flight state (in trim) following disengagement so that a manual landing can be accomplished without undue difficulty.

Fail passive systems are not authorised for very low visibility operations where intervention by the pilot in the event of a failure of the system would be inappropriate. However, a technology known as head-up display (HUD) is being developed to make the transition to manual flight less critical, and as a result, may lead to lower minima for fail passive systems.

Note: It is important to appreciate when considering an autoland system that a total system is being described, i.e. autopilots, autothrottle, navigation receivers, radio altimeters and in some cases, nosewheel steering. Also, special survey and ATC requirements apply with respect to the runway and runway environment.

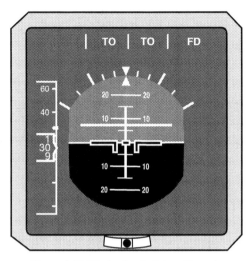

Figure 4-31 **FD display in take-off mode**

Typical Autoflight Operation

Let us consider a flight in a B767 from Melbourne to Sydney using the same FMS profile shown in chapter 3. During cockpit preparation, the three IRSs are aligned, which takes about ten minutes, and then selected to the NAV mode. Selection of one or both flight directors to ON whilst on the ground will bring up the FD display in the take-off mode on the ADI, as shown in figure 4-31. The roll bar will be centred, and the pitch command bar at about 8° nose-up.

The FMS can be programmed in accordance with the flight plan, and ATC clearance. When both pilots are satisfied that the FMS is properly set up, the active route can be selected, and the map range on the HSI adjusted to a scale which will give the best guidance after take-off.

At the same time, the autothrottle thrust mode can be selected on the thrust mode control panel. In this case, a reduced thrust take-off is planned, and the amount of derate is chosen by entering an assumed temperature, say 40°C, as shown in figure 4-32, using the TEMP SEL knob on the TMCP to set the value shown on the EICAS display.

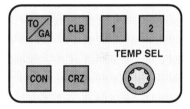

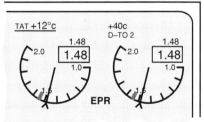

Figure 4-32 **Setting 40°C with the temperature select knob**

Note that setting a temperature higher than the total air temperature sensed by the air data computer will cause the thrust mode to read D-TO. *The amount of derate is usually determined by reference to company-specific runway charts,* which account for performance factors such as aircraft weight, air temperature, runway length, obstacle clearance and flap setting. Arm the autothrottle by switching it to ARM on the mode control panel.

During taxiing, the flight controls, including the yaw dampers, can be checked, and the take-off flap set. Remember, the selection of flap beyond FLAPS 1 will signal the centre air-driven hydraulic pump to run (in readiness for the rapid retraction of the landing gear after take-off).

After receiving take-off clearance, with the aircraft nearly lined up, advance the throttles a little, perhaps to about 1.1 EPR, ensuring an even response, and then select EPR mode to engage the autothrottle. The power levers will advance to accelerate the engines to the reference EPR displayed on EICAS. Be careful not to press the EPR switch too early, particularly in case the aircraft is not properly lined-up, or the rapid engine acceleration may overcome the nosewheel steering. The autothrottle mode will be shown as EPR on the ADI, shown in figure 4-33.

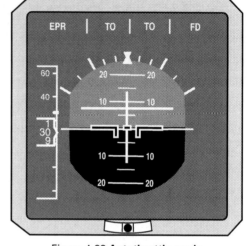

Figure 4-33 **Autothrottle mode shown as EPR on ADI**

The take-off is flown manually, using the control column and the rudders, with the autothrottle engaged (although the captain's hand is on the throttle, in case of a rejected take-off).

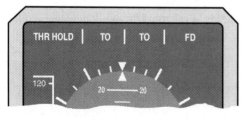

Figure 4-34 **THR HOLD displayed on ADI**

As the aircraft accelerates beyond 80 kt, the autothrottle mode will change to THR HOLD, and the pilots can adjust the power if they wish. THR HOLD will be displayed on the ADI, as shown in figure 4-34.

As the aircraft leaves the ground, the FD command bars will give roll guidance in the TO mode to maintain centreline, with the pitch command increasing from 8°ANU to about 17°ANU.

THR HOLD will remain the active autothrottle mode while the flaps are retracted in stages, when climb thrust can be selected on the TMCP, as shown in figure 4-35. The EPR will again become the autothrottle mode displayed on the ADI.

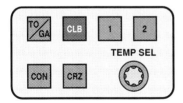

Figure 4-35 **Climb thrust selected and EPR as the autothrottle mode**

Figure 4-36 **Using HDG SEL to steer towards LNAV track**

At a safe height, say 400 ft, LNAV can be selected, and the FD mode will be displayed as LNAV (white – armed). If the aircraft track does not intercept the LNAV track, it will be necessary to use HDG SEL as the action mode (in green) to steer the aircraft towards the LNAV track, as shown in figure 4-36.

At any time above 400 ft AGL (autopilot limitation), the autopilot can be selected *in command* (CMD). If it is safe, CLB power can be selected on the thrust mode control panel, and the A/T will deliver climb EPR as shown in figure 4-37. The pitch mode is commanding VNAV PTH, in this case a profile climb, with the IAS increasing to a maximum of 250 kt, until above 10,000 ft, and then an ECON climb to the cruising level.

Figure 4-37 **Command mode**

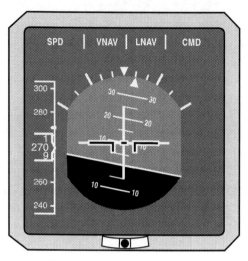

Figure 4-38 **ADI as aircraft turns to intercept LNAV track**

As the aircraft closes on, and captures the LNAV track, the roll command will change to LNAV (green), and the autopilot will turn the aircraft to make a smooth interception. The ADI will look like figure 4-38.

It is quite usual for ATC to restrict the climb to something less than the FMS programmed flight level. For instance, FL330 may be the planned level, but the ATC clearance is only to FL310. Set FL310 in the altitude select window on the MCP, but leave the FMS program unchanged. The AFDS will level off at the first level reached, either that in the altitude window, used to set the ATC clearance level, or the FMS level.

As FL310 is approached, the AFDS pitch mode will change from VNAV to ALT CAP (altitude capture), the AFDS will pitch the nose down to maintain FL310, and the autothrottle will change to SPD, reducing power to maintain the current airspeed, as shown in figure 4-39.

Figure 4-39 **Altitude capture**

As the aircraft levels off and maintains FL310, the AFDS pitch mode will change to ALT HOLD, see figure 4-40.

Subsequent ATC clearances to the planned level, recorded in the altitude window, will allow the reselection of VNAV, when the aircraft will climb to the planned level of FL330, and the autothrottle will adjust power to meet first, the climb requirement, and the ECON cruise speed.

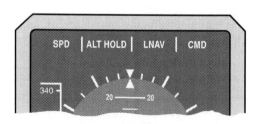

Figure 4-40 **Altitude hold**

It is a little quicker to use flight level change (FL CH) to trigger an AFDS response, and initiate the climb first, changing to VNAV a little later on. At the cruising level, the AFDS modes will be as in figure 4-41.

Figure 4-41 **VNAV**

Apart from responding to navigation requirements, the next task on a short leg like MELSYD is planning and programming the descent. Let us assume that we are advised to expect a straight-in approach to RWY 07 at Sydney. Program this data into the FMS, as shown in chapter 3, and, remembering that the aircraft will not leave the cruising level until a lower altitude has been set in the MCP altitude window, request a descent clearance in plenty of time (some 150 nm from SY). Keep an eye on the distance to run to the VNAV descent point, so you don't get too much of a shock when the throttles close quite suddenly and the nose pitches down! The A/T will initially show IDLE, and then THR HOLD. During the descent, the AFDS modes will be as shown in figure 4-42.

Figure 4-42 **VNAV path**

Whenever the aircraft gets above the VNAV descent profile, there will be a message to increase drag, usually achieved by extending speedbrakes. If the aircraft is below the profile, the autothrottle will respond by increasing power. The reported weather conditions will give some idea of the amount of autobraking to set up.

If you fly with your feet up on the rudder pedals, be advised that it is very easy to disarm the autobrakes by touching the brake pedals, so keep an eye on the brake status.

As the aircraft comes within range of the approach aid, the ILS equipment can be tuned – in the B767, all three ILS units are tuned by the one tuning head. After identifying the aid, and ensuring that the LNAV track will intercept the ILS centreline, the AFDS on the MCP can be programmed to intercept the

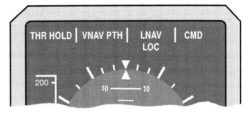

Figure 4-43 **Localiser**

localiser, by selecting LOC on the MCP, and LOC will appear as armed (amber) mode in the roll display on the ADI. See figure 4-43.

Figure 4-44 **Glideslope armed**

Airspeed can be controlled using the speed control function of the autothrottle, and by extending flap and landing gear. With the gear down, the ground spoilers can be armed to extend on landing.

Once the localiser has been captured, glideslope capture can be armed in a similar manner, as shown in figure 4-44.

With the glideslope getting closer, all three autopilots can be selected on the MCP; only the first autopilot is in CMD, with the other two in an armed mode, until below 1,500 ft AGL, and after an autoland system self check.

For autoland, the three electrical buses become isolated, so that each autopilot has a separate power supply. By about 1,200 ft AGL, all the automatic checks will be completed, and all three autopilots are active, as shown by the CMD3 caption on the ADI. The autoland annunciators will show LAND 3. The autothrottle will be in an SPD mode, as shown in figure 4-45.

Figure 4-45 **Glideslope capture**

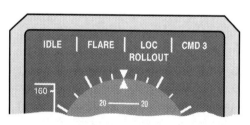

Figure 4-46 **Flare**

Approaching the runway, the pitch trim datum will shift to provide sufficient elevator authority for the flare. As the touchdown point gets closer, the autothrottle will close the throttles, going into IDLE mode, and then THR HOLD. FLARE becomes the active pitch mode, and the rollout mode is armed in the roll mode display (not really a roll mode, but ailerons are used to keep the wings level, with rudder and nosewheel steering tracking the centreline of the localiser). See figure 4-46.

The pilots must monitor the progress of the landing manoeuvre, and be ready to go around, by pressing the go-around (GA) buttons (not the autothrottle disconnect!). We have landed safely and are ready to apply reverse thrust to ease the strain on the automatic brakes. When convenient, the pilot flying can cancel reverse thrust, disconnect the autopilots, retract the ground spoilers, retract the flaps and taxi to the ramp.

Chapter 5

Warning and Recording Systems

The complexity of modern aircraft systems has required the installation of numerous warning lights to alert the crew to system failure or malfunction. Until the 1960s it was common to position warning lights adjacent to the respective system control panel.

However, cockpit space limitations have meant that many system control panels are located out of the direct view of the pilots, on overhead or side panels. Placement of warning lights on these panels is clearly ineffective, and aircraft designers have wired the warning function of most systems through a centralised display. In addition, aural alerts are used to capture the crew's attention, some of them loud enough to be heard halfway down the cabin!

Master Warning and Caution Systems

To alert the crew to an operational problem, or a system malfunction, transport aircraft are required to be fitted with warning systems, which use visual, aural and tactile methods. In a typical cockpit, there will be alerting lights immediately in front of both pilots, set into the glareshield, as well as specific system malfunction lights, usually grouped together, in the centre of the instrument panel, on the overhead panel, or in aircraft with a 'glass' cockpit, messages and corrective actions displayed on a pair of CRTs.

In most systems, the degree of urgency provided by a problem is divided into three distinct classifications: warnings, cautions and advisories.

- Warnings indicate aircraft system or operational conditions that require immediate corrective action by the crew, and are the most urgent type of crew alert. Loss of cabin pressure or an engine fire are typical warnings.
- Cautions indicate aircraft system or operational conditions that require crew action within a reasonable period of time, and are less urgent than warnings. Engine overheat or low oil pressure are typical cautions.
- Advisories indicate conditions that require action only when you have time available (i.e. the least urgent warnings). A typical advisory would be a yaw damper fault (in some aircraft).

Note: Status messages (white) may appear elsewhere on another screen showing conditions that require crew awareness for dispatch, i.e. the minimum equipment list (MEL) may have to be consulted to note any special requirements for dispatch relief.

Master Warning and Caution Lights

The visual indications of the levels of alert are usually colour coded, using red lights for warnings and amber lights for cautions and advisories. The glareshield lights are called the *master warning and caution lights* and usually have the ability to silence any audio alerts when pressed, so that the crew can communicate without having to shout.

The appropriate master light illuminates whenever a system malfunctions and directs the crew's attention to the central warning panel to establish which system is faulty. Most checklist procedures call for resetting the master warning or caution light, by pressing it, when the failure has been identified. The master light will go out, but the specific system warning will remain illuminated until the problem is fixed. In some aircraft, additional engine fire warning lights are contained in the engine fire shut-off handles to assist in identification.

Visual Alerts

In glass cockpit aeroplanes, warning, caution and advisory messages are displayed on a dedicated portion of one of the CRTs. In the Boeing system, the messages on EICAS are colour coded and prioritised so that the most critical messages are displayed. Less critical messages that may already be displayed are pre-empted. If there are more messages than can be displayed on the screen (having a bad day!) the excess messages are retained in the computer memory for display when there is room, or when called up by the crew. Typical displays are shown in figure 5-1.

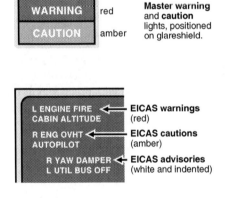

WARNING — red
CAUTION — amber

Master warning and **caution** lights, positioned on glareshield.

L ENGINE FIRE ← **EICAS warnings** (red)
CABIN ALTITUDE

R ENG OVHT ← **EICAS cautions** (amber)
AUTOPILOT

R YAW DAMPER ← **EICAS advisories** (white and indented)
L UTIL BUS OFF

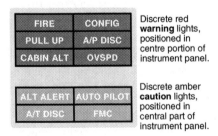

FIRE	CONFIG
PULL UP	A/P DISC
CABIN ALT	OVSPD

Discrete red **warning** lights, positioned in centre portion of instrument panel.

| ALT ALERT | AUTO PILOT |
| A/T DISC | FMC |

Discrete amber **caution** lights, positioned in central part of instrument panel.

Figure 5-1 **Typical visual alerts**

Aural Alerts

Various aural alerts are used to call attention to warnings and cautions.

Aural Warnings

Typically, there are four types of alarm – a bell, a computerised voice, a siren (or horn) and a wailer. The bell is used for fire warnings only, the voice for the GPWS and TCAS, the siren to indicate cabin altitude, overspeed, or configuration warnings, and the wailer for an autopilot disconnect. Generally the warnings will continue to sound until the condition is corrected, or until the crew cancel the aural warning, typically by pushing the master warning light.

Aural Cautions

Aural cautions typically consist of a voice and a beeper or clacker. The voice is used by the ground proximity warning system, and the beeper sounds for all other cautions. The beeper sounds a number of rapid tones, (bee-bee-bee-beep) and then stops. The crew can then scan the cockpit to identify the faulty system. The caution beeper may sound every ten seconds or so, unless the condition is rectified, or the crew cancel the alert, typically by pushing the master caution light.

Tactile Alert

The tactile alert in common use is the stick shaker of the stall warning system, discussed later in this chapter.

Inhibitions

Some of the crew alerting systems may be inhibited, or deactivated to prevent distraction during critical phases of flight. For instance, the fire warning bell and the master warning lights may be inhibited during take-off, from nosewheel lift-off to 400 ft radio altitude, or for 20 seconds, at which point the warnings will activate, if a fire exists. Similarly the beeper and the master caution light may be inhibited during the take-off, from 80 kt to 400 ft radio altitude, see figure 5-2.

During engine starting and shutdown, many of the alerts are inhibited, to avoid nuisance warnings as systems come on- or off-line.

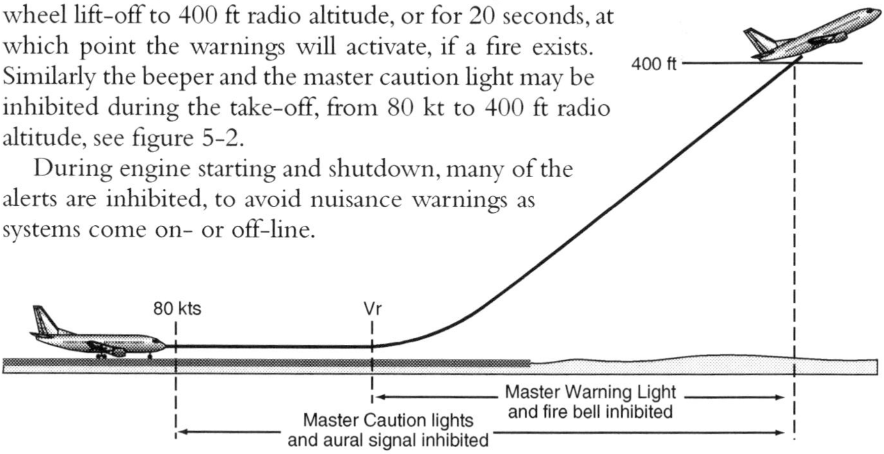

Figure 5-2 **Caution and warning inhibits during take-off**

Overspeed Warning Systems

This type of system is often referred to as an airspeed/Mach warning system since it simply provides warning to the pilots if V_{MO} or M_{MO} are exceeded. In transport aircraft, two separate warning systems must be provided, based on information from the two air data computers which give airspeed/Mach readings to the two pilot positions.

At low altitudes, generally below about 25,000 ft, the V_{MO} limit will be reached first. This is typically about 360 KIAS for most transport jets. Above that altitude the M_{MO} limit will be reached before V_{MO}. M_{MO} is typically between M 0.82 and 0.87. Exceeding either of these limits activates an aural caution in the cockpit, generally in the form of a 'clacker' or horn.

Certification standards demand that this warning cannot be cancelled by the pilots, who must reduce speed to below the limiting value to silence the 'clackers'. In some aircraft the aural warning may be accompanied by a warning light adjacent to the airspeed indication or on the EFIS displays. Also in some aircraft, the overspeed warning value can be varied by switching to suit certain conditions of weight, fuel distribution or CG.

Stick-Shaker Systems

Certification requirements demand that transport aircraft are either designed or equipped so that the pilot has clear warning of an approaching stall at a speed that is equivalent to seven per cent above the stall speed, i.e. at 107% stall speed. Most swept-wing transport aircraft cannot provide natural warning of an approaching stall of this margin, so artificial warning is required.

The artificial warning is normally in the form of an audio warning and a *stick shaker* that physically shakes the pilot's control column at a high frequency (or even pushes the control column forward – a *stick pusher*). The vibration is created by a small electric motor attached to the control column that rotates an out-of-balance rotor.

Activation of the stick shakers is not simply a function of airspeed since with more than normal load factor (1g), the stall will occur at a higher airspeed.

To handle various combinations, a small computer is fitted to the system which typically receives inputs from the following sources:
- angle-of-attack sensor on fuselage;
- flap position transmitter;
- N_1 or EPR indicator;
- air/ground switch; and
- air data computer.

Outputs from the computer are sent to the EFIS display, which can provide marks on the speed tape showing stall speeds in the various configurations.

With a sufficiently powerful processor, the stall warning computer can combine the various inputs to determine a maximum pitch attitude on the EADI. Maintaining aircraft pitch attitude less than this position will ensure that the aircraft remains free of the stall and stick-shaker warnings.

Figure 5-3 shows a typical stall warning system.

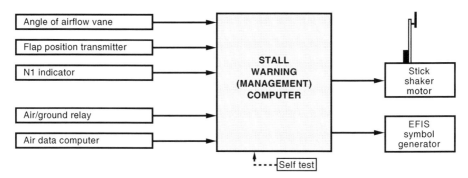

Figure 5-3 **Stall warning system**

Since the safe operation of an aircraft depends on the correct functioning of warning systems such as stall warning, checklist actions normally require that a test be conducted prior to each flight. Test buttons are provided for each stall warning system (pilot and co-pilot position) that check circuit integrity and the operation of the stick shakers.

Take-off Configuration Warning System

A number of accidents have occurred that have been directly attributed to take-off configuration errors. Most commonly, the pilots fail to select flap for take-off.

The take-off configuration warning system fitted to the majority of large aircraft consists of an audible warning horn which sounds intermittently if the engine thrust levers are advanced for take-off and certain configuration problems exist.

Configuration errors that will initiate a warning are typically:
- stabiliser trim not in take-off band;
- parking brake set;
- trailing edge flaps not selected in take-off range;
- leading edge slats not in take-off range; and
- speed brake extended.

Evacuation Signals

On older transport aircraft, evacuation signals were usually made over the public address system (PA), or by using the cabin attendants' call chimes in a pre-arranged pattern. On the latest aircraft, with wide-body cabins, multiple exits, and large numbers of people to be evac-uated, a dedicated evacuation signal is provided. Figure 5-4 shows a control

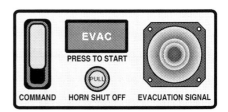

Figure 5-4 **Evacuation signal control panel**

panel for such a system. Control panels are usually located in the cockpit and at each of the cabin attendant stations, i.e. close to each exit.

Each panel has a command switch, an evacuation light, a horn, and a horn shut-off switch. Positioning any of the command switches to on will cause the horns to sound, and the EVAC light to illuminate at all locations. The horn at each panel may be silenced by using the horn shut-off switch.

Company procedures will indicate who has the authority to give the evacuation signal, and what action is required subsequently.

Ground Proximity Warning Systems

Despite the significant advances in aeronautical technology and the operational standards of modern airlines, fatal accidents involving airline aircraft continue to occur throughout the world. Most fatalities in airline accidents result from controlled flight into terrain (CFIT).

Ground proximity warning systems (GPWSs) are used as a method of alerting pilots to abnormal descent rates that they may otherwise not detect. Bad weather, poor cockpit coordination, and dealing with abnormal situations can distract crews at a time when proximity to terrain presents the greater hazard.

A typical GPWS computes closure rate with terrain and then compares that result with acceptable values that have been pre-programmed.

Inputs to the GPWS are typically:
* radio altitude;
* airspeed/Mach;
* barometric altitude;
* landing gear position;
* flap position; and
* glideslope deviations.

Some modern GPWSs are equipped to provide windshear warning as well. For this function the GPWS must also have inputs of angle of attack from the stall warning computer and sensitive acceleration inputs from the inertial reference system (IRS).

Typical warnings provided by a modern GPWS are in the form of aural alerts, where a synthesised voice makes the appropriate aural statement *(pull-up, pull-up)* or a buzzer/horn is activated.

GPWS Alert Modes

The various situations that can initiate a GPWS alert are normally called 'modes'. Most modes provide two levels of alert as terrain is approached and safe margins are infringed. When initial limits are exceeded the first warning that is given is usually termed a *soft warning* (i.e. a caution). If the aircraft then gets closer to terrain and exceeds the next level set by the system, a *hard warning* is given. Hard warnings are usually sufficient to wake the dead.

Typical alert modes are described as follows.

Excessive Descent Rate

This mode is normally independent of aircraft configuration and provides an alert on the basis of excessive rates of descent at low altitude.

In most installations, this mode does not become active until below 2,500 ft radio altitude. Below that height, a repeated aural alert of *sink rate* is sounded when the rate of descent exceeds the set limits.

The rate of descent is typically around 5,000 fpm at 2,500 ft radio altitude, reducing to 1,000 fpm as the aircraft descends further. In other words, the system does not allow high rates of descent at low radio altitudes without sounding the alert.

This mode also has another setting of a higher descent rate for each altitude which sounds a more intense aural warning of *'whoop whoop pull-up'*. Most systems also have a warning light marked 'pull-up' which illuminates if the higher warning rate is exceeded.

Figure 5-5 shows a typical relationship of radio altitude to sink rate which activates the two warnings. This mode generally provides protection from descent into all level or undulating terrain.

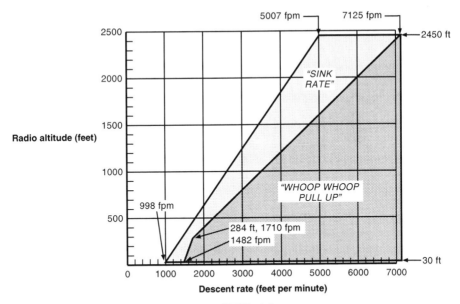

Figure 5-5 **GPWS sink rate**

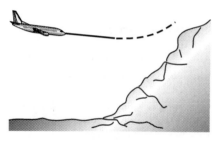

Figure 5-6 **Flight into rising terrain**

Excessive Terrain Closure

This mode monitors airspeed, radio altitude and rate of altitude change, barometric altitude and configuration. It provides protection from flight into rising terrain, as illustrated in figure 5-6. A submode allows closer proximity to rising terrain with landing gear and flaps selected before warnings are sounded. A typical system provides an aural 'terrain' warning when initial limits are exceeded, and *'whoop whoop pull-up'* command when final limits are reached.

Take-off/Go-Around Sink Rate

This mode is active when the landing gear or flaps are selected, and during take-off. If the aircraft loses altitude during a go-around or after take-off, or if the flaps are raised at a low radio altitude, an aural warning of *'don't sink'* accompanied by the pull-up warning light is activated. The amount of altitude loss permitted before the warning is activated is dependent on radio altitude. At 50 ft radio altitude, a loss of only 20 ft is typical of that needed to initiate the warning. However, at 1,000 ft radio altitude, a loss of about 100 ft is generally the limit value. This mode is normally deactivated above about 1,500 ft radio altitude.

Configuration

There are normally two separate modes: one for landing gear, and the other for flaps not being at a normal landing setting, which initiate warnings when the aircraft is too close to terrain and below a set airspeed, without the configuration selected. The warning for landing gear is normally set at about 500 ft radio altitude and gives a *'too low gear'* aural warning accompanied by the pull-up light. At higher speeds without the gear, normally above about 200 KIAS, the system gives the *'too low terrain'* aural warning. The low altitude without flaps in the landing configuration mode normally allows the aircraft to descend to about 250 ft radio altitude before giving a *'too low flaps'* aural warning and the pull-up light.

Below Glideslope

Inputs from the ILS glideslope receiver that are processed by the GPWS provide warnings when the aircraft is a specified number of dots (1.3 dots for the B767) below the glidepath on ILS and below a set radio altitude, normally about 1,000 ft. Soft warnings in the form of an aural *'glideslope'* and illumination of a below G/S light are usually given when more than 1.3 dots below glidepath. When the aircraft is more than two dots below glidepath at a low radio altitude (usually 300 ft), the hard warning is initiated. This normally consists of more volume for the aural warning but may also be accompanied by a whooping sound.

Below Minima (Minimums)

During preparation for an instrument approach, the pilot can program the GPWS for the minimum published altitude of the approach. This will be the ceiling on instrument approach charts. When the radio altimeter senses this value, the GPWS gives an aural *'minimums, minimums'* warning. This mode will only operate with the landing gear down and only values below 1,000 ft radio altitude can normally be set.

Windshear

If windshear is encountered on approach or after take-off, an aural warning consisting of a two-tone siren and a voice warning *'windshear, windshear, windshear'* is triggered. Also a visual warning is usually provided by windshear warning lights on the main instrument panel. Windshear warnings take priority over all other GPWS modes and are available from rotation to a radio altitude of 1,500 ft. As previously stated, a windshear condition sufficient to trigger a warning is detected using comparisons of angle of attack, IRS accelerations, and airspeed from the air data computer.

GPWS Control Panel

Figure 5-7 shows a typical GPWS control panel. This panel normally has a warning light to indicate if the system is inoperative, a test switch to confirm system integrity prior to take-off, and isolation switches for gear/flaps. The gear/flaps isolation switches prevent warnings being initiated that are based on low altitude/speed without those services selected. The inhibiting functions of these switches are only used in special circumstances, e.g. the flap isolation is selected on an engine-out approach because of the less than normal flap setting used.

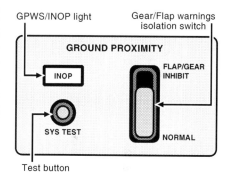

Figure 5-7 **Typical GPWS control panel**

Traffic Alert and Collision Avoidance Systems

The traffic alert and collision avoidance system (TCAS) is designed to provide protection against collision with other aircraft.

At the time of writing, there are two systems in use, TCAS I and TCAS II. Both are required to actively interrogate other aircraft (rather than listen to replies elicited by ground interrogators) to allow TCAS to accurately measure the range of proximate aircraft and to make TCAS operation independent of ground facilities. Such independence is necessary in oceanic and other non-radar airspace.

TCAS I System

Many of the basic features of the TCAS I system are common with TCAS II.

TCAS I systems are the least complex of TCAS equipment since they are only required to provide traffic advisories, i.e. do not need to give any resolution advisories. *Traffic advisories* (TA) simply show the presence of other aircraft. *Resolution advisories* (RA) suggest action to be taken to avoid conflict. TCAS I systems do not require a Mode S transponder.

Display to the pilot is in a plan view which shows the relative position of target aircraft together with symbology that gives an altitude differential relative to the host aircraft (i.e. above or below) and a vertical trend. Figure 5-8 shows a typical TCAS I display which may be provided on a separate TCAS CRT display or on an existing radar display tube.

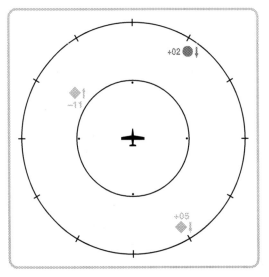

Note:

The numerals against the target display show height above or below host aircraft in hundreds of feet.

The arrow indicates vertical trend.

Different symbol shapes can be used to show varying levels of urgency.

Figure 5-8 **TCAS I display**

Specifications for TCAS I require provision of a traffic advisory (TA) when an intruder aircraft comes within 30 seconds of the host aircraft. However, TCAS I also provides display of target aircraft outside the 30-second time frame. Most systems use a 'box' of airspace 4 nm in radius and 1,200 ft above and below the host aircraft to display proximate advisories (PA), and different symbology to show aircraft outside that box.

Accuracy standards of TCAS I require measurement within 10° of bearing and 0.1 nm range. Although some TCAS equipment may provide detection of target aircraft at greater ranges, TCAS I systems must provide detection at a minimum of 8 nm. Thus a TCAS I system may use three types of display symbology to show the three different levels of urgency given to target aircraft:

* visual symbology of aircraft outside the 4 nm box;
* visual symbology of aircraft inside the PA box; and
* visual symbology plus an audible warning of TAs within the 30-second time frame.

As TCAS I systems actively interrogate target aircraft transponders, communications authorities have been concerned about the possibility of transponder frequency congestion. Consequently a *whisper-shout* variable transmission power feature has been developed.

Whisper-Shout

Whisper-shout is one technique used to elicit separate replies, one at a time, from multiple aircraft in sufficiently close proximity to one another that their transponder replies would otherwise be garbled. It is based on transponders not all having identical receiver sensitivity and the use of controlled power allows a degree of selective interrogation. Whisper-shout is not primarily intended to reduce or limit interrogations.

TCAS II System

The main differences of a TCAS II system compared to a TCAS I system are:

* installation of a Mode-S transponder;
* provision of vertical resolution advisories; and
* 45-second shield (rather than a 30-second one as for TCAS I).

A resolution advisory (RA) provides positive information to the pilot in the form of action to be taken to avoid the other (threat) aircraft.

Use of Mode-S Transponder

A new type of transponder, known as Mode S, will become increasingly common during the next few years. This new system is also referred to as the *discrete address beacon system,* and promises to reduce the workloads of both controllers and pilots, as well as reducing the congestion on normal radio communications frequencies.

In addition to the altitude information provided by the Mode C stem, Mode S transponders will automatically transmit an aircraft's registration and type whenever it is interrogated by ground-based radar. This eliminates the need for the controller to manually enter the identification of each aircraft into the ATC computer, and means that a pilot does not have to select a discrete code. This improvement is significant enough on its own, but fully optioned Mode S installation will provide further benefits.

By a process known as *select addressing,* it will also be possible for ATC to transmit other information, such as weather reports, ATIS, and clearances to a specific aircraft, which can then be displayed on a suitable screen or printer inside the cockpit. This promises to decrease the volume of radio transmissions considerably.

The Mode-S transponder provides the two-way data link which allows TCAS II-equipped aircraft to coordinate their RAs.

This data link may also be used to seek stale data from other aircraft to aid in accurate determination of the level of threat. The calculations to support RAs is performed in the TCAS II unit.

Antenna Diversity

TCAS II installations require top and bottom antennae. The top antenna must be directional. The bottom antenna may be either omni-directional or directional. The associated Mode-S transponder installations also require top and bottom antennae. The Mode-S transponder has two complete receivers, one per antenna. The reply to an interrogation is transmitted via the antenna that received the interrogation with greater signal strength. The combination of two top and two bottom antennae is required to ensure timely detection and adequate communication reliability regardless of the closure speed and relative position of the aircraft to each other.

Operation of TCAS II Systems

Once a target aircraft is acquired, the TCAS II unit continuously monitors time-to-collision. Since TCAS II systems provide both a visual and an aural indication of approaching aircraft, the crew must be trained to respond to these combined inputs. In many situations the first indication would be an aural warning of 'traffic, traffic' as the target aircraft enters the traffic advisory limit, which for TCAS II is 45 seconds from collision.

Resolution Advisory

A traffic advisory (TA) is normally issued 5 to 20 seconds in advance of the resolution advisory (RA). The RA is issued when time-to-collision is between 15 and 35 seconds. (The term *collision* is not usually used, rather the term 'closest point of approach', abbreviated CPA, is generally used.) It is rare, but possible, for an RA to be issued without being preceded by a TA. TCAS II generates RAs in combined aural and visual commands to create a vertical miss distance of 400–700 ft. This is to minimise the generation of additional encounters with aircraft on adjacent flight levels. TCAS II reassesses the encounter once per second. As the situation changes both the sense and required vertical rate of the RA may change. Changes to the sense of a RA are most likely to occur if the threat aircraft changes its vertical rate or an additional threat aircraft is detected. For TCAS II to be effective the pilot must respond to changes to the RA.

For example, in a situation where the target aircraft is approaching from below, the TCAS II system will command a climb. In such a case the aural instruction would be 'climb, climb' accompanied by VSI indications showing red for all negative and positive rates up to +1,500 fpm and green from +1,500 fpm. In this case the pilot should smoothly establish a rate of climb of at least 1,500 fpm. In such an example, as the geometry of the two flightpaths changes, so too will the value of the red and green vertical rate VSI sectors. To maintain adequate separation, the pilot must maintain vertical speed in the green sector. As the conflict is being controlled, aural warnings will change to *'maintain vertical speed'*, and finally, *'clear of conflict'*.

Pilot Response

For TCAS II to be effective, the pilot:
- must not manoeuvre on the basis of the traffic display or traffic advisory;
- must not manoeuvre horizontally;
- must obey all TCAS RAs and RA changes including sense reversals;
- must initiate the first manoeuvre required by an RA within 5 seconds of the RA being given;
- must initiate any subsequent manoeuvres required by RA changes within 2.5 seconds of the RA change;
- when *'clear of conflict'* is given, return to assigned level; and
- conduct all manoeuvres so as to generate a vertical acceleration of $0.25g$ (i.e. a total of $+1.25g$ pull up or $+0.75g$ push down).

RA Accuracy

RA accuracy is essentially independent of the equipment fitted to the threat aircraft. A TCAS II will generate RAs against threat aircraft equipped with:
- a Mode A/C transponder which is reporting pressure altitude; or
- a Mode S transponder which is reporting pressure altitude.

While a Mode A/C transponder reports pressure altitude in increments of 100 ft, a Mode S transponder reports pressure altitude in increments of either 100 ft or 25 ft, depending on the type of pressure altitude source. If the threat aircraft has 25 ft reporting, the accuracy of the RA in the vertical plane is obviously improved.

The presence, or absence, of TCAS I or TCAS II in the threat aircraft does not, in itself, affect the accuracy of the RA. However, 25 ft reporting is usually available on aircraft equipped with TCAS II.

The Mode S transponder allows complex calculations required for resolution advisories to be completed in a very short time. TCAS II aircraft can operate against TCAS I aircraft although the quality of resolution information is not as high as that provided in a full TCAS II environment. When two TCAS II-equipped aircraft are interrogating each other using Mode S, the highest degree of resolution accuracy is achieved. The fitment of a Mode S transponder also allows the TCAS II system to supply information to Mode S-compatible air traffic radar systems.

TCAS II Display

TCAS II systems provide the same types of display as TCAS I, although the dimensions of the TA box may vary. Interrogation of other aircraft uses the same whisper-shout transmission concept as TCAS I. TCAS II systems provide the same type of display to the pilot for relative position of target aircraft but also need to show vertical climb information for vertical resolution advisories.

This type of information is generally in the form of a VSI-type instrument generated on a CRT with the plan view information also provided in the centre of the instrument. Figure 5-9 shows a typical TCAS II display for an aircraft without EFIS instrumentation.

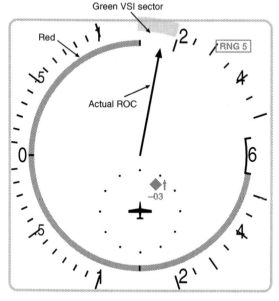

An intruder is located inside the dotted 2 nm range ring.
It is 300 ft low and climbing.

A green sector on the VSI is displayed between +1500 and +2000 fpm.
The aircraft is now climbing at 1800 fpm.

Figure 5-9 **TCAS II display**

Control for the TCAS II system is normally provided on a combined transponder/TCAS controller. Figure 5-10 shows a typical control panel.

EFIS-equipped aircraft can display TCAS II RA pitch commands on the ADI, and TA and RA traffic on the HSI, when traffic (TFC) is selected on the EFIS control panel.

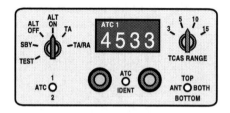

Figure 5-10 **TCAS II control panel**

Problems with TCAS II

Although TCAS II systems have gained the confidence of many airline crews, air traffic organisations are concerned that host aircraft resolution advisories will lead aircraft to leave cleared flight levels without notification.

Tests in the United States have already shown that at least one situation can lead to a climbing RA when normal separation exists. This is shown in figure 5-11, where a target aircraft planning to level 1,000 ft below the host aircraft is climbing at a high vertical rate.

The host aircraft issues an RA when the target aircraft is still 1,500 ft below, causing an uncleared climb by the host aircraft. Solutions to such procedural problems are still being resolved.

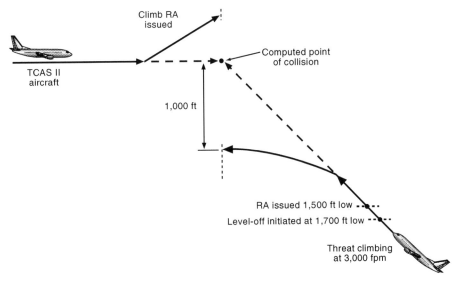

Figure 5-11 **TCAS false warning**

The problem depicted in figure 5-11, and generally known as the *'Dallas bump'*, was addressed by a change to the TCAS II in logic version 6.04A. This version has been deployed worldwide and operational experience indicates the change has been largely effective.

If the threat aircraft approaches its assigned level with a vertical rate of 500 ft/min or less for the last 1,000 ft, then TCAS II (version 6.04A) will not generate an RA.

Thus it is important in busy airspace for pilots to limit vertical rate to 500 ft/min for the last 1,000 ft when levelling off at assigned level. It is worth noting that some flight management systems do not behave in this manner!

TCAS and Altimetry Errors

TCAS uses the altitude information, from both own and threat aircraft transponder pressure altitude encoders, to determine the most appropriate escape manoeuvre. Should either of these encoders provide erroneous data, the accuracy of TCAS I/II TA display and TCAS II RAs will be adversely affected.

TCAS Levels of Protection

Figure 5-12 summarises the various levels of protection available.

Threat aircraft	Own aircraft – TCAS I	Own aircraft – TCAS II
No Xpdr or Xpdr Off	None	None
Mode A/C Xpdr pressure encoder not fitted	TA	TA
Mode A/C Xpdr with pressure encoder	TA	TA, RA
Mode S Xpdr	TA	TA, RA
TCAS I	TA	TA, RA
TCAS II	TA	TA, RA, TTC
Key: XPDR = transponder TA = traffic advisory RA = resolution advisory TTC = TCAS to TCAS coordination of resolution advisories		

Figure 5-12 **TCAS levels of protection**

Note: If the pilot of the threat aircraft disables pressure altitude reporting, then TAs will be displayed without relative altitude and RAs, and TTC will not be generated.

Summary

The following points summarise the use of TCAS.

- TCAS I/II provides no protection against aircraft that do not have a transponder or in which the transponder is not switched on.
- To maximise the effectiveness of TCAS, all aircraft should be equipped with a transponder and the transponder should be used whenever the aircraft is in flight.
- A Mode A/C transponder with pressure altitude encoder is sufficient to provide maximum protection in an encounter with a TCAS I/II-equipped aircraft.
- TCAS I/II can only display the relative altitude of a threat aircraft and TCAS II can only generate RAs if the threat aircraft is transponding pressure altitude (Mode C).
- Transponder control panels have provision to switch off pressure altitude reporting. This provision is used to allow pilots to disable pressure altitude reporting when the pressure altitude data is known to be erroneous.
- To maximise the effectiveness of TCAS, all aircraft should operate at all times with their transponder on and altitude reporting enabled (Mode C).
- Altitude-reporting accuracy is verified by ATC. When an aircraft enters controlled airspace, and is radar identified, the controller uses actual altitude reported by the pilot to validate the pressure altitude which is received by ground radar and displayed by the controller. Should this validation fail, the pilot is instructed to disable altitude reporting, but the transponder should remain on. The failure should be recorded in the maintenance log.

Weather Radar

Purpose

Weather radar systems are used primarily for airborne weather detection, ranging and analysis, but may also be used in a ground-mapping mode as an aid to navigation.

Equipment

The major components of a typical system are:
- radar antenna;
- receiver/transmitter unit;
- control panel; and
- display unit.

Operation

Weather radar systems operate in the X-band, with power outputs in the order of 125 W. Maximum range of modern radars is about 300 nm. The antenna is normally stabilised using attitude signals from one of the vertical gyros, or inertial references (to avoid clutter from ground returns during turns).

The antenna sweeps (scans) the pencil-shaped radar beam about 60° either side of the nose, and can be tilted up and down to about ±15°. Radar returns, or *echoes,* are processed to provide range and azimuth data, which is then displayed in the cockpit.

Control

There are various types of control panel for the weather radar. One fitted in the B767 is shown in figure 5-13.

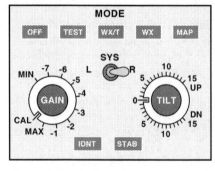

The panel provides controls for *gain* (sensitivity – like squelch on the radio) and antenna tilt. There is a switch to select left or right system, an IDNT button for suppressing ground return suppression, and a STAB button for activating antenna stabilisation. The mode switches are as follows:

Figure 5-13 **Weather radar control panel**

- OFF removes power from system;
- TEST displays maintenance test pattern;
- WX/T displays weather and turbulence returns;
- WX activates display of detected precipitation; and
- MAP activates display of ground returns.

Display

The weather radar information can be displayed on a single dedicated indicator, accessible to both pilots, on a multi-function display, or on an electronic HSI, such as that shown in figure 5-14.

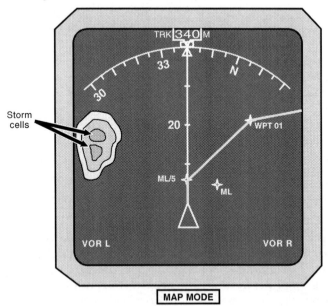

Figure 5-14 **Weather display on an HSI**

Generally the strongest radar returns are shown in red, and less intense in amber and lowest intensity in green. This makes it easier to plan avoidance manoeuvre priorities. When turbulence is indicated, the returns will be shown in magenta. By adjusting tilt and range, the vertical extent and severity of a storm cell can also be gauged.

The weather radar returns will be displayed on the HSI, when WXR is selected on, on the EFIS control panel, and the HSI mode is set to MAP, EXP VOR or EXP ILS.

Recording Systems

Flight Data Recorder (FDR)

All transport aircraft above 5,700 kg must be fitted with a flight data recorder that automatically records various engine and airframe conditions from engine start-up to engine shut-down.

Operation of the FDR must be fully automatic and not require pilot switching. Most importantly, pilots are not able to turn the FDR off in flight or erase data after landing (to ensure data that may be relevant to an accident or incident is protected for use by accident investigation officers).

The FDR provides a permanent record on tape of selected parameters such as altitude, heading, speed, load factor and engine readings. To protect the tape in the event of an accident, the recorder is housed in a sealed fire- and impact-resistant container. The FDR is normally located in a part of the airframe that is likely to suffer least in the event of an impact. Consequently, they are normally installed in the tail or roof of the aircraft.

Digital flight data recorders (DFDR) are fitted to many modern transport aircraft, and have the capacity to record as many as 300 parameters, including control positions and systems performance. This data is retained for 25 hours.

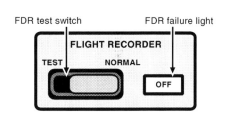

Cockpit controls for the FDR are limited to a warning light which illuminates in the event of FDR failure, and a test switch for use only on the ground. Figure 5-15 shows a typical FDR control panel.

Figure 5-15 **FDR control panel**

Cockpit Voice Recorder (CVR)

A cockpit voice recorder is fitted to all transport aircraft above 5,700 kg to record a full audio record of cockpit conversation and background noise. A CVR typically records 60 or 30 minutes of audio information on a continuous tape. This means it should always be able to provide the last 60 or 30 minutes of information. CVRs have proved very valuable in listening in to crew conversation for the last few minutes prior to a major accident.

Either one or two sensitive microphones are fitted to the ceiling of the cockpit which pick up voice and other noise. The normal background noise of engine, landing gear and other services being operated can be compared with an accident tape to detect abnormalities or identify certain stages of flight. When an accident is being investigated, the simultaneous analysis of both the FDR and CVR is highly desirable.

Controls for the CVR, like the FDR, are limited to prevent interference with recorded data. The system operates automatically whenever electrical power is provided to the cockpit.

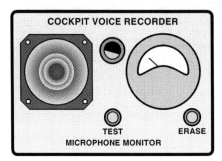

A small panel, as shown in figure 5-16, is located in the cockpit. The panel normally has a test switch for ground operation and some installations provide an erase button that allows the crew to wipe the tape after landing. If fitted, this button can only be operated on the ground, although many airlines forbid pilot erasure of CVR data.

Figure 5-16 **Cockpit voice recorder panel**

Abbreviations

AAL	above aerodrome level
ADC	air data computer
ADI	attitude director indicator
ADS	automatic dependent surveillance
AFCS	automatic flight control system
AFDS	autopilot flight director system
AGL	above ground level
AHRS	attitude heading reference system
AHRU	attitude heading reference unit
ANU	aircraft nose up (attitude)
ARINC	Aeronautical Radio Incorporated
ASCB	avionics standard communications bus
ASI	airspeed indicator
A/T	autothrottle
ATC	air traffic control
CDI	course deviation indicator
CDU	control display unit
CFIT	controlled flight into terrain
CPU	central processor unit
CRT	cathode ray tube
CVR	cockpit voice recorder
DA	decision altitude
DFDR	digital flight data recorder
DGPS	differential GPS
DH	decision height
DME	distance measuring equipment
DR	dead reckoning
EADI	electronic attitude director indicator
ECAM	electronic centralised aircraft monitoring
EET	estimated elapsed time
EFIS	electronic flight instrument system
EHSI	electronic horizontal situation indicator
EICAS	engine indicating and crew altering system
EPR	engine pressure ratio
FAA	Federal Aviation Administration (US)
FBWS	fly by wire system

FCC	flight control computer
FD	flight director
FDR	flight data recorder
FMC	flight management computer
FMGS	flight management guidance system
FMS	flight management system
GA	go around
GDOP	geometric dilution of precision
GHz	gigahertz
Glonass	Russian global navigation satellite system
GPS	global positioning system
GPWS	ground proximity warning system
HF	high frequency
HI	heading indicator
HSI	horizontal situation indicator
HUD	head-up display
IAS	indicated airspeed
ICAO	International Civil Aviation Organisation
IFR	instrument flight rules
ILS	instrument landing system
IMU	inertial measurement unit
Inmarsat	International Maritime Satellite
INS	inertial reference system
IRU	inertial reference unit
IVSI	instantaneous vertical speed indicator
kHz	kilohertz
LF	low frequency
LNAV	lateral navigation
LOC	locator
LOP	line of position
Loran	long range navigation
LRN	long range navigation
MASI	
(or Mach ASI)	Machmeter/airspeed indicator
MCP	mode control panel
MEL	minimum equipment list
MF	medium frequency
MFD	multi-function display
MHRS	magnetic heading reference system
M_{MO}	maximum operating Mach number
MHz	megahertz

NMS	navigation management system
PA	pressure altitude
PA	proximate advisory
PCD	polar cap disturbance
PDOP	position dilution of precision
PPS	precise positioning service
RA	resolution advisory
RA	radio altitude
RAIM	receiver autonomous integrity monitoring
RCU	receiver computer unit
RDMI	radio distance magnetic indicator
RF	radio frequency
RMI	radio magnetic indicator
RNAV	area navigation
RPU	receiver processor unit
S/A	selective availability
SG	symbol generator
SID	standard instrument departure
SID	sudden ionospheric disturbance
SPA	sudden phase anomaly
SOP	standard operating procedure
SPS	standard positioning service
STAR	standard arrival route
TA	traffic advisory
TACAN	tactical air navigation aid
TAS	true airspeed
TCAS	traffic alert and collision avoidance system
TMCP	thrust management control panel
TMS	thrust management system
UTC	coordinated universal time
UHF	ultra high frequency
VG	vertical gyro (or vortex generator)
VHF	very high frequency
VLF	very low frequency
V$_{MO}$	maximum operating airspeed
VNAV	vertical navigation
VOR	VHF omni-directional radio range
VSI	vertical speed indicator
WADGPS	wide area differential GPS
WGS	world geodetic system
WX	weather

Index